First World War
and Army of Occupation
War Diary
France, Belgium and Germany

5 CAVALRY DIVISION
Headquarters, Branches and Services
Adjutant and Quarter-Master General
1 January 1917 - 29 April 1918

WO95/1162/2

The Naval & Military Press Ltd
www.nmarchive.com
Published in association with The National Archives

Published by

The Naval & Military Press Ltd

Unit 10 Ridgewood Industrial Park,

Uckfield, East Sussex,

TN22 5QE England

Tel: +44 (0) 1825 749494

www.naval-military-press.com

www.nmarchive.com

This diary has been reprinted in facsimile from the original. Any imperfections are inevitably reproduced and the quality may fall short of modern type and cartographic standards.

© Crown Copyright
Images reproduced by permission of The National Archives, London, England, 2015.

Contents

Document type	Place/Title	Date From	Date To
Heading	WO95/1162/2		
Heading	1917-1918 5th Cavalry Division Adjt & Quartermaster Jan 1917-Mar 1918 28.3.18 To Egypt Division Ceased to Exist 29.4.18		
War Diary	Dargnies	01/01/1917	28/02/1917
Miscellaneous	Relief of Canadian Pioneer Battalion by Sec bad Pioneer Battalion. Appendix "A"	05/02/1917	05/02/1917
Miscellaneous	March Table		
War Diary	Dargnies	08/02/1917	28/02/1917
Miscellaneous	Relief of Canadian Pioneer Battalion by Sec bad Pioneer Battalion. Appendix A	05/02/1917	05/02/1917
Miscellaneous	March Table		
War Diary	Dargnies	07/03/1917	21/03/1917
War Diary	Pont De Metz	22/03/1917	23/03/1917
War Diary	Peronne	24/03/1917	30/03/1917
War Diary	Villers Bretonneux	01/04/1917	15/04/1917
War Diary	Guizancourt	16/04/1917	27/04/1917
Miscellaneous	List of Bivouacs-5th Cavalry Division Appendix "A"		
War Diary	Guizancourt	02/05/1917	15/05/1917
War Diary	Nobescourt Farm	15/05/1917	31/05/1917
Miscellaneous	Brigades and Divisional Troops. Appendix "A"	13/05/1917	13/05/1917
Miscellaneous	Administrative Instructions Reference No. G.S.573/1 dated 11th May and No. 531 dated 13th. May 1917.		
Miscellaneous	List of Bivouacs-5th. Cavalry Division. Appendix "B"		
Miscellaneous	Ammunition Supply (S.A.A. and Bombs) Appendix "C"	20/05/1917	20/05/1917
Miscellaneous	Establishments		
Miscellaneous	Headquarters 5th Cavalry Division May 1917. Ammunition Supply.		
Miscellaneous	List of Units Attached Appendix "D"		
War Diary	Nobescourt Farm	01/06/1917	30/06/1917
Operation(al) Order(s)	Administrative Instructions Reference Operation Order No. 32 Appendix "A"	31/05/1917	31/05/1917
Miscellaneous	The Following is the amended establishment to be held in Brigade and Advanced Divisional Dumps. Appendix "B"	04/06/1917	04/06/1917
Operation(al) Order(s)	Administrative Instructions. Reference Operation Order No. 33 dated 9/6/17 Appendix "B"	09/06/1917	09/06/1917
Operation(al) Order(s)	Administrative Instructions. Reference Operation Order No. 34 dated 20/6/17 Appendix "D"	20/06/1917	20/06/1917
War Diary	Nobescourt Farm	01/07/1917	10/07/1917
War Diary	Bouvincourt	10/07/1917	14/07/1917
War Diary	St Pol	16/07/1917	28/07/1917
War Diary	Heuchin	31/07/1917	31/07/1917
Operation(al) Order(s)	Administrative Instructions. Reference Operation Order No 35, dated 4/7/17 and No. G/552/15, dated 5/7/17. Appendix "A"	06/07/1917	06/07/1917
Miscellaneous	List of Bivouacs 5th Cavalry division Appendix "B"		
Operation(al) Order(s)	Administrative Instructions. Reference Operation Order No. 36 dated 10/07/17 Appendix "C"	12/07/1917	12/07/1917

Type	Description	Start	End
Miscellaneous	Appendix "D" Hdqrs 5th Cavalry Division 14 July 1917	14/07/1917	14/07/1917
Miscellaneous	Billoting List 5th Cavalry Division. Appendix "E"	23/07/1917	23/07/1917
War Diary	Hedchin	01/08/1917	06/10/1917
War Diary	Poperinghe	07/10/1917	14/10/1917
War Diary	Renescure	15/10/1917	15/10/1917
War Diary	Fressin	16/10/1917	31/10/1917
Miscellaneous	List of Bivouacs-5th Cavalry Division. Reference Sheet 27-1/40,000. Appendix "A"		
Miscellaneous	List of Billets-5th. Cavalry Division. Reference Sheet No.8 5A, 11,13 and 14 Appendix "B"	18/10/1917	18/10/1917
Miscellaneous	List of Billets-5th Cavalry Division. Reference Sheet No.8 5A, 11,13 and 14-1/100,000.	27/10/1917	27/10/1917
Miscellaneous	List of Bivouacs-5th Cavalry Division. Reference Sheet 27-1/40,000. Appendix "A"	12/10/1917	12/10/1917
Miscellaneous	List of Billets-5th. Cavalry Division. Reference Sheet No.5A, 11,13,and 14-1:100,000. Appendix "B"	18/10/1917	18/10/1917
Miscellaneous	List of Billets-5th Cavalry Division. Reference Sheets No.5A, 11,13 & 14-1/100,000.	27/10/1917	27/10/1917
War Diary	Fressin	02/11/1917	09/11/1917
War Diary	Occoches	10/11/1917	10/11/1917
War Diary	Querrieu	11/11/1917	11/11/1917
War Diary	Bouvincourt	12/11/1917	12/11/1917
War Diary	Suzanne	26/11/1917	26/11/1917
War Diary	Monchy Lagache	28/11/1917	30/11/1917
Miscellaneous	List of Bivouacs-5th. Cavalry Division. Reference Map Sheet 62c 1:4000. Appendix "A"	14/11/1917	14/11/1917
Miscellaneous	Administrative Instructions. Reference to the move of the Division to the foward concentration area. Appendix "B"	17/11/1917	17/11/1917
Miscellaneous	Concentration Order Of B Echelon And Dismounted Reinforcements. Appendix "B"	17/11/1917	17/11/1917
Miscellaneous	March Table		
Miscellaneous	Water Arrangements in Forward Concentration Area. Reference plan of Camp N. of Fins. Appendix "B"	18/11/1917	18/11/1917
Miscellaneous	List of Bivouacs-5th Cavalry Division. Appendix "C"	25/11/1917	25/11/1917
Miscellaneous	List of Bivouacs-5th Cavalry Division. Reference Map Sheet 62c-1/40,000. Appendix "D"	28/11/1917	28/11/1917
Miscellaneous	5th Cavalry Division	01/01/1918	01/01/1918
War Diary	Monchy Lagache	01/02/1918	29/02/1918
Miscellaneous	List of Bivouacs-5th Cavalry Division. Reference Map Sheet 62c.1/40.000. Appendix "A"	13/12/1917	13/12/1917
Miscellaneous	List of Bivouacs-5th Cavalry Division. Reference Map Sheet 62c.1/40.000. Appendix "B"	24/12/1917	24/12/1917
Miscellaneous	Memorandum. 5th Cavalry Division	08/03/1918	08/03/1918
War Diary	Monchy Lagache	03/02/1918	27/02/1918
War Diary	Bouvincourt	27/01/1918	30/01/1918
Miscellaneous	Brigades and Divnl. Troops. Administrative Instructions. Reference O.O. No.51 dated 26th instant. Appendix "A"	26/01/1918	26/01/1918
Miscellaneous	Proposed Billeting Area-5th Cavalry Division. Ref. Map Lens 11, Abbeville 14 and Amiens 17.	25/01/1918	25/01/1918
Miscellaneous	Divisional Orders by Major-General H.J.M. Macandrew, C.B., D.S.O. Commanding 5th Cavalry Division	15/01/1918	15/01/1918

Type	Description	Date 1	Date 2
Miscellaneous	Divisional Orders by Major-General H.J.M. Macandrew, C.B., D.S.O., Commanding 5th Cavalry Division.	23/01/1918	23/01/1918
War Diary	Domart	04/02/1918	15/02/1918
War Diary	Pont-De-Metz	16/02/1918	28/02/1918
Miscellaneous	List of Billets-5th Cavalry Division. Ref. Map. Lens 11, Abbeville 14 & Amiens 17 Appendix "A"		
Operation(al) Order(s)	Dismounted Divisions Order No. 7 Appendix "B"	12/02/1918	12/02/1918
Miscellaneous	Reference Dismounted Divisional Order No. 7. dated 12th February 1918. Appendix "C"	13/02/1918	13/02/1918
Miscellaneous	5th Cavalry Division Rear Headquarters will march From Domart to Pont de Metz on the 16th instant. Appx D	15/02/1918	15/02/1918
Miscellaneous	Reference para 1 of Cavalry Corps No. C.R/6 dated 21-2-18 for-warded with my Q-531/R/2 of date. Appendix "E"	21/02/1918	21/02/1918
Miscellaneous	The Following amendment are made to this office No. Q531/R/3 of 21st February. Appendix "E"	22/02/1918	22/02/1918
Miscellaneous	Cav. Corps "Q" Roar No. C.R./12 dated 22-2-18, forwarded for guidance with reference to my No. Q-531/11 of 22-2-18. Appendix "F"	23/02/1918	23/02/1918
Miscellaneous	Reference move of Division Eastward (Overseas) Appendix "F"	22/02/1918	22/02/1918
Miscellaneous	Reference my Q.531/11, of 22.02.18 Appendix "F"	25/02/1918	25/02/1918
Miscellaneous	Brigades & Divisional Units. Administrative Instructions No. 2. Appendix "F" i	22/02/1918	22/02/1918
Miscellaneous	Appendix "G"	22/02/1918	22/02/1918
Miscellaneous	Appendix "H" Headquarters 5th Cavalry Division	25/02/1918	25/02/1918
Miscellaneous	9th Hodsons Horse. Will commence entraining at Saleux on the 27th as follows:- Appendix "H" i	26/02/1918	26/02/1918
Miscellaneous	O.C. 9th Hodson's Horse. In continuation of this office Q.531/R/8 dated 26th inst. Appendix H 2	27/02/1918	27/02/1918
Miscellaneous	Appendix "I"	26/02/1918	26/02/1918
Miscellaneous	The Following personnel from this Division will entrain at Saleux Railhead for TARANTO on the 28th February:- Appendix "J"	27/02/1918	27/02/1918
Miscellaneous	Brigades and Divisional Units. Administrative Instructions. No. 3. Appendix "K"	25/02/1918	25/02/1918
Miscellaneous	Fifth Army. G.O.C., L.Of C.Area. Appendix "L"	24/02/1918	24/02/1918
Miscellaneous	Detail of Units that will embark at Taranto on 10th March, 1918. Appendix "A"		
Miscellaneous	Appendix "B"		
Miscellaneous	Appendix "M"	25/02/1918	25/02/1918
Miscellaneous	Headquarters, 5th Cavalry Division. Appendix "O"	28/02/1918	28/02/1918
Miscellaneous	Reference my No. Q-531/R/7 dated 25th February 1918. Appendix "P"	28/02/1918	28/02/1918
Miscellaneous	Fifth Army Reference C.H.Q. letter O.B/2160 dated 20/1/13. Appendix "N"	07/02/1918	07/02/1918
Miscellaneous	Headquarters, 5th Cavalry Division. 12th February 1918		
Miscellaneous	Headquarters, 5th Cavy Divn 1st March 1917	01/03/1917	01/03/1917
War Diary	Domart	04/02/1918	15/02/1918
War Diary	Pont-De-Metz	16/02/1918	28/02/1918
Miscellaneous	List of Billets-5th Cavalry Division. Ref.Map. Lens 11, Abbeville 14 & Amiens 17. Appendix "A"	06/03/1918	06/03/1918
Operation(al) Order(s)	Dismounted Divisions Order No. 7 Appendix B	12/02/1918	12/02/1918

Miscellaneous	Reference Dismounted Divisional Order No. 7. dated 12th February 1918. Appendix "C"	13/02/1918	13/02/1918
Miscellaneous	5th Cavalry Division Rear Headquarters will march from Domart to Pont de Metz on the 16th instant. Appendix D	15/02/1918	15/02/1918
Miscellaneous	Reference para 1 of Cavalry Corps No. C.R/6 dated 21-02-18 forwarded with my Q-531/R/2 of date. Appendix "E"	21/02/1918	21/02/1918
Miscellaneous	The Following amendments are made to this office No. Q531/R/3 of 21st February. Appendix "E"	22/02/1918	22/02/1918
Miscellaneous	Cav. Corps "Q" Roar No C.R./12 dated 22-2-18, forwarded for guidance with reference to my No Q-531/11of 22-2-18 Appendix "F" i	23/02/1918	23/02/1918
Miscellaneous	Reference move of Division Eastwards (Overseas) Appendix "F"	22/02/1918	22/02/1918
Miscellaneous	Sec"bad Cavalry Brigade. Reference my Q.531/11 of 22.02.18 Appendix "F"	24/02/1918	24/02/1918
Miscellaneous	Brigades & Divisional Units. Administrative Instructions No. 2. Appendix "F" i	22/02/1918	22/02/1918
Miscellaneous	Appendix "G"	22/02/1918	22/02/1918
Miscellaneous	Headquarters, 5th Cavalry Division. Appendix "H"	25/02/1918	25/02/1918
Miscellaneous	Appendix "H" 1	26/02/1918	26/02/1918
Miscellaneous	In continuation of this office Q.531/R/8 dated 26th inst. Appendix "H" 2	27/02/1918	27/02/1918
Miscellaneous	Appendix "I"	26/02/1918	26/02/1918
Miscellaneous	Appendix "J"	27/02/1918	27/02/1918
Miscellaneous	Administrative Instruction. No. 3. Appendix "K"	25/02/1918	25/02/1918
Miscellaneous	In continuation of my 6925/1/5 (Q.A.1) dated 20/2/1918 Appendix "L"	24/02/1918	24/02/1918
Miscellaneous	Detail of Units that will embark at Taranto on 10th March 1918. Appendix "A"		
Miscellaneous	Appendix "B		
Miscellaneous	Appendix "M"	25/02/1918	25/02/1918
Miscellaneous	Appendix "O"	28/02/1918	28/02/1918
Miscellaneous	Appendix "P"	28/02/1918	28/02/1918
Miscellaneous	Headquarters, 5th Cavalry Division. 12th February 1918	12/02/1918	12/02/1918
Miscellaneous	5th Cavalry Division	20/04/1918	20/04/1918
War Diary	Pont-De-Metz	01/03/1918	20/03/1918
Miscellaneous	Appendix "A"	01/03/1918	01/03/1918
Miscellaneous	O.C. Det. Sialkot Bde. at Bacouel. O.C. Ind. Vot. Sect. at Bacouel. A.D.V.S.	27/02/1918	27/02/1918
Miscellaneous	Appendix "B"	02/03/1918	02/03/1918
Miscellaneous	Appendix "C"	03/03/1918	03/03/1918
Miscellaneous	Appendix "D"	05/03/1918	05/03/1918
Miscellaneous	Appendix "E"	08/03/1918	08/03/1918
Miscellaneous	Appendix "F"	15/03/1918	15/03/1918
Miscellaneous	Appendix "A"	01/03/1918	01/03/1918
Miscellaneous	O.C. Det. Sialkot Bde. at Bacouel.	27/02/1918	27/02/1918
Miscellaneous	Appendix "B"	02/03/1918	02/03/1918
Miscellaneous	Appendix "C"	03/03/1918	03/03/1918
Miscellaneous	Appendix "D"	05/03/1918	05/03/1918
Miscellaneous	Appendix "E"	08/03/1918	08/03/1918
Miscellaneous	Appendix "F"	15/03/1918	15/03/1918
Miscellaneous	5th Cavalry Divn	26/04/1918	26/04/1918
War Diary	Tel-El-Kebir	05/03/1918	27/03/1918

Heading	War Diary H.Q. 5th Cav Division E.E. Force April 1st To April 30th 1918		
War Diary	Tel-El-Kebir	04/04/1918	29/04/1918
Miscellaneous	Appendix "A"	14/04/1918	14/04/1918
Miscellaneous	Appendix "B"	15/04/1918	15/04/1918
Miscellaneous	Appendix "C"	17/04/1918	17/04/1918
Miscellaneous	Appendix "D"	21/04/1918	21/04/1918
Miscellaneous	Appendix "E"	26/04/1918	26/04/1918
Miscellaneous	Appendix "F"	23/04/1918	23/04/1918
Miscellaneous	Appendix "G"	26/04/1918	26/04/1918
Miscellaneous	5th Cavalry Division	26/04/1918	26/04/1918
Miscellaneous	Reference No. G.178 of to-day; s date. Appendix "H"	27/04/1918	27/04/1918
Miscellaneous	Reference this Office No. G.178 and Q.609 of to-day's date.	27/04/1918	27/04/1918
Miscellaneous	Appendix		
Miscellaneous	Headquarters, 5th Cavalry Division (Administrative) Appendix		
Miscellaneous	Appendix "H"	27/04/1918	27/04/1918

No 95/1162/2

1917-1918
5TH CAVALRY DIVISION

ADJT & QUARTERMASTER
JAN 1917 - ~~FEB~~ MAR 1918

28.3.18. To EGYPT

DIVISION CEASED TO EXIST 29.4.18

AA & QMG 55th Div
5 CAV DIV

WAR DIARY
or
INTELLIGENCE SUMMARY.
(Erase heading not required.)

Army Form C. 2118.

Hour, Date, Place	Summary of Events and Information	Remarks and references to Appendices
DARGNIES January 1st 1917.	Grant by Government of India of interest gratuity to Indian ranks with effect from 1st August 1916 and issue to Indian troops under this head of Indian Officers 17 Rs/various Ranks, Indian Cavalry, announced. Casualties for 12 noon – Lord Strathcona's Horse – 1 wounded. 1 OR, accidentally.	
January 2nd	Captain Pierce Battalion 8th LONGROY GAMACHES by the at 10.81 hours to XII Corps to relieve Secunderabad Pioneer Regiment – Strength of Cavalry Pioneer Regiment as follows:- 18 B.Os. 10 I.Os. 790 OR. 71 Horses. 20 Followers. Two animal vehicles. Two Parent's vehicles. Casualties to 12 noon :- Kitchener's Horse 1 For Gang Horse	

Army Form C. 2118.

WAR DIARY
or
INTELLIGENCE SUMMARY.
(Erase heading not required.)

Instructions regarding War Diaries and Intelligence Summaries are contained in F.S. Regs., Part II. and the Staff Manual respectively. Title pages will be prepared in manuscript.

Hour, Date, Place	Summary of Events and Information	Remarks and references to Appendices
DARGNIES.		
January 3rd	Seconded Pioneer Battalion arrived at LONGROY-GAMACHES at 18.30 hrs from XIV Corps on relief by Ambala Pioneer Battalion.	
" 5th	Canadian Cav. Division	
	19th Lancers, Hodsons, 3rd O.P.I.	
" 7th	Ambala Pioneer Battalion transferred from XIV Corps to 9th Division VI Corps and located at AGNEZ-LES-DURANS	
" 12th	Canadian Cav. Pioneer Battalion transferred from XIV Corps to XIII Corps today	
" 13th	Orders issued to O.C. 3rd Field Squadron to inspect as regards horsemanship of regiments.	
" 15th	I.G.M. Canadian Corps examined at BEAUCHAMPS into No. 48 battery Outward journey to Railway Station 8¾ No. 2nd train a.a. R.C.H.A. Par/ogre.	

(73989) W4141-463. 400,000. 9/14. H.&J. Ltd. Forms/C. 2118/10.

Army Form C. 2118.

WAR DIARY
or
INTELLIGENCE SUMMARY
(Erase heading not required.)

Place	Date	Hour	Summary of Events and Information	Remarks and references to Appendices
DAGNIES	January 21st		Approval given by G.H.Q. to the training of Indian Cavalry Regiments with the British Cavalry Sword. They will be be armed in the undermentioned order:— 20th Deccan Horse, 9th Hodson's Horse, 34th Poona Horse, 18th Lancers.	Walter Lynden Bell Lt Col. G.S.O. 5th Cavalry Div.

WAR DIARY

INTELLIGENCE SUMMARY

Place	Date	Hour	Summary of Events and Information	Remarks and references to Appendices
DARGNIES	February			
	8th		The designation of the undermentioned units changed as follows:- Secunderabad Machine Gun Squadron to No 13 Squadron M.G.C (Cavalry) Ambala Machine Gun Squadron to No 14 Squadron M.G.C (Cavalry)	Appendix "A" (overleaf)
	8th 9th 10th		Relief of Canadian Pioneer Battalion by Secunderabad Pioneer Battalion	
	18th		Thaw set in. Came into the thaw having.	
	22nd		98 Remounts received from Remount Depot DIEPPE. (3 Riding, 1st L.D. hints. 94 L.D mules)	
	24th		Designation of 2nd Indian R.H.A. Bde. changed to 17th Brigade R.H.A.	
	25th		Intimation received from Cavalry Corps that the duration of changes at present allowed by the establishments to General and Staff Officers with Cavalry is being looked into thus:- Brigade Commanders from 5 to 4. This change of all Staff Officers (G.O.C. except) to be reduced to 1 in every 2 Officers.	

Army Form C. 2118.

WAR DIARY
or
INTELLIGENCE SUMMARY
(Erase heading not required.)

Instructions regarding War Diaries and Intelligence Summaries are contained in F. S. Regs., Part II. and the Staff Manual respectively. Title Pages will be prepared in manuscript.

Place	Date	Hour	Summary of Events and Information	Remarks and references to Appendices
DARGNIES	February 26"		Three Brunei lemon) few turning. One L.G.S. began during at to Carriage of Rent to to Flying Corps personnel attached to this Division. Casualty to 12 noon :- Lt H.W. LUTTMAN-JOHNSON wounded, accidentally (Flight at duty.)	
	27"		The following regiments completed w/s British Country Pattern Gunner's :- 20th Deccan Horse 34th Poona Horse 9th Hodson's Horse	
	28"		Casualties to 12 noon :- L^t (T/Capt) G.R. REEVES killed, accidentally.	

W.M. Colley Col
a/a on 9
5th Cav. Div.

Appendix 'A'

No.Q/39/c.   Headquarters 5th Cavalry Division.

Dated 5th February, 1917.

TO/:

Canadian Cav.Bde.   A.D.P.S.
Sec'bad   "   "   A.D.M.S.
Field Squadron.   Anti-gas Officer
O.C. A.S.C.   Canadian Pioneer Bn., attd.,
D.A.D.O.S.   XIII Corps.

SUBJECT:- Relief of Canadian Pioneer Battalion by Sec'bad Pioneer Battalion.

1. RELIEF.

The relief of the Canadian Pioneer Battalion by the Sec'bad Pioneer Battalion will be carried out in lorries on the 8th, 9th and 10th February, in accordance with the attached Table, *15 lorries being provided daily.*

2. TRANSPORT & RIDING HORSES.

The Transport & Riding Horses of both Battalions will move by road in three marches. Dates & billets will be notified later.

3. STRENGTHS.

Strength of the Sec'bad Pioneer Battalion will be as laid down in War Establishment, except that the strength of officers will be the same as ordered in this Office No.Q/8052, dated 23rd January 1917.

4. MARCHING OUT STATES.

Nominal rolls, etc., will be furnished by the Sec'bad Brigade on the departure of the Battalion.

5. RATION LORRIES.

O.C. A.S.C. will arrange to relieve the Canadian lorries attached to XIII Corps for supply.

6. TOOLS.

No tools or trench stores will be taken.

7. POSTAL.

The postal arrangement for the Sec'bad Battalion will be the same as that, when the Battalion was previously detached. Bags should be clearly labelled :-

Regiment _____.

Sec'bad Pioneer Battalion, attached
XIII Corps.

8. ORDNANCE.........

8. ORDNANCE.

O.C. Sec'bad Pioneer Battalion will indent for any Ordnance stores which they may require on the Ordnance Officer of the Formation to which they are attached.

9. GAS HELMET RESERVE.

The D.A.D.O.S. will collect 100 Smoke Helmets from the Anti-gas Officer at the Divisional School on the 6th February, and hand them over to the Staff Captain, Sec'bad Brigade, to form a reserve for the Pioneer Battalion.

10. RATION STRENGTH.

Are as follows :-

Sec'bad Pioneer Battalion.

British..310.
Indians (307 Hindus, 240 Mahdns.)............547.
Animals.. 71

Canadian Pioneer Battalion.

British..834.
Horses... 71

11. Acknowledge.

[signature]

Lt-Colonel.

A.A. & Q.M.G. 5th Cavalry Division.

Copy to :-

    Cavalry Corps "Q".

    XIII Corps "Q".

    R.C.E, III, DOULLENS.

    General Staff, 5th Cav.Divn.

MARCH TABLE.

Date.	Relieving Parties.	Starting Times & Places	Relieving Parties rejoining Divn. on returning lorries.	Remarks.
8th February.	Sec'bad Bn.Hdqrs. Deccan Horse Coy. Medical Detachment.	7 a.m. (a). HARCELAINES & MAISNIÈRES.	1 Company Canadian Pioneer Battalion.	(a). 7 lorries to MAISNIERES and remainder to HARCEL- AINES. Lorries for HARCELAINES will pick up Medical Party at BOUVAINCOURT at 6-30 a.m. en route.
9th February.	Poona Horse Coy. R.E. Detachment.	7 a.m. (b). AIGNEVILLE.	1 Company Canadian Pioneer Battalion. Medical Detachment.	(b) Lorries will pick up R.E. Detachment at EMERLVILLE at 6-30 a.m. en route to AIGNEVILLE.
10th February.	7th D.Guards Coy.	7 a.m. (c) FRUGUIERES.	Canadian Battalion Hdqrs. 1 Company Canadian Pioneer Battalion. R.E. Detachment.	(c) Lorries will pick up detachment from HOCQUELUS en route to FEUQUIERES.

NOTE:- Relieved Parties must be ready to start in returning lorries at 2 p.m. each day.

WAR DIARY A.Q. ~~or~~ **INTELLIGENCE SUMMARY**

(Erase heading not required.)

Army Form C. 2118.

Headquarters Vol VIII
5th Cavalry Division

Place	Date	Hour	Summary of Events and Information	Remarks and references to Appendices
DARGNIES	February			
	9th		The designation of the undermentioned units changed as follows:— Secunderabad Machine Gun Squadron to No. 12 Squadron M.G.C. (Cavalry) Ambala Machine Gun Squadron to No. 14 Squadron M.G.C. (Cavalry)	
	8th 9th 10th		Relief of Canadian Pioneer Battalion by Secunderabad Pioneer Battalion.	Appendix "A" (Orders)
	18th		Thaw set in. Came into the thin horse lines.	
	22nd		98 Remounts received from Remount Depot DIEPPE. (3 Rams, 1 L.D. mule, 94 L.D. horses)	
	24th		Designation of 2nd Indian R.H.A. Bgde changed to 17th Brigade R.H.A.	
	25th		Information received from Cavalry Corps that the number of chargers at horses allowed to the Establishment of General and Staff Officers with Cavalry is being reduced as follows:— Brigade Commanders from 5 to 4. That chargers of all Staff Officers (G.O.C. scale) to be reduced to 1 for Every 2 officers.	

Army Form C. 2118.

WAR DIARY
or
INTELLIGENCE SUMMARY

(Erase heading not required.)

Place	Date	Hour	Summary of Events and Information	Remarks and references to Appendices
DARGNIES	26th January		Three Battalions learned the howitzer. One L.G.S began Gunnery Int. the Gunnery of Pilots i.e. to Flying Corps personnel attached to the Division. Casualties to 12 noon :- Lt. H.N LUTTMAN JOHNSON wounded accidentally (slightly at duty)	
	27th		The following regimental completed into British Cavalry Regiments Rumor :- 2 Lt Deegan horse 3 Lt Dunn horse 4 Lt Stewart horse	
	28th		Casualties to 12 noon :- Lt (T/Capt) G.B REEVES killed accidentally	

McCullough Col
A.I.O.M.G
5th Corps Div?

Appendix A

No. Q/39/2.   Headquarters 5th Cavalry Division.

Dated 5th February 1917.

TO/
    Canadian Cav.Bde.   A.D.P.S.
    Sec'bad "   "   A.D.M.S.
    Field Squadron.   Anti-gas Officer
    O.C. A.S.C.   Canadian Pioneer Bn., attd.,
    D.A.D.O.S.   XIII Corps.

===

SUBJECT:-   Relief of Canadian Pioneer Battalion by
              Sec'bad Pioneer Battalion.

1. RELIEF.

      The relief of the Canadian Pioneer Battalion by the Sec'bad Pioneer Battalion will be carried out in lorries on the 8th, 9th and 10th February, in accordance with the attached Table, 15 lorries being provided daily.

2. TRANSPORT & RIDING HORSES.

      The Transport & Riding Horses of both Battalions will move by road in three marches.   Dates & billets will be notified later.

3. STRENGTHS.

      Strength of the Sec'bad Pioneer Battalion will be as laid down in War Establishment, except that the strength of officers will be the same as ordered in this Office No.Q/8052, dated 23rd January 1917.

4. MARCHING OUT STATES.

      Nominal rolls, etc., will be furnished by the Sec'bad Brigade on the departure of the Battalion.

5. RATION LORRIES.

      O.C. A.S.C. will arrange to relieve the Canadian lorries attached to XIII Corps for supply.

6. TOOLS.

      No tools or trench stores will be taken.

7. POSTAL.

      The postal arrangements for the Sec'bad Battalion will be the same as that, when the Battalion was previously detached. Bags should be clearly labelled :-

              Regiment _____.

                Sec'bad Pioneer Battalion, attached
                    XIII Corps.

                                    8. ORDNANCE.........

8. ORDNANCE.

O.C. Sec'bad Pioneer Battalion will indent for any Ordnance stores which they may require on the Ordnance Officer of the Formation to which they are attached.

9. GAS HELMET RESERVE.

The D.A.D.O.S. will collect 100 Smoke Helmets from the Anti-gas Officer at the Divisional School on the 6th February, and hand them over to the Staff Captain, Sec'bad Brigade, to form a reserve for the Pioneer Battalion.

10. RATION STRENGTH.

Are as follows :-

Sec'bad Pioneer Battalion.

British.....................................310.
Indians (307 Hindus, 240 Mahdns.)...........547.
Animals.....................................71

Canadian Pioneer Battalion.

British.....................................834.
Horses......................................71

11. Acknowledge.

Lt-Colonel.
A.A. & Q.M.G. 5th Cavalry Division.

Copy to :-

Cavalry Corps "Q".

XIII Corps "Q".

R.C.E. III, DOULLENS.

General Staff, 5th Cav.Divn.

MARCH TABLE.

Date.	Relieving Parties.	Starting Times & Places.	Relieved Parties.	Remarks.
8th February.	Sec'bad Bn.Hdqrs. Deccan Horse Coy. Medical Detachment.	7 a.m. (a). HARCELAINES & MAISNIÈRES.	Relieved Parties rejoining Divn. on returning lorries.	(a). 7 lorries to MAISNIÈRES and remainder to HARCELAINES. Lorries for HARCELAINES will pick up Medical Party at BOUVAINCOURT at 6-30 a.m. en route.
9th February.	Poona Horse Coy. R.E.Detachment.	7 a.m. (b). AIGNEVILLE.	1 Company Canadian Pioneer Battalion. Medical Detachment.	(b) Lorries will pick up R.E. Detachment at EMREVILLE at 6-30 a.m. en route to AIGNEVILLE.
10th February.	7th D.Guards Coy.	7 a.m. (c) FLUQUIÈRES.	Canadian Battalion Hdqrs. 1 Company Canadian Pioneer Battalion. R.E.Detachment.	(c) Lorries will pick up detachment from HOCQUELUS en route to FLUQUIÈRES.

NOTE:- Relieved Parties must be ready to start in returning lorries at 2 p.m. each day.

Vol IX

WAR DIARY
or
INTELLIGENCE SUMMARY

Army Form C. 2118.

(ADMINISTRATIVE)
5TH. CAVALRY DIVN
HDQRS.

Place	Date	Hour	Summary of Events and Information	Remarks and references to Appendices
DARGNIES.	March 7th		92 OR despatched to Ambala Pioneer Batn as reinforcements & reliefs and party of 52 OR relieved, required to return to Brigade. Approval given by G.H.Q. to the grant of leave to England, India, the Sine Creations as Indian Officers, to Senior Indian ranks of Indian Departmental Services in France.	
	12th		Division ordered to be prepared to move at 48 hours notice.	
	14th		Secunderabad Pioneer Battalion arrived back from XIII Corps.	
	17th		Ambala Pioneer Battalion arrived back from VII Corps.	
	19th		Canadian Cavalry Brigade and RHA Pors. moved into 9 hundred billets and bivouacs about SENARPONT.	
	20th		Remainder of Division moved into 9 billets and bivouacked together with Canadian Cav Bde and 17th RHA Bde to traverse to an area around HORNOY. Following animals received between March 13th and 20th: 10 received from ROUEN, 78 " 1st Cav Divn	
	21st		Division marched to an area about PONT DE METZ, just S.W. of AMIENS. Report Centre Closed at DARGNIES at 12 noon and opened at PONT DE METZ same hour.	
PONT DE METZ	22nd		Division marched to an area about CERISY and bivouacked there	

Army Form C. 2118.

WAR DIARY
or
INTELLIGENCE SUMMARY

(Erase heading not required.)

Instructions regarding War Diaries and Intelligence Summaries are contained in F. S. Regs., Part II. and the Staff Manual respectively. Title Pages will be prepared in manuscript.

Place	Date	Hour	Summary of Events and Information	Remarks and references to Appendices
PONT DE METZ	March 23rd		Ambala and Canadian Cav Bde moved to Amiens about PERONNE and Secourt (incomplete) Cav Bde just N. of the BOIS DE MEREAU COURT - Report Centre closed at PONT DE METZ at 12 noon and opened at PERONNE Somme km. Summer Time introduced today. At 11pm clocks advanced 1 hour.	
PERONNE	24th			
	25th		7th L.D. Arrived licens from Remonts. Ambala and Canadian Cav Bdes moved up and took over the line held by XIX Corps Cav. Regt. 1 Company Corps Cyclists attached to Sup from IV Corps. 2 Hampshire Corps Cyclists attached from III Corps. XIV Corps Cav Regt and Cyclist Battalion came under orders of the Division. Casualties to 12 noon:-	
			For Army HQrs. 1 Officer injured accidentally 5 O.R. wounded (includes 3 missing)	
			R.C. Dragoons. 1 O.R. wounded.	
			9th Hussars. 1 O.R.I wounded.	
			18th Lancers. 4 O.R.I missing 1 O.R.I missing	
			5th Cavalry Divn Recon Patrol reported the Division and intersection road ≠ 1000 yds N.W. of BIACHES	

2449 Wt. W14957/M90 750,000 1/16 J.B.C. & A. Forms/C.2118/12.

War Diary or Intelligence Summary

Army Form C. 2118.

Place	Date	Hour	Summary of Events and Information	Remarks and references to Appendices
PERONNE	March 26th		Ammunition Expenditure to 12 noon :- 13h Shrapnel 379 rds. " H.E. 52 rds. " S.A.A. 8,700 rds. Casualties to 12 noon :- R.C. Dragoons. 1 OR wounded. Fd. Gunny Horse. 3 OR wounded. 18th Lancers. 1 OR wounded. Horse Casualties. 12.	
	27th		(Secunderabad) Cav Bde moved up to bivouacs about HALLE - AH.T. Company to bivouacs 1800 yds N.W. H RIACHES - Reserve Park to I 23 at 8.4. - Main Ammunition Column to I.23.a.8.4.- Ammunition Expenditure to 12 noon :- 13h Shrapnel - 426 rds. " H.E. - 96 rds. " S.A.A. - 1528 rds. Casualties to 12 noon :- R.C. Dragoons - 1 OR killed - Lieut P.F. ARNOLD and 5 OR wounded. L. Strathcona Horse - Major J.A. CRITCHLEY - M.C and 4 OR wounded. 9th Horse. 1 OR wounded. 18th Lancers. 7 OR wounded (includes 1 missing) Horses. 26 Casualties.	

Army Form C. 2118.

WAR DIARY
or
INTELLIGENCE SUMMARY
(Erase heading not required.)

Place	Date	Hour	Summary of Events and Information	Remarks and references to Appendices
PERONNE	March 27th		Prisoners taken. 1 German Officer and 19 OR by 8th Hussars at VILLERS FAUCON. 13 OR by Canadian Cav Regt. just N of VILLERS FAUCON.	
	28th		Approval given by G.H.Q. to the establishment of M.M.P. into an Indian Cavalry Division to be increased to 4 Sergeants and 36 Lance Corporals in addition to the Indian Police Establishment.	
			Ammunition Expenditure to 12 noon :-	
			13 pr. Shrapnel — 817.	
			H.E. — 377.	
			S.A.A. — 19,571.	
			Casualties to 12 noon :-	
			R.C. Dragoons — 6 OR wounded.	
			L.S. Horse — 1 OR killed — 16 OR wounded.	
			Fort Garry Horse — Capt S.H. LEE & Lieut G.H. TAYLOR wounded (slightly, at duty) 10 OR wounded — 2 OR missing.	
			8th Hussars — 2 OR killed — Lieut R.F. HORNBY and 10 OR wounded.	
			9th L.A.C. Battery — Capt J. RONAN and 4 OR wounded.	
			Horse Casualties — 80 —	
			Canadian Cav Bde. withdrawn to a bivouac between CLERY and HEM.	

Army Form C. 2118.

WAR DIARY
or
INTELLIGENCE SUMMARY

(Erase heading not required.)

Place	Date	Hour	Summary of Events and Information	Remarks and references to Appendices
PERONNE	March 29		Whole Division Watchman to position of assembly between CLERY - HEM - and CAPPY. Ammunition Expenditure to 2 hours :- S.A.A. 500 rds. Casualties to 12 noon :- 9th Hrs. - 1 OR killed. 1 OR wounded.	
	30		210 animals arrived from Remounts as reinforcements. Division less Canadian Cavalry Bde. marched westward : Secundrabad Bde. to bivouacs about WARFUSÉE - bivouacs about BAYONVILLERS and Ambala Bde. to bivouacs at CAPPY. Canadian Bde. remains at CAPPY. Report Centre closed at PERONNE at 2 pm and opened at VILLERS BRETTONEUX same hour.	

W.W.O'Keefe Lt.Col.
A.A. & Q.M.G.
3rd Cavalry Div.
1/4/17

Vol 10

Hdqrs. 5th Cavalry Divn
(Administrative)

Army Form C. 2118.

WAR DIARY
or
INTELLIGENCE SUMMARY.
(Erase heading not required.)

Instructions regarding War Diaries and Intelligence Summaries are contained in F. S. Regs., Part II. and the Staff Manual respectively. Title pages will be prepared in manuscript.

Place	Date	Hour	Summary of Events and Information	Remarks and references to Appendices
VILLERS BRETONNEUX	April 1st		14th Animals received as reinforcements from ROUEN	
	5th		No.5 Section 16th Reserve Park joined the Division consisting of 53 L.G.S. wagons loaded with oats. Diamond has brought up from GAMACHES and are now concentrated about FOUCAUCOURT HAMEL CAPPY + CHUIGNES - Strength 357 Indian and 622 British Ranks. They will be employed in road work under III Corps until further orders	
	9th		Dismounted men concentrated = Canadians at ESTREES. Remainder at FOUCOURT. All are employed on road repair under III Corps.	
	10th	2 am	Reported to 18th Ammunition changed to O.B. MERIGNOLLES - Our 13th Amm. Park from O1 PLATEAU and O1 BEAUCOURT to O.B. hamstrung by Amm Park from O1 PLATEAU to more East.	
	11th	10 am	Orders received to Division to move East. Orders to move cancelled and Division remains at 2 hours notice.	
	12th		Application made for return of 2 extra machine guns by 8th Hussars. (Sanctioned. 18.6.17)	

Army Form C. 2118.

WAR DIARY
or
INTELLIGENCE SUMMARY.
(Erase heading not required.)

Instructions regarding War Diaries and Intelligence Summaries are contained in F.S. Regs., Part II. and the Staff Manual respectively. Title pages will be prepared in manuscript.

Place	Date	Hour	Summary of Events and Information	Remarks and references to Appendices
VILLERS BRETONNEUX	April 15th		During moved East towards Secundahabad Bgd. in bivouacs between TREFCON and MONCHY LAGACHE. Ambala Bde. " " " CAULAINCOURT and TERTRY. Canadian Bde. " " about ATHIES. Report Camp closed at VILLERS BRETONNEUX at 8 hrs and fixed at GUIZANCOURT same hour. Railhead for Supplies - NESLE. 344 Animals arrived from ROUEN as reinforcements.	Appendix "A"
GUIZANCOURT	16th		List of bivouacs. Disamand Bde. came up to bivouacs in LE MESNIL and Camp near BRIE (approx 53).	
	18th		Disamand Reinforcements to L.S.H. proceeded to Camp at AALON (1 mile south of CAIX) to the number of thirteen forty kart in this area.	
	26th		Ammunition Railhead O.J. (1½ kilometres NE PEURCHY). Our 13th Ammn haversack by Ammn Park from O.B. MERIGNOLLES h.O.S. Two days rations and 20 lbs oats per horse drawn from Supply Depot and dumped in Reserve in TREFCON.	
	27th		Reserve Park moved to bivouac but East of Am ponds in W.II.e. (sheet 62.e.)	

H.M. Mulfer (?)
Lt Col
A.D.V.S. Canadian

(Appendix "A")

LIST OF BIVOUACS — 5TH. CAVALRY DIVISION.

```
Divisional Hdqrs..................GUIZANCOURT.
Field Cashier.....................HERLY.
Signal Squadron...................GUIZANCOURT.
Field Squadron (Hdqrs.)...........S.W. of TERTRY (W.8.b.3.9.)
C.R.H.A...........................GUIZANCOURT.
17th Bde.RHA.Amn:Col.(Main).......FALVY.
Ammunition Park...................ETALON.
Supply Column.....................HERLY.
Sanitary Section..................GUIZANCOURT.
No.9 L.A.C.Battery................-----do-----
Aux: H.T.Company..................EPENANCOURT.
5th Cav.Reserve Park..............-----do-----

Railhead (Supplies,etc)...........NESLE.
   "     (Gun Amn).................O.B.MERIGNOLLES. (near PROYART).
   "     (S.A.A. )
```

AMBALA CAVALRY BRIGADE.
```
Brigade Hdqrs.....................Wood E. of CAULAINCOURT (W.5.a.9.7.)
8th Hussars.......................)
9th Horse.........................)
18th Lancers......................)  Bivouacs between CAULAINCOURT
"X" Battery R.H.A.................)
M.G.Squadron......................)      &  TERTRY.
Mhow I.C.F.A......................)
M.V.Section.......................)
Lt: Section Amn:Col.             )
Dismounted Reinfcements...........Camp near BRIE (O.20.d.5.9.)
```

SEC'BAD CAVALRY BRIGADE.
```
Brigade Hdqrs.....................TREFCON (W.10.a.5.7.)
7th D.Guards......................)
20th Horse........................)
34th Horse........................)  Bivouacs between TREFCON and
"N" Battery R.H.A.................)
M.G.Squadron......................)  MONCHY LAGACHE.
M.V.Section.......................)
Sec'bad I.C.F.A...................)
Lt. Section Amn: Col..............)
Dismounted Reinfcements...........Camp near BRIE (O.20.d.5.9.)
```

CANADIAN CAVALRY BRIGADE.
```
Brigade Hdqrs.....................ATHIES (Northern exit)
F.G.Horse.........................)
R.C.Dragoons......................)
L.S.Horse.........................)  Bivouacs about
R.C.H.A.Brigade...................)
Can.Lt.Section Amn:Col............)       ATHIES.
M.G.Squadron......................)
Can. C.F.A........................)
Can. M.V.Section..................)
Dismounted Reinfcements...........LE MESNIL.
```

****

No.Q/213/2.   Headquarters 5th. Cavalry Division.
                                         Dated 16th April 1917.
TO/
     Fourth Army "Q".

               For information.   Lieut-Col.,
                                         for G.O.C. 5th Cav. Division.
Copies to :-
     Usual Billeting List distribution.

ADMINISTRATIVE
5TH. CAVALRY DIVISIONAL
HEADQRS

WAR DIARY
INTELLIGENCE SUMMARY

Place	Date	Hour	Summary of Events and Information	Remarks and references to Appendices
GUIZANCOURT	MAY 2nd		Dismounted Reinforcements of Canadian Cav. R.R. (less LSH) proceeded by M.T. to HALTE. Parties to HAMAGE on W. Edge of BOIS D'HOLNON for N.R. to HALTE. in X.10.b. to work on defences there.	
	6th		Leave allotment to England increased from 45 to 90 per month with effect from May 6th.	
	8th		17th R.H.A. Brigade, R.C.H.A. Brigade and Gun Section of Ammunition Column left to attachment to VII Corps, but continues to be administered by this division.	
	10th		17th R.H.A. Brigade, R.C.H.A. Brigade and Gun Section of Ammunition Column rejoins the division.	
	13th		Following moves took place. Limbered Trans. to Rouvrae Inst. E.9.X. roads in W.11.d Ammunition Column to W.2.b. (sheet 62:SE) A.M.T. Company to W.1.d. 77.C. Ammunition Park to POTTE Supply Column to MORCHAIN.	
	14th-15th		Relieved 104th Infantry Brigade in the line on night 7 14th-15th	

Canadian Cav. R.R.
9th Hussars
16th R+A R.R.
Own Fiscal Troop " No 9 LAC Railway

WAR DIARY
or
INTELLIGENCE SUMMARY.

(Erase heading not required.)

Army Form C. 2118.

Place	Date	Hour	Summary of Events and Information	Remarks and references to Appendices
GUIZANCOURT	May 15th		Administrative Instructions. Report Centre closed at GUIZAN COURT at 6 hrs. and opened at NORESCOURT FARM same hour.	Appendix "A"
NORESCOURT FARM	15th/16th		Secunderabad Cav Bde. — 9th Horse, 18th Lancers, No 14 Machine Gun Squadron, 17th Bde RHA, RCHA Bde, 1 Field Troop } Relieved 177th Infantry Brigade in the Line night 15th-16th.	
	17th		Casualties to 12 hours :— R.C. Dragoons — wounded 1 OR. 2/5th Notts Staffs — killed 1 OR — wounded 2 OR	
	18th		Casualties to 12 hours :— R.C.H.A. Bde — wounded 3 OR accidentally. L.S. Horse — wounded 1 OR. F.G. Horse — wounded 1 OR. 8th Hussars — wounded 1 OR. 34th Horse — wounded 1 Ind. Offr. and 6 OR. (Ind. Offr. Jemadar RANJIT SINGH). 1/5th Notts Staffs — wounded 1 OR. 2/6th " " — wounded 1 OR.	

Army Form C. 2118.

WAR DIARY
or
INTELLIGENCE SUMMARY.
(Erase heading not required.)

Instructions regarding War Diaries and Intelligence Summaries are contained in F.S. Regs., Part II. and the Staff Manual respectively. Title pages will be prepared in manuscript.

Place	Date	Hour	Summary of Events and Information	Remarks and references to Appendices
NORESCOURT FARM	May. 19th		Allotment of Bomb to the U.K increased to 5 daily from today. Casualties to 12 noon :- wounded 1. O.R. 7th D.Guards - wounded 2. O.R. F.G. Horse -	
			Expenditure of Ammunition to 12 noon :- Nil. Dump of SAA + Bombs at VERMAND taken over from 35th Division. 2 OR captured by L.S. Horse - Prisoners. - Allotment of Leave to the U.K increased to 10 daily from today.	N. 143. N.X. 14. SAA 5344 Grenades No.5. 17.
	20.		Lot of Bismarck - F.G. Horse. wounded Lieut J.M FLOWERDEW (slightly at duty). Casualties to 12 noon :- Expenditure of Ammunition to 12 noon :-	N. 242. N.X. 42. SAA. 2010	Appendix "B"
	21		2 R.H.A. moved from Penruch ROUEN. Casualties to 12 noon :- 20th Horse. wounded 4. O.R. F.G. Horse. wounded Lieut. R.B. HILLS (slightly at duty) (including 1 slightly at duty)		
			Expenditure of Ammunition to 12 noon :- and 4 OR 5th Cavalry Divl. Amn. Park amalgamated in One Corps Amn. Park. but continued to be administered by the Division. Instructions in regard Supplies of SAA + Bombs	N. 107. 20% 20% Following horses took place. N.X. 7 2R. Supply between MORCHY LAGACHE SAA. 308 2R. Ammn Park to TINCOURT (J.10 c 53) and heavier Corps Troops	Appendix "C"

Army Form C. 2118.

WAR DIARY
or
INTELLIGENCE SUMMARY.
(Erase heading not required.)

Instructions regarding War Diaries and Intelligence Summaries are contained in F. S. Regs., Part II. and the Staff Manual respectively. Title pages will be prepared in manuscript.

Place	Date	Hour	Summary of Events and Information	Remarks and references to Appendices
MORESCOURT FARM	May 22nd		Casualties to 12 noon :— XX Hrs. Wounded 1 ORI. 18th Squadron M.G.C. (Cav) Wounded 1 ORB. F.G. Arse. Killed 1 ORB. 9th Arse. Wounded 1 ORI Expenditure of Ammn. to 12 noon :— N. 95 rds. NX. 31 rds. SAA 1030 rds. Grenades Nos. 25.	
	23rd		Casualties to 12 noon :— F.G. Arse. Wounded 1 ORB. (Slightly at duty) 9th Arse. Wounded 1 Ind Off. (Risaldar SIRDAR KHAN) 1 ORI. 34th Arse. Killed 1 ORI. Wounded to 12 noon :— N. 140 rds. NX. 78 rds. Wagon Lines RCHA Ride moved to W.B.d. SAA. 310 rds. Grenades Nos. 16.	
	24th		Supply Railhead changed to POISEL. Main SAA + Bomb Dump BEAUMETZ and Advanced Dump HERVILLY taken over from 5th Div. List of Units attached to 4th Div. 40 "PB" men allotted to the Division to Employment, Mainly into Area Commandants. "Q" + "U" Batteries RHA rejoined 4th Cav Div. this morning. A/295th Brigade RFA attached to 4th Div from today.	Appendix "J"

Army Form C. 2118.

WAR DIARY
or
INTELLIGENCE SUMMARY.
(Erase heading not required.)

Place	Date	Hour	Summary of Events and Information	Remarks and references to Appendices
NOBESCOURT FARM	May 24th		Expenditure of Ammunition to 12 noon:- N. 108 $\frac{1}{2}$rds A.47 $\frac{1}{2}$rds A/249 Bde came into action N of the Div at 9am { NX.71 " A.X.58 rds SAA.160 rds Casualties to 12 noon:- F.G. Horse. killed 1 OR. wounded 1 OR. Can M.G. Squadron. wounded 1 OR. (slightly at duty) 8th Hussars " 3.O.R. (includes 2 accidentally) 7th D. Guards " 1 OR. 20th Horse " 1 ORT. (slightly at duty). Prisoner 3 OR captured by 20th Horse.	
	25th		SAA & Petrol Dump HERVILLY handed over to 4th Cavalry Div. See 2nd Bde Entrance to dump in this Summary. Expenditure of Ammunition to 12 noon:- N.50 $\frac{1}{2}$rds - NX. 82 rds - SAA 60 rds - A.17 rds A.X. 10 rds - Casualties to 12 noon:- 2nd D Guards. wounded. 1 OR. (slightly at duty) R.C. Dragoons " 3.OR. (includes 2 slightly at duty) 2/5th Nork + Derby " 1 OR. (accidentally)	
	26th		Railhead (Supplies) changed to PERONNE - LA CHAPELETTE D/248 Battery RFA attached to the Division. Expenditure of Ammunition to 12 noon:- A.45 rds - AX.21 rds - N.64 rds - NX 180 rds - Casualties to 12 noon:- R.C. Dragoons - wounded. 1 OR. F.G. Horse - " 1 OR. (slightly at duty) 8th Hussars - " 3.OR. (includes 1 slightly at duty) 9th Horse. - Missing 1.ORT	

1577 Wt.W10791/1773 500,000 1/15 D. D. & L. A.D.S.S./Forms/C. 2118.

Army Form C. 2118.

WAR DIARY
or
INTELLIGENCE SUMMARY.
(Erase heading not required.)

Instructions regarding War Diaries and Intelligence Summaries are contained in F.S. Regs., Part II. and the Staff Manual respectively. Title pages will be prepared in manuscript.

Place	Date	Hour	Summary of Events and Information	Remarks and references to Appendices
NORRESCOURT FARM	May 27		152 Remounts received from ROUEN - 8 Remounts received from 4th Cav Divn - Ammunition Expenditure to 12 noon:- A. 40 rds - AX 16 rds - N. 771 rds - NX 767 rds - Box 23 rds - SAA - 35,150 rds - Grenades No 5 - 92 - Casualties to 12 noon:- L.S. Horse - Killed 1 OR - Wounded 2 OR - Canadian MG Sqdn - Wounded 1 OR -	
	28th	2.15 am	Prisoners: 17 OR captured by L.S. Horse & F.G. Horse. A successful raid was carried out by 3 troops belonging to L.S. Horse & F.G. Horse against FISHER CRATER - Sunken Road in G.32.d.10.1. and DOG'S LEG. and resulted in the capture of 17 Mausers and 12 killed, all belonging to 164th Infantry Reg. Our casualties 1 killed & 2 wounded. Ammunition Expenditure to 12 noon:- A. 36 rds - AX 37 rds - N. 173 rds - NX 128 rds - SAA 8296 rds - Grenades No 5 - 1 - Casualties to 12 noon:- R.C. Dragoons - Wounded 1 OR (slightly at duty) 7th D. Guards - Wounded 1 OR (slightly at duty) Strath - Killed 3 ORI. Wounded 4 ORI 9th Horse - Wounded 5 ORI. (includes 1 slightly at duty)	
	29th		February latest trips here were night 28th-29th (a) Canadian Cav Regt took over from 4th Cav Divn held by Secret Cav Regt. (b) Mhow Cav Regt of 4th Cav Divn took over part of the line held by Seebal Cav Regt. The 4 Carbine Regt line in the line interchange (less 3 Sub Sections 14th MG Sqdn) and returned to bivouacs between CAULIN COURT and TERTRY on Divisional Reserve. The 3 Sub-sections 14th MG Sqdn remain at the disposal of Secret Cav Regt. LAC Battery joined Canadian Cav Brigade. 3rd Artillery Group.	

Army Form C. 2118.

WAR DIARY
or
INTELLIGENCE SUMMARY.
(Erase heading not required.)

Place	Date	Hour	Summary of Events and Information	Remarks and references to Appendices
NOBESCOURT FARM	May 29th		Ammunition Expenditure to 12 noon:- A.36 - AX.22 - N.149 - NX.164 - SAA. 2600 - Grenades No 5 - 10 - 7th D. Grenades - Wounded - 2Lieut L.G. Ross and 1. O.R.B.	
	30th		Casualties to 12 noon:- Ammunition Expenditure to 12 noon:- A. 13 - AX - 27 - N. 186 - NX. 66 - RX. 57 - SAA - 7600 & - Casualties to 12 noon; - F.G. Jones - Killed 1. O.R.B. Wounded - Lieut E. Mc I HOLIDAY and 4 O.R.B. 31st A.H.E. - Wounded 4 O.R.I. 14th Squadron M.G.C. Killed 1. O.R.B.	
	31st		Disbandment of Reinforcements at Amiens Gas Bde. Commenced at VENDELLES h.L. Employed to work on the Intermediate Line. Ammunition Expenditure h 12 noon:- A.41 - AX. 22 - N. 137 - NX. 140 - RX - 85. SAA. 2710 & - Grenades No 5 - 1. O.R.B. (Slightly at duty) Casualties to 12 noon :- 7th D. Grenades - Wounded - 1. O.R.B.	

M.M. Lambton
a/c S. Lambton Inst 1/6/17
S. Coy

(Appendix "A")

No.Q/392   Headquarters 5th.Cavalry Division.

Dated 13th.May 1917.

SECRET

To/
Brigades and Divisional Troops.
===============================

The attached Administrative Instructions are forwarded for information and necessary action.

Lieut-Colonel
A.A.and Q.M.G.
5th.Cavalry Division

Copies to :-

General Staff
"A" Section
Field Cashier
Gas Officer

ADMINISTRATIVE INSTRUCTIONS

Reference No.G.S.573/1 dated 11th.May and No. G.531 dated 13th.May 1917.

1. **SUPPLY ARRANGEMENTS.**

	Canadian Brigade and other units in same sector.	Secbad Brigade and other units in same sector.
(a) Brigade Supply Officer	Capt. THOMAS	Lt. PEMBERTON
---------do--------- (for troops in back area)	Lieut. HALL	Capt. SHORT
Brigade Transport Officer	Capt. BROWN	Lieut. KEEFE
---------do--------- (for troops in back area)	Lieut. HALL	Capt. SHORT
Refilling Point	X Rds.in W.11.c	X Rds.in W.11.c.
Transport Lines	VERMAND	MONTIGNY Farm. (Essential vehicles only. Remainder to return to Back area).

(b) Supplies will be taken from the refilling point to units in L.G.S. Wagons of the Reserve Park. The load in each wagon will not exceed 1000 lbs and animals will be changed daily.

(c) B.T.O's will be in charge of Supply Trains and will join the Reserve Park (West of X rds.in W.11.c.) as under :-

    B.T.O. Canadian Brigade on the 14th.May 1917, at 6 pm.
    B.T.O. Secbad Brigade on the 15th.May 1917 at 6 pm.

Regiments and Batteries will detail 1 N.C.O. and 1 man, and other units 1 N.C.O. or 1 reliable man to report to the B.T.O's at the same time and place.
These men will be attached to the Supply Trains.
Their duties are to take over the supplies of the units at the refilling point, help to load them and be responsible for their safe custody, until delivered.

(d) The Supply trains will start daily from the refilling point so as to arrive at the following places at 8 pm where they will be met by guides sent by each unit.

    (i) X Rds in BIHECOURT for...(Canadian Brigade, 2 Batteries of
                                    (16th.Brigade R.H.A.*,
                                      (Adv.Dressing Station, Canadian
                                      (Field Ambulance.

(2) Road Junction at Western   (Secbad Brigade, "X" and
    Entrance of ~~HANCOURT~~ for...   ("N" Batteries, R.C.H.A.
~~via MONTIGNY Farm where sup-~~   (Brigade(including wagon
~~plies will be delivered for~~   (lines), Advanced Dressing
~~Bde.Hdqrs~~   (Station, Secbad Field Ambce.
~~Field Sqdn(less 2 Troops)~~
~~Wagon Lines R.C.H.A. Bde.)~~

(circled: VENDELLES)
(circled: battery) — replacing "each"

* On the 15th., one section each~~each~~ only. Remainder draw direct from Refilling Point.

From these points supplies will be delivered to Units under Brigade Arrangements.
B.S.O's are responsible for the delivery of supplies at Unit Hdqrs; beyond this point they will be delivered under regimental arrangements.

(e) These arrangements will come into force for :-

    (1) Canadian Brigade and other units in the same sector, on the 15th, for supplies of the 16th.
    (2) Secbad Brigade and other units in the same sector, on the 16th, for supplies of the 17th.

(f) Brigades and other units will take with them supplies for the day following the night on which they take over the line.

(g) Supplies for the remainder of the Division will be delivered as follows :-

    (1) Divisional Headquarters   (By Lorry.
    (2) Tent Section, Secbad Field Ambce. (
        (At BOUVINCOURT).

    (3) ~~17th.Bde R.H.A. Wagon Lines~~   (On unit's transport
    (4) 17th.Bde Ammunition Column   (wagons from the Re-
    (5) 16th.Bde Ammunition Column   (filling Point W. of
    (6) Troops in back area   (MONTECOURT.

    (7) Wagon lines of 2 batteries,   (Direct from Refilling
        16th.Brigade R.H.A.   (Point at W.11.c. on their
    17th Bde. R.H.A. wagon lines   (own transport.

2. <u>TRENCH STORES.</u>
                         After taking over the line, Brigades will send to Divisional Headquarters a list of Trench Stores, and also tentage and trench covers taken over.
        All petrol tins used for water must also be taken over from relieved units.

3. <u>WATER.</u>
                    Water carts will be detailed as under :-

    (a) For duty with the Secbad Brigade...(1 from Secbad Fd.Ambce.
                                              (1 from Mhow Fd.Ambce.
    (b) For duty with the Canadian Brigade.(1 from Can.Fd.Ambce.
                                                  (1 from a regiment of
                                                 (the brigade.*

                                                            *Will..............

* Will be replaced by a
G.S.Wagon fitted with
tank at present in
charge of A.S.C.Hdqrs.

The O.C. A.S.C. will supply extra petrol tins for carriage of water. Brigades and other units will inform him as soon as possible how many they will require.

A list of wells and other sources from which drinking water can be obtained will be sent to all units.

4. AMMUNITION.

    (a) <u>13 pdr.</u>
        A dump is established at X rds.Q.8.c.8.3. (3000 N.
                                                                                         (3000 N.X.
        A second dump will be formed near the Ammunition Column.

    (b) Small Arm, Bombs, Grenades, Very Pistol Ammn etc,:-

        Brigade Dump at R.10.d.9.6.
        Brigade Dump at JEANCOURT.

These dumps will be taken over by Brigades from the relieved infantry brigades.

The amount of S.A.A., bombs, etc., taken over in the line and in the dumps will be reported to Divisional Headquarters as soon as possible.

Brigade dumps will be replenished from advanced Divisional dumps. The position of these dumps will be notified later.

5.   R.E.Dump is at MONTIGNY.

(Appendix "B")

LIST OF BIVOUACS - 5TH. CAVALRY DIVISION.

Divisional Hqrs............	NOBESCOURT FARM.
Field Cashier.............	MORCHAIN.
Signal Squadron...........	NOBESCOURT FARM.
Field Squadron, R.E.......	MONTIGNY.
Field Sqdn.(Back Area)....	S.W. of TERTRY (W.8.b.3.9.)
C.R.H.A..................	NOBESCOURT FARM.
17th. R.H.A.Bde.Amn.Col... (	E. of TERTRY.(W.2.a/b.)
R.C.H.A.Bde.Amn.Col....... (	
Ammunition Park...........	POTTE.
Supply Column.............	MORCHAIN.
Sanitary Section..........	NOBESCOURT FARM.
No.9 L.A.C.Battery........	att'd Canadian Cav. Bde.
" " (Lorries),,	E. of TERTRY.(W.2.b.)
A.H.T.Coy................	W.1.d.7.9.
5th.Cav.Reserve Park......	(E. of X Roads in W.11.c.
No.5 Sec.10th.Res.Park.... (	
Railhead Supplies.........	NESLE.

AMBALA CAVALRY BRIGADE.

Brigade Hqrs..............	Wood E. of CAULAINCOURT(W.5.a.9.7.)
8th. Hussars.)	
9th. Horse.)	
18th. Lancers.)......(Back Area)	Bivouacs between CAULAINCOURT & TERTRY.
No.14 M.G.Sqn.)	
M.V.Section.)	
"X" Battery........(Wagon Lines)	W.3.b.9.4.
Mhow I.C.F.A..............	CAULAINCOURT.

SEC'BAD CAVALRY BRIGADE.

Brigade Hqrs.(Back Area)...	TREFCON(W.10.a.5.7.)
7th. Dragoon Guards.)	
20th. Hodson.)	
34th. Horse.) (Back	
No.13 M.G.Sqdn.) Area)..	Bivouacs about TREFCON.
M.V.Section.)	
"N" Battery....(Wagon Lines)..,	W.11.a.(Central)
Sec'bad I.C.F.A.(Tent Section).	St.CREN.

CANADIAN CAVALRY BRIGADE.

Brigade Hqrs..............	MONCHY LAGACHE.
R.C.Dragoons.)	
L.S.Horse.)	
F.G.Horse.) (Back Area)	Bivouacs between
Can. M.G.Sqdn.)	DEVISE and MEREAUCOURT.
Can. M.V.Section.)	
R.C.H.A.Brigade(Wagon Lines....	V.4.a. & c.
Can.C.F.A................	MEREAUCOURT.

ATTACHED.

"Q" Battery, R.H.A.) (Wagon Lines)	W.6.d. & X.1.a.
"U" " " "	
16th. Bde. R.H.A. Am.Col.(2Sections)	E. of TERTRY(W.2.a. & b.)

No.Q/213/3.   Headquarters, 5th. Cavalry Division.
                                              20th. May 1917.
To/
  Cavalry Corps "Q".
              Forwarded.
                                            J H Cobbe
                                         Lieut-Colonel,
                              for G.O.C., 5th. Cavalry Division,

Copies to :-
    Usual Billeting List Distribution.

(Appendix "C")

Subject :- AMMUNITION SUPPLY (S.A.A. and BOMBS).

No.Q/392/a/7.   Headquarters 5th.Cavalry Division

20th.May 1917.

To/ Canadian Cavalry Brigade
    Sec'bad Cavalry Brigade
    Ambala Cavalry Brigade
    C.R.H.A.
    O.i/c Adv.Ammn.Dump, VERMAND.
    ---------do------ HERVILLY.
    O.i/c Main Ammn.Dump BEAUMETZ.
    O.C.17th.Brigade Ammn.Column.
    =========================

1.   Brigades will draw to complete their Brigade Dumps to establishment on the advanced Divisional Dumps i.e.,

    Canadian Cavalry Brigade...Adv.Dump VERMAND.
    Sec'bad Cavalry Brigade.... --do--- HERVILLY.

2.   Officers i/c Adv.Divnl.Dumps will meet all demands by brigades and will refill to establishment by indonting on the Divnl.Ammn.Column at CAUVIGNY FARM. O.C.Ammn.Col.will send one push bicycle to the O.i/c Dump at VERMAND, and one of the motor cycles attached to them from the Ammn.Park to O.i/c Dump HERVILLY, for purposes of communication.

3.   On receipt of demands from the Adv.Divnl.Dumps, the Ammn.Col.will draw the ammunition required from the main Divnl.Dump at BEAUMETZ, and deliver it to the Advcd.Dumps.

4.   Demands to complete Main Divnl.Dump, will be made by this office from the Daily Ammunition Return.

5.   Ammunition Returns will be rendered daily by the O.^{s} i/c Dumps to reach this office by 4pm daily. They will be made up from 12 noon to 12 noon.

                                J.S. Whitcombe
                                            Capt. for
                        A.A.and Q.M.G. 5th.Cavalry Division.

Copies to :-
            Ammunition Park.
            General Staff.

ESTABLISHMENTS

	Main Dump	Adv. Divl. Dump	Bde Dumps	Remarks
S.A.A	400,000	300,000	250,000	
Grenades No. 5	20,000	10,000	4,000	
Grenades No. 23	1,500	750	500	
Grenades Nos. 3 & 20	3000	1,500	1000	80% of each.
Pistol Webley	5,064	2,532	2,532	
Very Lights 1"	30	15	8	Boxes
Very Lights 1½"	40	20	12	Boxes
Ground Flares	700	400	300	
S.O.S. Tins	30	17	10	Tins "A" Variation 4 Red Stars
Smoke Candles	700	400	150	
"P" Bombs	700	400	—	

Headquarters 5th. Cavalry Division.
May, 1917.

AMMUNITION SUPPLY.

5th. Cavalry Divisional Artillery.	Canadian Cavalry Brigade (Sector A.1).	Sec'Bad Cavalry Bde. (Sector A.2).
	Brigade Dump (S.A.A. and BOMBS). R.16.b.9.9.	Brigade Dump. (S.A.A. and BOMBS). JEANCOURT.
Wagon Lines.		
	Advanced Divnl. Dump. (S.A.A. and BOMBS). VERMAND.	Advanced Divnl. Dump. (S.A.A. and BOMBS). HERVILLY.
Ammn. Column. CAUVIGNY FARM.		
	Main Divisional Dump. (S.A.A. and BOMBS). BEAUMETZ.	
REFILLING POINT. HANCOURT.		
	Ammunition Park. J.15.d.6.0.	
	Railhead O.J. OURCHY.	

Note. Ammunition Column draws on Main Ammn. Dump and delivers to Advanced Divnl. Dumps.
For Gun Ammunition, works between Wagon Lines of Batteries and A.R.P. HANCOURT.

(Appendix D)

LIST OF UNITS ATTACHED.

To Cavalry Corps.   Location.
109th. Siege Battery.   Draw direct from R.P.
282nd. A.H.T.Coy.   BETHENCOURT.
~~145th. Labour   "~~   ~~MARCHELPOT.~~
8th. Labour Battalion.   ~~NESLE & ROUY LE GRAND.~~ Mons en Chaussee
No.36 M.A.C.   LANGUEVOISIN.
"D" Coy.21st.Gn.Bn.K.O.Y.L.I.

To 5th. Cavalry Division.
62nd. H.A.Group.   FORESTE.
89th. H.A.Group.   CAULAINCOURT.
1/1st.London (H) Battery.   VILLEVEQUE.
110th. H.Battery.   MARTEVILLE.
115th. H.Battery.   VAUX.
125th. H.Battery.   VAUX.
216th. Siege Battery.   Draw from R.P.
119th. Siege Battery.   -- do --
Hqrs. IV Corps H.A.   VOYENNES.
K.E.H.   EPANANCOURT.
IV Corps Cyclist Battalion.   ST.CHRIST.

For rations only.
9th. Squadron, R.F.C.   ESTREES EN CHAUSSEE.
14th. Wing, R.F.C.   GUIZANCOURT.
21st. C.C.Station.   NESLE.
21st. Hygiene Laboratory.   NESLE.
Railhead Party.   CURCHY.
50th. A.A.Battery.   I.13.c.6.4.
20th. Balloon Coy.   X.7.a.
7th. Squadron, R.F.C.   MATIGNY.
61st. Divnl. Sanitary Section.   TERTRY.
Lovat's Scouts.   TEMPLEUX LE GUERRARD.
~~Cable and Air Line.~~   ~~K.28.a.~~
"D" Corps Siege Park.   ?
34th Sqdn R.F.C.   VOYENNES
35th Ammn Sub Park.   ?

(Administrative)

Army Form C. 2118.

WAR DIARY
~~INTELLIGENCE SUMMARY~~
(Erase heading not required.)

HEADQUARTERS
5th CAVALRY DIVISION

Place	Date	Hour	Summary of Events and Information	Remarks and references to Appendices
NOBESCOURT FARM	JUNE 1st		Ammunition Expenditure to 12 noon :- A. 6. - AX. 38. - N. 211. - NX. 150. - RX. 85. Casualties to 12 noon :- 34th Hrse. Wounded 1. ORs. (Slightly at duty).	
	2nd		Ammunition Expenditure to 12 noon :- A. 32. - AX. 42. - N. 212. - NX. 132. - RX. 48. - SAA. 452. Casualties to 12 noon :- R.C. Dragoons Wounded 1. ORs. (Slightly at duty)	
	3rd		Administrative Instructions for the relief of the Canadian Cavalry Brigade by the Canadian Cavalry Brigade. Ammunition Expenditure to 12 noon :- A. 55. - AX. 31. - N. 942. - NX. 882. - RX. 47. - SAA - 4010 rds. - Grenades N°S - 6. Casualties to 12 noon :- 14th Squadron M.G.C. (Cav.) Wounded (gas) - 2Lt C.V.M. CHASE.	Appendix A
	4th		Ammunition Expenditure to 12 noon :- A. 7. - AX. 58. - N. 135. - NX. 142. - RX. 46. SAA (1624 rds) Casualties to 12 noon :- 34th Horse - Wounded 2. ORs. "N" Battery R.H.A. Wounded 1. OR.B (Slightly at duty) 9th LAC Battery Wounded 1. OR.B (accidentally)	
	5th		Main SAA + Bomb Dump at BEAUMETZ cleared by Cav Corps. New Establishment Ammunition Expenditure to 12 noon :- A. 12. - AX 30. - N. 70. - NX. 81. SAA - 5800 rds - Casualties to 12 noon :- 34th Hrse - Killed 3 ORs. Wounded 1 ORs. "X" Battery Wounded 1 ORs accidentally (Since died of wounds) "N" Battery Wounded 1 ORs.	Appendix "B"
	5th. 6th (night)		Ambala Cav. Regt. relieved the Canadian Cav. Bde in the Line.	

Army Form C. 2118.

WAR DIARY
or
INTELLIGENCE SUMMARY.
(Erase heading not required.)

Instructions regarding War Diaries and Intelligence Summaries are contained in F. S. Regs., Part II. and the Staff Manual respectively. Title pages will be prepared in manuscript.

Place	Date	Hour	Summary of Events and Information	Remarks and references to Appendices
MORESCOURT FARM	JUNE 6th		Canadian Dismounted men encamped at VENDELLES to take on Junior medical Leave allotment to the United Kingdom reduced from 10 to 9 per day. Ammunition Expenditure to 12 noon:- A. 46 - AX 42 - N. 159 - NX. 192. Bx. 26. SAA. 769 Rds. - Grenades N°5. 9 - Grenade N°20. 3 -	
	7th		Casualties to 12 noon:- 2nd Horse. Killed. 1 ORI. Wounded. Lt. A.S. GODFREE (slightly at duty) 7th D Guards. Wounded. 1. ORR. Ammunition Expenditure to 12 noon:- A. 18 - AX 39 - N. 102 - NX. 46 - BX 33 - SAA. 562 - Grenade N°20 - 6.	
	8th		Casualties to 12 noon:- 7th D Guards. Killed. 1 ORR. Wounded. 3. ORR. R.C.H.A. Batt. Wounded. 3. ORB. (slightly at duty) Ammunition Expenditure to 12 noon:- A. 20 - AX. 8 - N. 116 - NX. 82 - BX. 33 - SAA 45 Rds. - Grenades N°23. 4 -	
	9th		Casualties to 12 noon:- Nil. 2nd additional P.B. men attached to the Division to take into the Dual Aux. Command* Ammunition Expenditure to 12 noon:- A. 79 - AX. 7 - N. 167 - NX. 118 - BX. 20 - SAA. 255 Rds. - Grenades N°23. 1 - Casualties to 12 noon:- "B" Battery R.C.H.A. Killed. 1 ORR. Wounded. Lt. J.C. MURCHIE and 2 ORR.	
	10th		Ammunition Expenditure to 12 noon:- A. 125 - AX 196. N. 554 - NX. 721 - BX. 98 - SAA. 1620 Rds. N°5 Grenade - 29 - Casualties to 12 noon:- 8th Hussars Wounded Capt. E.G. WELDON & 4 ORA (includes 1 slightly at duty) 18th Lancers Killed 1 ORI Wounded Lt. D.W.M. PRINSEP (3rd Horse attd 18th L) 20th Horse Killed 1 ORI and 4 ORI (includes 2 slightly at duty) 3 Chargers and 37 LDH arrived from Remount ABBEVILLE -	

Army Form C. 2118.

Instructions regarding War Diaries and Intelligence Summaries are contained in F.S. Regs., Part II. and the Staff Manual respectively. Title pages will be prepared in manuscript.

WAR DIARY
or
INTELLIGENCE SUMMARY.
(Erase heading not required.)

Place	Date	Hour	Summary of Events and Information	Remarks and references to Appendices
NOBESCOURT FARM	JUNE 11th		Ammunition Expenditure to 12 noon :- A. 54 - AX - 107 - N. 470 - NX. 5335 - BX. 63 - SAA 170 rds. Casualties to 12 noon :- 18th Lancers, wounded. 1. ORI. Aux. H.T. Coy. wounded 1. ORB (accidentally) since died.	
	12th		100 OR of the Indian Cavalry Entrenching Battalion allotted to the Division to work in loads. Ammunition Expenditure to 12 noon :- A.28 - AX 9 - N.227 - NX 168 - BX. 22 - Casualties to 12 noon :- 8th Hussars - 1. ORB reported wounded (slightly at duty) on 10th June since admitted to hospital on return of wounds.	
	13th		Ammunition Expenditure to 12 noon :- A.218 - AX.217 - N.472 - NX.470 - BX. 166 - SAA. 18139 rds - Grenades Nº5. 147 - Casualties to 12 noon :- 20th Jnrs. Killed. 4 ORI. wounded. Capt (T/Major) A.C. Ross. D.S.O. (Secunderabad Cav. Bde.), I.A.R (slightly at duty), Lieut. L.A. GLASSPOOL - I.A.R (slightly at duty) and 22 ORI (includes 5 slightly at duty). Ressaidar DALIP SINGH, I.A.R. and 4 ORI. Lieut. E.E. LAWFORD. I.A.R. wounded. 2. ORI. 34th Horse wounded. 2. ORI. 12th Cavalry ath 18th Lancers - wounded. 1. ORI. 8 Chargers received from Remount ROUEN Following horse took place to-day :- 5th Cavalry Reserve Park h V.6 d 5th Section to Reserve Park h V.6 d "N" Railway head Line to Q. 33.6. Adv Refilling Point (Supplies) h V.11.a 9.8.	
	14th		Ammunition Expenditure to 12 noon :- A. 36 - AX - 289 - N. 281 - NX. 292 - BX. 1114 - SAA. 28 rds. Grenades Nº5 - 36.	

Army Form C. 2118.

WAR DIARY
or
INTELLIGENCE SUMMARY.
(Erase heading not required.)

Instructions regarding War Diaries and Intelligence Summaries are contained in F. S. Regs., Part II. and the Staff Manual respectively. Title pages will be prepared in manuscript.

Place	Date	Hour	Summary of Events and Information	Remarks and references to Appendices
NOBESCOURT FARM	June 14th		Casualties to 12 noon :- 18th Lancers - Wounded - Lt (Ty Capt) D.S. FRAZER; Jemadar KEHAR SINGH (39th Horse att) and 5 ORI. 20th Horse - Killed - 4 ORI. Wounded - 2 ORI.	(Adminiature Instructions "Armour C")
	14th/15th Night		Canadian Cav RDR relieved Secunderabad Cav Bde in the Line. Ammunition Expenditure to 12 noon :- A. 52 - AX. 87 - N. 272 - NX. 245 - BX. 197 - No 5 Grenades - 12 - "P" Bombs - 6 -	
	15th		Casualties to 12 noon :- A/295 Brigade RFA. Wounded 1 OR. (slightly at duty) 3rd Horse (att 18th Lancers) Killed 1 ORI. Wounded - 1 ORI. 20th Horse. Killed 1 ORI. Wounded - 1 ORI.	
	16th		Ammunition Expenditure to 12 noon :- A. 88 - AX. 12 - N. 114 - NX. 67 - BX. 61 - Casualties to 12 noon - 18th Lancers. Wounded - 1 ORI.	
	17th		8 Officer Riding Horses received from Remount ROUEN. "D" Battery RHA attached to the Division today into S.Sings. Ammunition Expenditure to 12 noon :- A. 168 - AX. 131 - N. 131 - NX. 90 - BX. 142 - SAA. 2050 rds - Grenades No 5 - 6 - F.G. Horse - Wounded - 2. ORR.	
	18th		Casualties to 12 noon :- Sailings via BOULOGNE. Embarked horse from their orders h. 12 noon :- A. 67 - AX. 38 - N. 153 - NX. 141 - BX. 163 - Ammunition Expenditure. SAA. 400 rds.	
	19th		Casualties to 12 noon :- Nil. BOULOGNE Sailing resumed - Ammunition Expenditure to 12 noon :- A. 297 - AX. 270 - N. 1337 - NX. 1222 - BX. 155 - SAA. 49,950 rds - Grenades No. 83 - "P" Bombs. 20 -	

WAR DIARY or INTELLIGENCE SUMMARY

Army Form C. 2118.

Place	Date	Hour	Summary of Events and Information	Remarks and references to Appendices
NOBESCOURT FARM	JUNE 19th		Early this morning a raid was carried out by the Right 2nd Sectn (9th Italian Infse) against the trench of a post in the vicinity of ST HELENE. The trench was entirely successful, the whole of the garrison of the section (18) being accounted for. 3 dugouts burnt, and 3 prisoners of the 186th Regt. being taken. Our casualties 3 slightly wounded. Casualties to 12 noon:- 8th Hussars - Wounded 1 ORR. 9th Hsrs - Bombed Lt. G. WILSON (slightly at duty) and 6 ORR. (includes 14 slightly at duty) Wounded Lt. F.G. BUTTERFIELD F.G. Horse. Killed 1 ORR - Wounded 1 ORR. "D" Battery 298 Bde RFA and "D" Battery R.H.A. returned to 4th Cavalry Div.	
	20th		Ammunition Expenditure to 12 noon:- A.19.- AX 1. - N. 239 - NX. 182 - RX. 26.- SAA. 1100 rds - Grenade Ns. 18.- Casualties to 12 noon:- F.G. Horse - Wounded 3 ORR. (Includes 1 slightly at duty). 64 animals received from Remounts ROUEN. Ammunition Expenditure to 12 noon:- A 57 - AX 11 - N. 101 - NX 104 - RX 25.- SAA. 1040 rds.	
	21st		Casualties to 12 noon:- 9th Hsrs - Wounded 1 ORI. Mhow I.C.F.A. Wounded 1 ORI. (accidentally) Ammunition Expenditure to 12 noon:- A. 15.- AX. 88.- N. 270 - NX. 181 - RX. 25.- SAA. 31750 rds	
	22nd		Casualties to 12 noon :- 8th Hussars - Wounded Lt. D.W. DALY (slightly at duty) and 3 ORR. Canadian M.G. Squadron - Wounded 1 ORR. (slightly at duty) West of Ambala Cav Bde in the line by Seebel Cav Bde on the night 23rd/24th inst.	Administrative Instructions issued for the Appendix "D"

Army Form C. 2118.

WAR DIARY
or
INTELLIGENCE SUMMARY.
(Erase heading not required.)

Place	Date	Hour	Summary of Events and Information	Remarks and references to Appendices
NORESCOURT FARM	JUNE 23rd	to 12 noon	Ammunition Expenditure to 12 noon :- A 50 - AX. 23 - N. 175 - NX. 237 - BX. 25 - Casualties to 12 noon :- 18th Lancers - Wounded 1. ORR (slightly, at duty) L/Dvr. W. DALY 8th Hussars, and 1. ORR Gun MG Squadron reported wounded (slightly at duty) on June 22nd, have since been admitted to hospital as a result of wounds.	
	23rd/24th	Night	Secunderabad Cav. Bde. relieved Ambala Cav. Bde. in Sub-Section A.I. and Ambala Bde. withdrawn to Back Area (Nainsel).	
	24th		N° 5 Section 10th Reserve Park amalgamates with 3rd Cavalry Reserve Park and its whole unit designates (by the taken name. The Park is now organised in two Sections, a Major Section, comprising 63 L.G.S. wagons, and a Heavy Section comprising 62 G.S. wagons. Ammunition Expenditure to 12 noon :- A.52 - AX. 35 - N. 135 - NX. 475 - BX. 25 - Casualties to 12 noon :- Nil.	
	25th		Ammunition Expenditure to 12 noon :- A. 66 - AX. 24 - N. 91 - NX. 279 - BX. 25 - Casualties to 12 noon :- 34th Horse - (Killed) 1. ORR - Wounded 2. ORR - Missing 1. ORR. "D" Battery 298 Bde. - Wounded 1. ORR.	
	26th		Ammunition Dump at VERMAND moved to Q.35.C.34. N of CAULAINCOURT. Ammunition Expenditure to 12 noon :- A.39 - AX. 19 - N. 265 - NX. 349 - BX. 25 - SAA 200 Rds. Grenades N°5. 9 - Casualties to 12 noon :- L.S. Horse - Wounded Lieut. J.G. TATLOW, M.C. (slightly at duty). 34th Horse - 1. ORR reported missing on June 25th since returned.	
	27th		Ammunition Expenditure to 12 noon :- A. 41 - AX. 28 - N. 117 - NX. 173 - BX. 25 - SAA 150 - Casualties to 12 noon :- Nil.	

WAR DIARY or INTELLIGENCE SUMMARY

Army Form C. 2118.

Place	Date	Hour	Summary of Events and Information	Remarks and references to Appendices
NOBESCOURT FARM	June 28th		2 Guns of No 9. L.A.C. Battery temporarily detached to 3rd Cav: Div: from H.Qrs. Ammunition Expenditure to 12 noon :- A.15 - AX.85 - N.163 - NX.264 - RX.9. SAA. 202 rds - Grenades Nos. 10.- Casualties to 12 noon :- 3 rd Horse - Killed. 1. ORT - L.S. Horse - Wounded. 1. ORR - (on 26.6.17, wounded today).	
	29th		Ammunition Expenditure to 12 noon :- A.40 - AX.11 - N.175 - NX.298 - RX.25. SAA. 6750 rds.- Casualties to 12 noon :- NIL	
	30th		Ammunition Expenditure to 12 noon :- A.36 - AX.25 - N.158 - NX.239 - RX.15.- SAA. 10218 rds.- Casualties to 12 noon :- 3rd Horse - Wounded - 1. ORT - Missing. 1. ORT.-	

J.P. Vincent Cpt
Lieut ? Signaller
for g.o.c. 5th Cavalry
for g.o.c.

SECRET.

(Appendix "A" June '17)
No. Q/392/1

ADMINISTRATIVE INSTRUCTIONS.

Reference Operation Order No.32 dated 31/5/17.

1. **SUPPLY ARRANGEMENTS.**

    (a) <u>Canadian Cavalry Brigade (less forward details of Hqrs. and 2 sections M.G. Squadron).</u>

    Supplies will be issued on the 5th. June (for the 6th.) and thereafter in the Back Area except for D.Rs (see (d) below).

    (b) <u>Ambala Cavalry Brigade.</u>

    Units going in to the line will take with them their supplies for the 6th. After this, the supply arrangements will be as before for this Sub-Sector. (Full details of these arrangements are forwarded separately to the Ambala Cavalry Brigade).

    (c) <u>Hqrs. and 2 Sections Canadian M.G.Sqdn.(Forward Details).</u>

    Supplies for the 5th. and thereafter will be sent up to the line as usual.

    (d) <u>Ambala Brigade D.Rs.</u>

    Supplies will be issued on the 5th. and thereafter in the Back Area.

    <u>Canadian Brigade D Rs.</u>

    Advanced Party will take its supplies for the 5th. and 6th. to VENDELLES. On the 6th. and thereafter supplies will be issued for the whole party at VENDELLES.

2. **RESERVE RATIONS.**

    2 days British rations are kept in advanced posts and 500 British rations at Brigade Headquarters. The O.C., A.S.C. will arrange, in communication with the Ambala Brigade, to substitute Indian Rations for British in those posts which are taken over by Indian Troops, and also to maintain a proportion of Indian Rations at Brigade Hqrs. to meet deficiencies.

3. After the relief has been completed, the Ambala Brigade will send to Divnl. Hqrs. statements showing :-

    (1) S.A.A. and Grenades, taken over in the line.
    (2) --- do --- --- do --- the Brigade Dump.
    (3) Reserve Rations taken over.
    (4) Trench Stores taken over.
    (5) Tents and Trench Covers taken over.
    (6) The number of Petrol Tins taken over. (All tins in possession of Canadian Brigade must be handed over).

4. The G.S.Wagon fitted with water tank at present with the Canadian Bde. Back Details will be handed over to O.C., Ambala Bde. Back Details.

Lieut-Colonel,
A.A.& Q.M.G., 5th. Cavalry Division.

To/
Canadian Cav.Bde.   O.C., Ambala Cav.Bde.Back.Details.
Ambala Cav.Bde.   O.C., A.S.C. A.D.M.S. "G".
O.C., Can.Cav.Bde.Back Details. D.A.D.O.S. A.D.V.S. "A".

3/6/17.

(Appendix 'B') June '17

No. Q/392/a/18.   Headquarters 5th.Cavalry Division.

                              4th. June 1917.

To/
    Canadian Cavalry Brigade.
    Ambala   "   "
    Sec'bad   "   "
    Officer i/c S.A.A. Dump VERMAND.
    =====================================

The following is the amended establishment to be held in Brigade and Advanced Divisional Dumps.

The Main Divisional Dump at BEAUMETZ is being cleared by Cavalry Corps on the 5th.instant. After this date, the Advanced Dump VERMAND will be kept up to establishment by this office, demands being based on the Daily Ammunition Return.

NATURE OF AMMN.	BRIGADE DUMPS.	ADVANCED DUMPS. (VERMAND & HERVILLY)
S.A.A.	250,000	500,000
Grenades No.5	4,000	10,000
" " 23	350	650
" " 3)		
" " 20 or 24)	350	650
" S.O.S. "A"	12 tins.	30 tins.
Pistol Webley	2,532	5,064
Very Lights 1" (White)	10 boxes.	20 boxes.
" " (Red)	-	150 cartridges.
" " (Green)	-	150 "
" " 1½"(White)	12 boxes.	25 boxes.
" " (Red)	-	90 cartridges.
" " (Green)	-	90 "
Rockets G.S. Rain	20	30
" Parachute, Red	-	50
" " Green	-	50
" " White	-	50
"P" Bombs	-	400

                              P. S. Whitcombe
                              Captain for
                   A.A. and Q.M.G. 5th.Cavalry Division.

Copy to :-
    4th. Cavalry Division "Q".

Will you kindly hold ammunition to the establishment shown in your dump at HERVILLY for this division.

As regards the Brigade Dump at JEANCOURT, the establishment shown is for the left subsector of this Division. Will you please say if you would like an equal amount held for your right subsector.

                              P. S. Whitcombe
                                   Captain
                   for G.O.C., 5th.Cavalry Division.

(Appendix "B")

No. Q/392/5.   S E C R E T.

Headquarters, 5th Cavalry Division,

15th June, 1917.

ADMINISTRATIVE INSTRUCTIONS.

Reference Operation Order No.33, dated 9/6/17.

1. SUPPLY ARRANGEMENTS.

   (a) Supplies for the 15th will be taken by the Canadian Brigade into the line.

   (b) Supplies for the 15th for Sec'bad Brigade and 1 Section No.13 M.G. Squadron will be delivered on the 14th in the Back Area.

   (c) Sec'bad Dismounted Reinforcements. The advance party referred to in para 3 (b) ii, will take with it supplies for the 14th and 15th. Supplies for the whole party for the 16th will be delivered in VENDELLES on the 15th.

   (d) Canadian Dismounted Reinforcements. Supplies for the 15th will be issued on the 14th in the Back Area instead of VENDELLES.

   (e) Supplies for the Hqrs. and 2 Sections No. 13 M.G. Squadron and the Canadian M.G. Squadron for the 15th will be sent into the line on the night 14/15th as usual.

   (f) After the above dates the issue of supplies will continue under normal arrangements. Details of these arrangements for Sub-Sector A-2 are sent separately to the Canadian Cavalry Brigade.

2. RESERVE RATIONS.

   The O.C., A.S.C. will arrange in communication with the Canadian Brigade to substitute two days British Rations for two days Indian Rations in those advanced posts which are taken over from Indian Units. All Indian Rations will be withdrawn from those posts, but left at Brigade Hqrs. in view of further reliefs.

3. After the relief has been completed, the Canadian Brigade will send to Divnl. Hqrs. statements showing:-
   (1) S.A.A. and Grenades, etc., taken over in the line (giving locations)
   (2) ---do---   ---do--- in the Bde Dump.
   (3) Quantities and location of Reserve Rations.
   (4) Trench Stores taken over.
   (5) Tents and trench covers taken over.
   (6) The number of petrol tins taken over. (All tins in possession of Sec'bad Brigade must be handed over.

4. WATER.

   The G.S. Wagon fitted with a water tank at present with Ambala Bde Back Area Details will be handed over on the 15th to O.C., Canadian Bde Back Area Details, and the water lorry at present with Mhow F. Ambulance for duty with Sec'bad Back Details will be handed over to Canadian F. Ambulance for duty with the Canadian Back Details.

   A.A.& Q.M.G., 5th Cavalry Division.
   Lieut-Colonel,

To/ Sec'bad Cav.Bde.
    Ambala   "   "
    Canadian   "   "
    Os.C., Back Area Details.

O.C.A.S.C.   D.A.D.O.S.   A.D.M.S.
A.D.V.S.   "G"   "A".

(Appendix D)

SECRET.

Headquarters, 5th Cavalry Division.
22nd June, 1917.

No.Q/392/2.

ADMINISTRATIVE INSTRUCTIONS.

Reference Operation Order No.34 dated 20/6/17

1. **SUPPLY ARRANGEMENTS.**

    (a) Supplies for the 24th will be taken by Sec'bad Brigade into the line.

    (b) Supplies for the 24th for Ambala Brigade and 1 Section No.14 M.G.Sqdn. will be delivered on the 23rd in the Back Area.

    (c) Ambala Brigade Dismounted Reinforcements. The advance party referred to in para 4 (b) (ii) will take with it supplies for 23rd and 24th. Supplies for the whole party for the 25th will be delivered in VENDELLES on the 24th.

    (d) Sec'bad Brigade Dismounted Reinforcements. Supplies for the 24th will be issued on the 23rd with the supplies of the remainder of the Brigade.

    (e) Supplies for the Hqrs. and 2 Sections No.14 M.G. Sqdn. and No. 9 L.A.C. Battery will be sent into the line on the night 23/24th as usual.

    (f) After the above dates the issue of supplies will continue under normal arrangements. Appendices "E" & "G" of the defence scheme, showing arrangements for supplies, ammunition and other administrative details are forwarded separately to the Sec'bad Brigade.

2. After the relief has been completed the Sec'bad Brigade will send to Divnl Hqrs a statement showing :-

    (1) S.A.A. & Grenades,etc., taken over in the line(giving locations)
    (2) --- do ---   --- do ---   --- do -- Bde Dump.
    (3) Quantities and locations of Reserve Rations.
    (4) Trench Stores taken over.
    (5) Tents and trench covers taken over.
    (6) The number of petrol tins taken over.(all tins in possession of Ambala Brigade must be handed over).

3. Ambala Brigade will hand over to Sec'bad Brigade 42 sets of Yukon Pack.

4. On being withdrawn to the training area, the G.O.C., Ambala Brigade will assume the duties defined in this Office No.Q/392/1, dated 14/5/17. Sec'bad Brigade will appoint an Officer to command their details left behind, and will notify his name to this Office and to the G.O.C., Ambala Brigade.

P.S. Whitcombe Capt for Lieut-Col
A.A.& Q.M.G., 5th Cavalry Division.

To/ Brigades.
    O.C., Brigade Details.
    O.C., Sec'bad Dis.Reinf.
    O.C., A.S.C.

A.D.V.S.
D.A.D.O.S.
A.D.M.S.
"G". "A".

WAR DIARY
or
INTELLIGENCE SUMMARY

Army Form C. 2118.

(Erase heading not required.)

(Ramondzahi)
Headquarters
8th Cavalry Bde

Place	Date	Hour	Summary of Events and Information	Remarks and references to Appendices
NOIRESCOURT FARM	JULY 1st		Ammunition Expenditure to 12 noon :- A.22 - AX - 18 - N 140 - NX - 58 - SAA 9210 rds. Casualties to 12 noon :- L.S. Jones - Wounded. 1.ORR. 3rd Horse - 1 ORR (whole) training on 25 [?] Pom Pom [?].	
	2nd		Ammunition Expenditure to 12 noon :- A.386 - AX.392 - N.332 - NX [?] 283 BX.192 - SAA 25,066 rds. Casualties to 12 noon :- 9th Horse - Wounded. 2.ORR. (includes 1 slightly at duty)	
	3rd		Ammunition Expenditure to 12 noon :- A.94 - AX.25 - N.262 - NX.315 - SAA.320 rds. Casualties to 12 noon :- RCHA B? - Wounded 1 ORB. (slightly at duty).	
	4th		Ammunition Expenditure to 12 noon :- A.61 - AX.11 - N.341 - NX.277 - BX.6 - SAA.1175 rds - Guncotton N5 - 5 - Casualties to 12 noon :- L.S. Horse - Wounded. 1 ORR.	
	5th		Ammunition Expenditure to 12 noon :- A.81 - AX.30 - N.243 - NX.207 - SAA.2560. Guncotton N5 - 10. Casualties to 12 noon :- L.S. Horse - Killed. 1 ORR. Wounded 1 ORR. F.G. Horse - Wounded 1 ORR. (slightly at duty) 7th D. Guards - Wounded 1 ORR. 3rd Horse - Wounded - Lieut. R. YATES. IAR - Jemadar TAJ MUHAMMAD KHAN (both slightly at duty) & 2 ORR. 14 Sqdn M.G.C. Wounded. Sowar Niaz Ood Camn Rambaksh. Under the NCR 101st Infantry Bde. B.N. Div. Fr. A.Q. at VRAIGNES.	

WAR DIARY
INTELLIGENCE SUMMARY.
(Erase heading not required.)

Army Form C. 2118.

NOEUX COURT FARM
JULY.

Hour, Date, Place	Summary of Events and Information	Remarks and references to Appendices
6/5	No. 2 gun of No. 9 LAC Battery attached with 31st Cav Div. Mental A&Q. Ammunition Formation to 12 noon - A 83. AK. 33. N 230. NX 289 - Box. 20 - SAA. 17200. VS. Grenades Nº 5 55. Casualties to 12 noon - Gun M.G. Section. wounded 1 OR. (slightly at duty) 1st Sqdn. M.G.C. wounded 1 OR. (slightly at duty)	
7/5	Ammunition Instructions issued to the West of the Division to be done by 3½ Div - in the 9th and 125 Inf. Ammunition Expenditure to 12 noon :- A. 19 - AK. 97 - N. 249 - NX. 469 - RX. 25 - SAA. 17260 etc - Grenades Nº 5. 111 - Grenades Nº 23 - 13 - 182 horses + 5 mules received to 12 noon. No. 1 from Nº1 Base Remount Depot. Casualties to 12 noon :- A. 285 - AK. 53 - N. 1092 - NX. 971 - BX. 170 - SAA. 1889 etc, Grenades Nº 5. 169. Grenades Nº 23 - 26 -	Appendix "A"
8/5	Casualties to 12 noon - F.G. Jones. wounded 1 OR. 7th S. Grenades. Khaut 2 ORs. wounded L.C.L. HASTINGS (slightly at duty) and 7 ORs (includes 4 slightly at duty) 34th Jas. wounded. Jemda. JATAN SINGH (31st Lancers) (slightly at duty) M.G.C. wounded 1 OR. 16 Sqdn. M.G.C. wounded 1 OR.	

WAR DIARY
INTELLIGENCE SUMMARY

Army Form C. 2118.

(Erase heading not required.)

Instructions regarding War Diaries and Intelligence Summaries are contained in F.S. Regs., Part II. and the Staff Manual respectively. Title Pages will be prepared in manuscript.

Place	Date	Hour	Summary of Events and Information	Remarks and references to Appendices
NOREUIL COURT FARM	June 9th		A successful raid was carried out last night by enemy. Two patrols by F.O. Irvine and L/Cpl Irvine. Parties from G20a28 to G21c41 by Fr. Officer out 65 OR and the trenches on entered in situation to return. A list NX 557 - N 1261 - NX 1478 - NX 185 - Ammunition situation to return SAA 148,950 N.Z. (includes M.G. 374) "B" Ron. 65. Casualties to 12 hrs. L.S. hore Wounded Capt. C.E. CONNOLLY (slightly at duty) and 6 ORs (including Lt./Sgt. W.H. STEWART) and 20 ORs.	
			F.G. Irvine. 1 ORs REHA P.M. (slightly at duty) 2nd Hine L/A.R. STEWART Wounded 1 OR. 3rd Irvine (att'd Div HQ) Wounded Private Log. MUHI-UD-DIN KHAN (sleeping at duty) Missing Pte. STEPHEN SEWARD.	
NOREUIL COURT	9.6.18 16.30 9pm	Nil Nil	Division returned to the line by the 101st Infantry Bde. Gnd Intercom in Posn. Guns sited at NOREUIL to cover RENINCOURT. Casualties K. 12 hors - A.C. STUART. Killed 1 men. Wounded 2 ORs (slightly at duty) 1 N.J.C.NON F.G. Irvine.	
	10.6.18 Nil		Ammunition situation to 12 hrs: = N 286 - NX 712 Cummergraphin 9.C. List of HFB5 7mm and Rt ass Rts in 1st Div. Australian Com. 16 BR 6th Coms in Situation to 12 hrs - N 3P - NX Graphite patrol - F.G. Irvine Recce Ltr T. Pulmer	signed

Army Form C. 2118.

WAR DIARY
or
INTELLIGENCE SUMMARY

(Erase heading not required.)

Instructions regarding War Diaries and Intelligence Summaries are contained in F. S. Regs., Part II. and the Staff Manual respectively. Title Pages will be prepared in manuscript.

Place	Date	Hour	Summary of Events and Information	Remarks and references to Appendices
BAUVINCOURT	July 11th,12, 13th	Night	Patrol of Ostham carried on. Ammunition refilling.	
	14th		Ammunition instructed to Operation Order No. 6. — Ammunition instructed to St Pol and Operation Order No. 36.	Appendix "C"
	15th, 17th		3a Section marched to St Pol area in accordance with Operation Order No. 2.	Appendix "D"
	16th		Ammunition to Refilling Quex 3. Submitted Men Concentrated in and about MONCHY LAGACHE	
	17th	10pm	Refill Point closed at BAUVINCOURT at 6am and billeted at ST POL. Base train from Submarine) train arrived at St Pol by 10 am and joined their train.	
	18th		4 Armoured) Cars of No.9 L.A.M. Battery	
			and the 4 Cars of No.7 Battery handed over to No.7 L.A.M. Battery in knowledge on orders taken on by No.9.	
	21st		4 Day lorries and 29 L.D. mules received from No.18 Reserve Spadan PRESENT	
	23rd		One Section 17 Suffolk (Colne horse) to RETRENCOURT COLINCAMPS and	
			MAILLCOURT to Salvage work under their army.	
	25th		List of Return in St Pol area. Section 17 Suffolk (Colne Horse) rejoined from Salvage work on Salvage with their Army.	Appendix "E"
	27th		17 RMA Brigade — RCHA Brigade gone with on Ammunition Columns and Park arrived to join Canadian Corps.	
	28th		75 L.D. horses drawn from ABBEVILLE as reinforcements.	

Army Form C. 2118.

WAR DIARY
or
INTELLIGENCE SUMMARY.
(Erase heading not required.)

Instructions regarding War Diaries and Intelligence Summaries are contained in F. S. Regs., Part II, and the Staff Manual respectively. Title pages will be prepared in manuscript.

Hour, Date, Place.	Summary of Events and Information.	Remarks and references to Appendices.
St. Pol. July 28th	Head Quarters and No. 2 Reserve Park Refinis Division	
HEUCHIN 31st	Divisional Head Quarters (excluding Gen & ADMS) Supplies, DAPOS, OC ASC, & ADMS) march from St Pol to HEUCHIN. Casualties to 12 noon :— "X" Battery RHA Rules 2 OR Wounded :- Capt. C.W.R. WHITE (since died of wounds) and 1 OR	H.M. Fuiger Brig General A.A. & Q.M.S.

(Appendix "A")

SECRET. Headquarters, 5th Cavalry Division.
No.Q/392/13. 6th July 1917.

ADMINISTRATIVE INSTRUCTIONS.

Reference Operation Order No.35, dated 4/7/17 and No. G/552/15, dated 5/7/17.

1. SUPPLY. Supplies for the 10th July will be delivered in the Back Area for all Units, except Hqrs. 17th Bde R.H.A. and R.C.H.A. Bde and for Battery positions.

2. RESERVE SUPPLIES.
(a) O.C.,A.S.C. will arrange to withdraw all Reserve Indian Rations.
(b) The Reserve British Rations in Advanced Posts, LE VERGUIER Keeps and at Bde Hqrs will be handed over to the Relieving Battalions.

3. TRENCH COVERS & TENTS.
(a) All trench covers and any tents, at present in the line and in Battery positions will be handed over to the relieving Battalions.
(b) Tents and trench covers in possession of the Dismounted Reinforcements at VENDELLES will be carefully packed and collected at the Hqrs of the detachment, where they will be taken over by the D.A.D.O.S. on the morning of the 9th July. One man will be left in charge until they are taken over.

4. HANDING OVER. Reference para 8 (b) of O.O. No.35 :-
The following handing over statements will be prepared and sent in duplicate with receipts to Divnl Hqrs after the relief has been completed:-

(a) S.A.A. & Grenades, etc., in the line (giving locations).
(b) ----- do -----   Bde Dumps.
(c) Reserve Rations in (1) Advanced Posts.
                      (2) LE VERGUIER Keeps.
                      (3) Brigade Headquarters.
(d) Tools and trench covers.(on A.F.W-3405).
(e) Trench covers and any tents in the line.
(f) Water tanks and petrol tins(all must be handed over).
(g) R.E.Stores at MONTIGNY and VERMAND Dumps.

5. REGTL. STORES. No Regimental or other Government Stores other than those mentioned in para 4 are to be left in the line.

6. SANITATION. All dug-outs, shelters and bivouacs must be left in an orderly and Sanitary condition. Short latrine trenches or pits into which soil from latrine buckets in the line has been emptied, will be filled in and marked. Latrine buckets will be left empty and clean and each will contain a small quantity of cresol.
All refuse, empty tins and garbage will be buried and the site of such pits will be marked FOUL ground.
Wagon lines or horse standings in the forward area e.g. at MONTIGNY FARM, VERMAND and VADENCOURT will be left clean and in good order, and in particular all manure will be close-packed and tamped with earth.

7. TRANSPORT All limbered G.S. Wagons belonging to the Reserve Park now at MONTIGNY and VERMAND will rejoin their Unit on the 10th July.

8............

8. The three Garford water lorries attached to Mhow and Canadian Field Ambulances for duty in the back areas will report to the O.C., Supply Column who will return them to the Cavalry Corps Troops Supply Column.

at 12 noon on/10

9. The G.S. wagon fitted with water tank will rejoin A.S.C. Headquarters from the Canadian Cavalry Brigade on the 10th July.

H.K. Cobbe
Lieut-Colonel,
A.A. & Q.M.G., 5th Cavalry Division.

To/
    Canadian Cavalry Brigade.
    Sec'bad Cavalry Brigade.
    Ambala Cavalry Brigade.
    Canadian Brigade Back Area Details.
    Sec'bad   "   "   "   "
    C.R.H.A.
    C.R.E.
    Signal Squadron.
    Ammunition Column.
    Aux.H.T.Coy.
    Reserve Park.
    A.D.M.S.
    A.D.V.S.
    D.A.D.O.S.
    O.C., A.S.C.
    A.P.M.
    Camp Commandant.
    D.A.A. & Q.M.G.
    General Staff.
    O.C., Ambala Dismounted Reinforcements
    Gas Officer.
    101st Infantry Brigade.
    34th Division "Q".
    O.C. Supply Column

(Appendix "B") July 17

LIST OF BIVOUACS - 5TH CAVALRY DIVISION.

Divisional Headquarters.........	BOUVINCOURT.
Field Cashier....................	MONCHY LAGACHE (V.18.a.6.9.)
Signal Squadron..................	BOUVINCOURT.
Field Squadron, R.E..............	S.W. of TERTRY (W.8.b.3.9.)
C.R.H.A..........................	NOBESCOURT FARM.
17th Bde R.H.A. Ammn Col.)	
R.C.H.A. Bde Ammn.Column.)	E. of TERTRY (W.2.a. & b.)
Ammunition Park..................	N.W. of TINCOURT (J.15.d.6.0.)
Supply Column....................	MONCHY LAGACHE (V.18.a.6.9.)
Sanitary Section.................	BOUVINCOURT.
No. 9 L.A.M. Battery.............	E. of TERTRY (W.2.b.)
A.H.T.Coy........................	W.1.d.7.9.
5th Cavalry Reserve Park.........	V.6.d.
Railhead Supplies................	PERONNE LA CHAPELLETTE.

AMBALA CAVALRY BRIGADE.

Brigade Headquarters.............	CAUVIGNY FARM.
8th Hussars.)	
9th Horse.)	
18th Lancers.)	Bivouacs between CAULAINCOURT
No.14 M.G.Sqn.)	and TERTRY.
M.V.Section.)	
"X" Battery (Wagon Lines)........	W.3.b.9.4.
Mhow I.C.F.A. (Tent Section).....	TERTRY.

SEC'BAD CAVALRY BRIGADE.

Brigade Headquarters.............	TREFCON (W.10.a.5.7.)
7th Dragoon Guards.)	
20th Horse.)	
34th Horse.).................	Bivouacs about TREFCON.
No.13 M.G.Sqdn.)	
M.V.Section.)	
"N" Battery (Wagon Lines)........	Q.33.b.
Sec'bad I.C.F.A. (Tent Section)..	TREFCON.

CANADIAN CAVALRY BRIGADE.

Brigade Headquarters.............	MONCHY LAGACHE.
R.C.Dragoons.)	
L.S.Horse.)	
F.G.Horse.)..............	Bivouacs between DEVISE & MERAUCOURT.
Can M.G.Sqn.)	
Can M.V.Section.)	
R.C.H.A. Bde (WagonLines)........	E. of CAULAINCOURT WOOD (W.6.d.)
Canadian C.F.A...................	MERAUCOURT.

No.Q/213/4.　　　　　　　　　　　　Headquarters, 5th Cavalry Division.
　　　　　　　　　　　　　　　　　　　　　　　　　　10th July 1917.

To/
　Cavalry Corps "Q".

　　　　　　　　　Forwarded.

　　　　　　　　　　　　　　　　　　　　　　　　P.S. Whitcombe Capt.
　　　　　　　　　　　　　　　　　　　　　　　　　　Lieut-Colonel,
　　　　　　　　　　　　　　　　　　　　for G.O.C., 5th Cavalry Division.

Copies to :-
　　　Usual Billeting List Distribution.
　　　34th Division "Q".
　　　III Corps "Q".

(Appendix 'C') July '17

SECRET

No.Q/444/3.   Headquarters 5th.Cavalry Division.

12th.July 1917.

ADMINISTRATIVE INSTRUCTIONS

To/
Brigades and Divisional Troops.

Reference Operation Order No.36 dated 10/7/17.

Divisional Headquarters will move to BRYAS and not to St.POL. Para.7a and 9c should be amended accordingly.

2.   Billetting Areas in the St.POL Area will be :-

CANADIAN BRIGADE........WAVRANS (Ex) - CROIX - RAMECOURT (Ex) -

ST.POL (Ex) - "W" in Chapp^{lle} WILLIAUME.

SEC'BAD BRIGADE........"W" in Chapp^{lle} WILLIAUME - ST.POL -

RAMECOURT - ROELLECOURT (Ex) - St.MICHEL

sur TERNOISE - TROISVAUX.

(Brigade Hdqrs, may be billetted in St.POL if desired, but no other units. Accommodation will be given by Town Major. Accommodation only for about 30 horses in ST.POL.

AMBALA BRIGADE.........ROELLECOURT - St.MICHEL sur TERNOISE (Ex) -

"T" in ARRET - OSTREVILLE - ORLENCOURT (Ex)

- MARQUAY (Ex).

FIELD SQUADRON R.E.)...LA THIEULOYE (Billets to be allotted by the
MUNITION COLUMN.   )   O.C.Field Squadron R.E.)

AUX.H.T.COMPANY.   )......ORLENCOURT (Billets to be allotted by the
RESERVE PARK.   )   O.C. A.S.C.)

DIVISIONAL HDQRS.   )....BRYAS (Billets to be allotted by the Camp
L.A.M.BATTERY.   )   Commandant D.H.Q.)
SANITARY SECTION.   )

SUPPLY COLUMN.   )....ST.POL (Town Major ST.POL will allot billets
AMMUNITION PARK.   )   to a representative of the O.C.
                                      A.S.C.)

3.   O.C. A.S.C. will issue instructions for the move of the Supply Column to the new area.

4.   The Ammunition Park will move to ST.POL on the 16th.July.

5............

5.　　　　In the billeting areas on the march and in the final area, all land which has been previously occupied must be used for horse standings. Information regarding these can be obtained at Mairies - new land, if required, must be taken up only in consultation with Maires. Attention is drawn to this office No.Q/2386, dated 3/4/16.

6.　　　　No grazing is permitted in the back areas except as laid down in G.R.O. 1028.

7.　　　　The greatest care must be taken to avoid damage to crops, pastures, and trees, and in villages.

8.　　　　Claims must be settled on the march by Units, an Officer remaining behind at each halt to do this. This officer will obtain a certificate from the Maire of the village stating that all claims have been handed in and that there are no others.

　　　　　　　　　　　　　　　　　　　　　　Lieut-Colonel,
　　　　　　　　　　　　　　　　　A.A.& Q.M.H., 5th Cavalry Division

Copies to :-
　　　　Town Major, ST. POL.
　　　　"G".　　"A".
　　　　A.D.P.S.
　　　　Field Cashier.
　　　　Claims Officer.
　　　　Gas Officer.

(Appendix "D") July 17.

No. Q/1414/4   Hdqrs. 5th Cavalry Division
                            14th July 1917

To
Brigades and Divl. Troops.

The following amendments are made to para 2 of my No. Q/1414/3 dated 12th July 17 (Administrative Instructions):-

BILLETING AREAS

SECBAD BRIGADE - "W" in Chapp"e WILLIAUMÉ - ST. POL - RAMECOURT - Point 150 - level crossing W. of ST. MICHEL - along railway to BRYAS (Chateau Ex) - TROISVAUX. (ST. POL not to be used for billeting).

AMBALA BRIGADE - BRYAS (Ex) - L'Abbé de Neuville Ime - ORLENCOURT (Exc) - MARQUAY (Exc) - ROELLECOURT - Point 150 - ST. MICHEL sur TERNOISE.

DIVL. HEADQRS
L.A.M. BATTERY   } - ST. POL.
SANITARY SECTION
Billets to be allotted by the Camp Commdt D.H.Q. Horse Standings outside the town to be arranged in communication with Sec! bad Bde.

2.   Para 1 of No. Q/1414/3 is hereby cancelled. Divisional Hdqrs. move to ST. POL.

                    H A Wolley
                    AA & QMG. 5th Cavy. Dn.

Copy to G.S.
Town Major ST POL   A.D.P.S.
Claims office   Field Cashier
                             Gas officer

(Appendix "C") July 17

CONFIDENTIAL

Billoting List - 5th. Cavalry Division.

Divisional Headquarters	St.POL
Field Cashier	-do-
Signal Squadron	-do-
Field Squadron R.E.	TROISVAUX
C.R.H.A.	St.POL
17th.Brigade Ammunition Column)	
R.C.H.A.Brigade Ammunition Column)	LA THIEULOYE
Ammunition Park	St.Pol (S. of town on St.POL - FREVENT Road)
Supply Column	St.POL (N.E. corner of town on St.POL - PERNES Rd).
Sanitary Section	St.POL
No.9 L.A.M.Battery	-do-
Aux:Horse Transport Company	RAMECOURT
Reserve Park	---do--- (Hdqrs and No 2 Section
Railhead (Supplies etc)	St.POL S.28.d.10.1 ALBERT combined sheet)

AMBALA CAVALRY BRIGADE

Brigade Headquarters	ROELLECOURT
8th.Hussars	St.MICHEL sur TERNOISE - ROCOURT St.LAURENT.
9th.Horse	OSTREVILLE
18th.Lancers	ROELLECOURT
No.14 M.G.Squadron	-do-
M.V.Section	-do-
"X" Battery R.H.A.	L'ABBAYE de NEUVILLE Fm.
Mhow I.C.F.A.	St.MICHEL sur TERNOISE.

SEC'BAD CAVALRY BRIGADE

Brigade Headquarters	MONCHY CAYEUX
7th.Dragoon Guards	ANVIN
20th.Horse	MONCHY CAYEUX
34th.Horse	EPS - HERBEVAL
No.13 M.G.Squadron	MONCHY CAYEUX
"N" Battery R.H.A.	SAUTRECOURT
Sec'bad I.C.F.A.	MONCHY CAYEUX

CANADIAN CAVALRY BRIGADE

Brigade Headquarters	CROIX
R.C.Dragoons	HERNICOURT - WAVRANS
L.S.Horse	GAUCHIN
F.G.Horse	St.MARTIN - BETHONVAL
Canadian M.G.Squadron	HERNICOURT
M.V.Section	GAUCHIN
R.C.Horse Artillery Brigade	CHAPPELLE ROCOURT
Canadian C.F.A.	St.POL

No.Q/213/5.   Headquarters 5th.Cavalry Division.
                   23rd.July 1917.

To/
    Cavalry Corps "Q".

                Forwarded.

Copy to :-   H H Cobbe
Usual Distribution.   Lieut=Colonel
Third Army "Q"   for G.O.C., 5th.Cavalry Division.
1st,2nd,3rd and 4th.Cavalry Divisions "Q".
Town Major and Area Commandant St.POL

WAR DIARY
INTELLIGENCE SUMMARY

Army Form C. 2118.

Place	Date	Hour	Summary of Events and Information	Remarks and references to Appendices
	1917			
HEUCHIN	Oct 1st		Canadian Cavalry Brigade (less 2 Sqns) moved to HAUTRECOURT Reconnaissances for ROUEN - Go Canals	
		At 9 AM Batty moved from its Rds @ HEUCHIN New Quarters are in 2 fields (about ½ mile) Park w.n.w. of BRYAS	
		At 1 seclor Reserve Park moved to BRYAS 13th Mobile vet section (Canadian) moved to BETHUNE Canadian Bde 2 wrms 5th Cavalry Supply Column - 1 GR 3 trucks (medically)	
	11		Canadian Bde 2 wrms - RCHA Brigade seconded A.D. MILLINGTON RCHA Alderson	

WAR DIARY or INTELLIGENCE SUMMARY

Army Form C. 2118.

Place	Date	Hour	Summary of Events and Information	Remarks and references to Appendices
HEUCHIN	1917 Aug. 15th		Casualties to 12 noon - "X" Battery RHA wounded (gas) 1 O.R.B	
	20th		Casualties to 2 noon - RHA Bde - wounded 1 O.R.B (dying on duty)	
	22nd		Casualties to 2 noon - "X" Battery RHA - wounded 3 O.R.B (includes 1 died later)	
	24th		Brig. Gen. N.R.R. T.E.B. SEELY assumed command of the Canadian Cavalry Brigade on return from sick leave	
	31st		Remounts received from Rouen 38 animals	

W.M.H. ffrench
Capt & Adjt

WAR DIARY or INTELLIGENCE SUMMARY

Army Form C. 2118

Administrative Headquarters 3rd Cavalry Division

Place	Date	Hour	Summary of Events and Information	Remarks and references to Appendices
HEUCHIN	1917 Sept. 2nd	12 noon	Casualties to 12 noon:— 3rd Dragoon Guards — Major B.H. ALDERSON Special hospital cases — names Though fatal. RHA Brigade	
"	" 3rd	12 noon	Casualties to 12 noon:— RCHA Brigade — Wounded 1 ORB	
"	" 4th	12 noon	Casualties to 12 noon:— 7th Machine Gun Squadron — Wounded 1 ORB (severely but slightly injured)	
"	" 5th	12 noon	Casualties to 12 noon:— RCHA Brigade — Killed 1 ORB, Wounded 2 ORB (accidentally slightly injured)	
"	" 6th	12 noon	Casualties to 12 noon:— 2nd Dragoon Guards — Wounded 1 ORB (accidentally at Rifle Range) 7th RHA Brigade and RHA Brigade not previously mentioned Clynes and Park reported this incident from Palaiseau Camp.	
"	" 12th	12 noon	Casualties to 12 noon:— Manning died at O.C. FITZPATRICK (accidentally slightly injured)	
"	" 13	"	Reinforcements received — 106 horses — 9 mules	

Instructions regarding War Diaries and Intelligence Summaries are contained in F. S. Regs., Part II. and the Staff Manual respectively. Title pages will be prepared in manuscript.

WAR DIARY
or
INTELLIGENCE SUMMARY.
(*Erase heading not required.*)

Army Form C. 2118.

Place	Date	Hour	Summary of Events and Information	Remarks and references to Appendices
[illegible]	Apl	20th	Reinforcements received: [illegible] [illegible] [illegible] 125 light draught horses from ROUEN	
	Apl	[illegible]th	Number 13 Machine [illegible] per Squadron issued to [illegible]	
	Apl	25th	Following horses returned to No 4 Cav. Remount Depot SERQUEUX as unsuitable for RHA [illegible] [illegible] RHA — 30 RCHA [illegible] — 18	

H H [illegible] Lieut Col.
AA & QMG
5th Cavalry Divn

8/10/17

(A7092). Wt. W12839/M1293- 750,000. 1/17. D. D. & L., Ltd. Forms/C.2118/14.

Army Form C. 2118.

WAR DIARY
INTELLIGENCE SUMMARY

(Erase heading not required.)

Headquarters *Administry*
5th Cavalry Bde

Place	Date	Hour	Summary of Events and Information	Remarks and references to Appendices
HEUCHIN	Oct 1st		Orders received for X Battery R.H.A. and an Ammn. waggons and an G.S. waggons (from gun Reserve) from Divison (Divn) to be held in readiness to entrain on the 6 inst. for the purpose of proceeding overseas.	
"	Oct 4th		5th Field Squadron R.E. (two troops detached in this Army area) proceeds to Second Army to be attached to that Army for operations.	
"	Oct 6th		Remainder men of this Division concentrated in GAUCHIN VERLOINGT.	
			Division commenced to move to WATOU area in accordance with Operation Order No 37.	
POPERINGHE	Oct 7th		Report Centre opened at HEUCHIN at 10.0 AM and reopened at POPERINGHE at the same hour.	
		10.0pm	Orders received for AMBALA Bde. to hold in SKENDECOUR area until further orders. CANADIAN and SECUNDERABAD Bdes. are now proceeding to the WATOU area.	
			5th Field Squadron R.E. rejoined the Division.	
			Railhead moved to TATINGHEM.	

WAR DIARY or INTELLIGENCE SUMMARY

Army Form C. 2118.

Place	Date	Hour	Summary of Events and Information	Remarks and references to Appendices
POPERINGHE	Oct 8th		"X" Battery RHA and "X" Section today at St Pol for MARSEILLES to serve overseas. They are struck off strength of this division from this date. All units were completed to establishment in Cavalry Horse Transport by over Cadre with 1748 M, 957 M and 549,000 SAA. For text of Divisional see Appendix "J"	
"	Oct 9th		Railhead changed to HIPPERSHOEK. Belgian Mission, consisting of an Officer and 15 interpreters, is attached to the division from this date.	
"	Oct 10th		Remainder of the Division moved from GAUCHIN VERLOINT and are now concentrated at BAILLEUL. Sixteen horses drawn for Interpreters of Belgian Mission from Cavalry Corps Adv. Remount Depot' BAILLEUL.	
"	" 11th		Twenty seven recruits drawn from BAILLEUL (60 for 1st Cav. Regt Brigade)	
"	" 11th		AMB9th A Cav. Bde. moved from the STEENBECQUE to HAZOUBROUCK	

WAR DIARY
or
INTELLIGENCE SUMMARY.

Army Form C. 2118.

Place	Date	Hour	Summary of Events and Information	Remarks and references to Appendices
POPERINGHE	Oct 14th		Reinforcement – 102 Reinforcements drawn from Cavalry Corps Card Reinforcement Depot BAILLEUL. Division commenced to move WESTWARDS. Ambala Bde. Queen's Coy. Reserve Park No 9 I.A.C. Battery } Moved to RENESCURE Area Divn Headquarters Divisional Report Centre closed, at POPERINGHE at 11 A.M. and opened at RENESCURE at the same hour.	
RENESCURE	Oct 15th		Ambala Bde Queen's Col Reserve Park } Moved to bivouacs near FAUQEMBERGUES Secunderabad Cav Bde moved from WATOU area to RENESCURE Area.	
FRESSIN	Oct 16th		Ambala Bde Queen's Col Reserve Park No 9 I.A.C. Battery } Moved to billets in Southern FRUGES area	

WAR DIARY
or
INTELLIGENCE SUMMARY.
(Erase heading not required.)

Army Form C. 2118.

Place	Date	Hour	Summary of Events and Information	Remarks and references to Appendices
FRESSIN	Oct	16th	Accumulators Cav. Bde. moved to bivouacs near FAUQUEMBERGUES. Canadian Cav. Bde. moved to RENESCURE Area. A.H.T. Co?	
"		17th	Divisional H.Qrs. Coyce opened at RENESCURE at 11.0 A.M. and joined at FRESSIN at the same hour. Accumulators Cav. Bde. moved to Northern FAUGES Area. Canadian Cav. Bde. moved to bivouacs near FAUQUEMBERGUES. A.H.T. Co?	
"		17th 18th	3rd Cavalry Battalion formed, comprising :- 2nd Machine Gun (with 2 horsed) G.S. Wagon and necessary transport. To be attached to 2nd Army for guard & police work. Canadian Cav. Bde. moved to Northern FAUGES area following now units are billet in Southern FAUGES area.	
"		20	Reinforcements expected :- 1/18 Hussars drawn from No 4 Cavalry Remount Depot BOULOGNE.	

WAR DIARY
INTELLIGENCE SUMMARY

Place	Date	Hour	Summary of Events and Information	Remarks and references to Appendices
FRESSIN.	Oct 23rd		No. 9 L.A.M. Battery left this Division & is attached to G.H.Q. Troops.	
	"	27th	Casualties 6-12 noon :- 5th Cavalry Supply Column, wounded 2 O.R's. 18th Lancers, wounded, 1 O.R. 9th Horse, wounded, 1 O.R.	
	"	28th	2nd Anzac Cavalry Regiment (Capts Coady) and cyclist Battalion joined to-day & be administered by this Division and billeted at RUSSEAUVILLE, AMBRICOURT, CANLERS, and AZINCOURT.	
	"	31st	58 remounts (riding horses) to No 5 Brown arrived.	

W M Gunnier
Lt. Col. S & Secy

1/11/17

SECRET (Appendix 'A')

LIST OF BIVOUACS — 5TH CAVALRY DIVISION.

Reference Sheet 27 - 1/40,000.

Divisional Headquarters............	POPERINGHE.
Field Cashier.....................	WATOU.
Signal Squadron...................	POPERINGHE.
Field Squadron....................	K.24.a.9.8.
C.R.H.A...........................	POPERINGHE.
Ammunition Column.................	K.10.d.5.2.
Ammunition Park...................	WINNEZELLE.
Supply Column.....................	WATOU.
Sanitary Section..................	WATOU.
9th L.A.C. Battery................	POPERINGHE.
A.H.T. Coy........................	L.16.c.3.3.
Reserve Park......................	L.17.a.9.6.
Dismounted Reinforcements.........	BAILLEUL.
Railhead (Supplies)...............	WIPPENHOEK.

CANADIAN CAVALRY BRIGADE.

Brigade Headquarters..............	L.9.b.6.4.
R.C.Dragoons......................	L.9.b.5.8. & L.9.c.6.6.
L.S.Horse.........................	L.15.b.3.7.
R.C.H.A. Brigade..................	L.15.b.7.3.
F.G.Horse.........................	L.9.b.3.7.
Canadian M.G. Squadron............	L.15.b.9.5.
Canadian C.F.A....................	L.10.c.8.1.
Canadian M.V. Section.............	L.8.d.6.5.

SEC'BAD CAVALRY BRIGADE.

Brigade Headquarters..............	WATOU.
7th Dragoon Guards................	K.3.d.6.6.
20th Horse........................	K.4.d.6.5. & K.4.d.4.4. (SCOTS FARM).
34th Horse........................	K.3.d.7.2.
"N" Battery R.H.A.................	K.3.c.2.2.
No. 13 M.G. Squadron..............	K.3.d.5.1.
Sec'bad I.C.F.A...................	K.4.c.4.4.
M.V. Section......................	K.5.d.8.7.

AMBALA CAVALRY BRIGADE.

Brigade Headquarters..............	K.10.d.7.2.
8th Hussars.......................	K.17.b.2.1.
9th Horse.........................	K.9.a.6.4.
18th Lancers......................	K.15.b.3.8.
No. 14 M.G. Squadron..............	K.9.b.7.5.
Mhow I.C.F.A......................	K.16.d.9.7.
M.V. Section......................	K.10.d.7.2.

No.Q/213/8.

Headquarters, 5th Cavalry Division.
12th October 1917.

To/
Second Army "Q".

Forwarded.

for Lieut-Colonel,
for G.O.C., 5th Cavalry Division.

Copies to :-
    Cavalry Corps "Q".
    Usual Billeting List Distribution.
    1st, 2nd, 3rd and 4th Cavalry Divisions "Q".
    Area Commandant, WATOU.
    O.C., Dismounted Reinforcements, 5th Cavalry Division.

SECRET (Appendix B)

LIST OF BILLETS - 5TH. CAVALRY DIVISION.

Reference Sheets Nos. 5A, 11, 13 and 14 - 1:100,000.

Divisional Headquarters.......FRESSIN.
Field Cashier................LA LOGE.
Signal Squadron..............FRESSIN.
Field Squadron...............KENTY.
C.R.H.A......................PLANQUES.
Ammunition Column............VERCHOCQ.
Supply Column................LA LOGE - WAMIN.
Sanitary Section.............LA LOGE.
Ammunition Park..............FRUGES.
No.9 L.A.M.Battery...........PLANQUES.
A.H.T.Company................Pt.BEAURAIN.
Reserve Park.................RUMILLY.
Railhead (Supplies)..........HESDIN.

CANADIAN CAVALRY BRIGADE.
Brigade Headquarters.........AIX en ISSART.
R.C.Dragoons.................BOUBERS - EMBRY - RIMBOVAL.
L.S.Horse....................MARLES - MARENT - MARENLA.
F.G.Horse....................SEMPY - HUMBERT - ST.MICHEL - QUILEN.
R.C.H.A.Brigade..............HERLY - AVESNES.
Canadian M.G.Squadron........LESPINOY.
Canadian C.F.A...............RENOVILLE.
Canadian M.V.Section.........ST.WANDRILLE.

SEC'BAD CAVALRY BRIGADE.
Brigade Headquarters.........FRUGES.
7th.Dragoon Guards...........COUPELLE VIELLE - WAILLY.
20th.Deccan Horse............ROYON - OFFIN - LEBIEZ - IOISON - HESMOND.
34th.Poona Horse.............CREQUY - TORCY.
"N" Battery R.H.A............FRUGES.
No. 15 M.G.Squadron..........--do--
Sec'bad I.C.F.A..............--do--
Sec'bad M.V.Section..........--do--

AMBALA CAVALRY BRIGADE.
Brigade Headquarters.........MARESQUEL.
8th.Hussars..................BEAURAINVILLE - BEAURAIN c^h - MARESQUEL.
9th.Hodson's Horse...........GAVROL ST.MARTIN.
18th.Lancers.................AUBIN ST.VAAST - BOUIN.
No.14 M.G.Squadron...........WAMBERCOURT.
Mhow I.C.F.A.................CONTES.
Ambala M.V.Section...........--do--

No.Q/215/9

Headquarters 5th.Cavalry Division.
18th.October 1917.

To/
   Cavalry Corps "Q".

Forwarded.

/for Lieut-Colonel
for G.O.C., 5th.Cavalry Division.

Copies to :-
   2nd.Army "Q".
   1st, 2nd, 3rd and 4th.Cavalry Divisions "Q".
   Usual Billeting List distribution.
   O.C.5th.Cavalry Battalion.

S.E.C.R.E.T.

LIST OF BILLETS - 5TH CAVALRY DIVISION.

Reference Sheets Nos.5A, 11, 13 & 14 - 1/100,000.

Divisional Headquarters	FRESSIN.
Field Cashier	LA LOGE.
Signal Squadron	FRESSIN.
Field Squadron	RENTY.
C.R.H.A.	PLANQUES.
Ammunition Column	VERCHOCQ.
Supply Column	LA LOGE - WAMIN.
Ammunition Park	FRUGES.
Sanitary Section	LA LOGE.
A.H.T. Company	WICQUINGHEM.
Reserve Park	RUMILLY - ERGNY.
5th Cavalry Battalion	Sheet 28 - H.6.c. Central.
Railhead (Supplies)	HESDIN.

CANADIAN CAVALRY BRIGADE:

Brigade Headquarters	AIX en ISSART.
R.C. Dragoons	BOUBERS - EMBRY - RIMBOVAL.
L.S. Horse	MARLES - MARENT - MARENLA.
F.G. Horse	SEMPY - HUMBERT - ST.MICHEL - QUILEN.
R.C.H.A. Brigade	HERLY - AVESNES.
Canadian M.G. Squadron	LESPINOY.
Canadian C.F.A.	BRIMEUX.
Canadian M.V. Section	ST.DENOEUX.

SEC'BAD CAVALRY BRIGADE.

Brigade Headquarters	FRUGES.
7th Dragoon Guards	COUPELLE VIELLE - WAILLY - ROLLEZ.
20th Deccan Horse	ROYON - OFFIN - LEBIEZ - LOISON - HESMOND.
34th Poona Horse	CREQUY - TORCY.
"N" Battery R.H.A.	FRUGES.
No. 13 M.G. Squadron	COUPELLE NEUVE - AVONDANCE.
Sec'bad I.C.F.A.	FRUGES.
Sec'bad M.V. Section	FRUGES.

AMBALA CAVALRY BRIGADE.

Brigade Headquarters	MARESQUEL.
8th Hussars	BEAURAINVILLE - BEAURAIN C^h - MARESQUEL.
9th Hodson's Horse	CAVRON ST.MARTIN - AUBIN.ST.VAAST.
18th Lancers	AUBIN ST.VAAST - BOUIN - ECQUIMCOURT.
No. 14 M.G. Squadron	WAMBERCOURT.
Mhow I.C.F.A.	CONTES.
Ambala M.V. Section	CONTES.

Headquarters of Units underlined.

No. Q/213/10.   Headquarters, 5th Cavalry Division.
                                                  27th October 1917.
To/
    Cavalry Corps "Q".

                    Forwarded.

                                                    [signature]
                                                    Lieut-Colonel,
                                        for G.O.C., 5th Cavalry Division.

Copies to :-   Second Army "Q".
                1st, 2nd, 3rd & 4th Cavalry Divisions "Q".
                Usual Billeting List Distribution.
                O.C., 5th Cavalry Battalion (attached Canadian Corps).

SECRET (Appendix "A")

LIST OF BIVOUACS - 5TH CAVALRY DIVISION.

Reference Sheet 27 - 1/40,000.

Divisional Headquarters	POPERINGHE.
Field Cashier	WATOU.
Signal Squadron	POPERINGHE.
Field Squadron	K.24.a.9.8.
C.R.H.A.	POPERINGHE.
Ammunition Column	K.10.d.5.2.
Ammunition Park	WINNEZEELE.
Supply Column	WATOU.
Sanitary Section	WATOU.
9th L.A.C. Battery	POPERINGHE.
A.H.T. Coy	L.16.c.8.3.
Reserve Park	L.17.a.9.6.
Dismounted Reinforcements	BAILLEUL.
Railhead (Supplies)	WIPPENHOEK.

CANADIAN CAVALRY BRIGADE.

Brigade Headquarters	L.9.b.6.4.
R.C.Dragoons	L.9.b.5.8. & L.9.c.6.6.
L.S.Horse	L.15.b.3.7.
R.C.H.A. Brigade	L.15.b.7.3.
F.G.Horse	L.9.b.3.7.
Canadian M.G. Squadron	L.15.b.9.5.
Canadian C.F.A.	L.10.c.8.1.
Canadian M.V. Section	L.8.d.6.5.

SEC'BAD CAVALRY BRIGADE.

Brigade Headquarters	WATOU.
7th Dragoon Guards	K.3.d.6.6.
20th Horse	K.4.d.6.5. & K.4.d.4.4.(SCOTS FARM).
34th Horse	K.3.d.7.2.
"N" Battery R.H.A.	K.3.c.2.2.
No. 13 M.G. Squadron	K.3.d.5.1.
Sec'bad I.C.F.A.	K.4.c.4.4.
M.V. Section	K.5.d.8.7.

AMBALA CAVALRY BRIGADE.

Brigade Headquarters	K.10.d.7.2.
8th Hussars	K.17.b.2.1.
9th Horse	K.9.a.6.4.
18th Lancers	K.15.b.3.8.
No. 14 M.G. Squadron	K.9.b.7.5.
Mhow I.C.F.A.	K.16.d.9.7.
M.V. Section	K.10.d.7.2.

No. Q/213/8.

Headquarters, 5th Cavalry Division.
12th October 1917.

To/
Second Army "Q".

Forwarded.

for Lieut-Colonel,
for G.O.C., 5th Cavalry Division.

Copies to :-
Cavalry Corps "Q".
Usual Billeting List Distribution.
1st, 2nd, 3rd and 4th Cavalry Divisions "Q".
Area Commandant, WATOU.
O.C., Dismounted Reinforcements, 5th Cavalry Division.

(Appendix B.)

SECRET

LIST OF BILLETS - 5TH. CAVALRY DIVISION.

Reference Sheets Nos. 5A, 11, 13 and 14 - 1:100,000.

```
Divisional Headquarters......FRESSIN.
Field Cashier................LA LOGE.
Signal Squadron..............FRESSIN.
Field Squadron...............RENTY.
C.R.H.A......................PLANQUES.
Ammunition Column............VERCHOCQ.
Supply Column................LA LOGE - WAMIN.
Sanitary Section.............LA LOGE.
Ammunition Park..............FRUGES.
No.9 L.A.M.Battery...........PLANQUES.
A.H.T.Company................Pt.BEAURAIN.
Reserve Park.................RUMILLY.
Railhead (Supplies)..........HESDIN.
```

CANADIAN CAVALRY BRIGADE.
```
Brigade Headquarters.........AIX en ISSART.
R.C.Dragoons.................BOUBERS - EMBRY - RIMBOVAL.
L.S.Horse....................MARLES - MARENT - MARENLA.
F.G.Horse....................SEMPY - HUMBERT - ST.MICHEL - QUILEN.
R.C.H.A.Brigade..............HERLY - AVESNES.
Canadian M.G.Squadron........LESPINOY.
Canadian C.F.A...............HENOVILLE.
Canadian M.V.Section.........ST.WANDRILLE.
```

SEC'BAD CAVALRY BRIGADE.
```
Brigade Headquarters.........FRUGES.
7th.Dragoon Guards...........COUPELLE VIELLE - WAILLY.
20th.Deccan Horse............ROYON - OFFIN - LEBIEZ - LOISON - HESMOND.
34th.Poona Horse.............CREQUY - TORCY.
"N" Battery R.H.A............FRUGES.
No. 13 M.G.Squadron..........--do--
Sec'bad I.C.F.A..............--do--
Sec'bad M.V.Section..........--do--
```

AMBALA CAVALRY BRIGADE.
```
Brigade Headquarters.........MARESQUEL.
8th.Hussars..................BEAURAINVILLE - BEAURAIN Ch - MARESQUEL.
9th.Hodson's Horse...........GAVROL ST.MARTIN.
18th.Lancers.................AUBIN ST.VAAST - BOUIN.
No.14 M.G.Squadron...........WAMBERCOURT.
Mhow I.C.F.A.................CONTES.
Ambala M.V.Section...........--do--
```

No.Q/213/Q

Headquarters 5th.Cavalry Division.
18th.October 1917.

To/
   Cavalry Corps "Q".

             Forwarded.

                                        for Lieut-Colonel
                            for G.O.C., 5th.Cavalry Division.

Copies to :-
       2nd.Army "Q".
       1st, 2nd, 3rd and 4th.Cavalry Divisions "Q".
       Usual Billeting List distribution.
       O.C.5th.Cavalry Battalion.

S E C R E T.

LIST OF BILLETS - 5TH CAVALRY DIVISION.

Reference Sheets Nos. 5A, 11, 13 & 14 - 1/100,000.

Divisional Headquarters	FRESSIN.
Field Cashier	LA LOGE.
Signal Squadron	FRESSIN.
Field Squadron	RENTY.
O.R.H.A.	PLANQUES.
Ammunition Column	VERCHOCQ.
Supply Column	LA LOGE - WAMIN.
Ammunition Park	FRUGES.
Sanitary Section	LA LOGE.
A.H.T. Company	WICQUINGHEM.
Reserve Park	RUMILLY - ERGNY.
5th Cavalry Battalion	Sheet 28 - H.6.c. Central.
Railhead (Supplies)	HESDIN.

CANADIAN CAVALRY BRIGADE.

Brigade Headquarters	AIX en ISSART.
R.C. Dragoons	BOUBERS - EMBRY - RIMBOVAL.
L.S. Horse	MARLES - MARENT - MARENLA.
F.G. Horse	SEMPY - HUMBERT - ST.MICHEL - QUILEN.
R.C.H.A. Brigade	HERLY - AVESNES.
Canadian M.G. Squadron	LESPINOY.
Canadian C.F.A.	BRIMEUX.
Canadian M.V. Section	ST. DENOEUX.

SEC'BAD CAVALRY BRIGADE.

Brigade Headquarters	FRUGES.
7th Dragoon Guards	COUPELLE VIELLE - WAILLY - ROLLEZ.
20th Deccan Horse	ROYON - OFFIN - LEBIEZ - LOISON - HESMOND.
34th Poona Horse	CREQUY - TORCY.
"N" Battery R.H.A.	FRUGES.
No. 13 M.G. Squadron	COUPELLE NEUVE - AVONDANCE.
Sec'bad I.C.F.A.	FRUGES.
Sec'bad M.V. Section	FRUGES.

AMBALA CAVALRY BRIGADE.

Brigade Headquarters	MARESQUEL.
8th Hussars	BEAURAINVILLE - BEAURAIN C^h - MARESQUEL.
9th Hodson's Horse	CAVRON ST.MARTIN - AUBIN ST.VAAST.
18th Lancers	AUBIN ST.VAAST - BOUIN - ECQUIMCOURT.
No. 14 M.G. Squadron	WAMBERCOURT.
Mhow I.C.F.A.	CONTES.
Ambala M.V. Section	CONTES.

Headquarters of Units underlined.

No. Q/213/10. Headquarters, 5th Cavalry Division.
 27th October 1917.

To/
Cavalry Corps "Q".

Forwarded.

Lieut-Colonel,
for G.O.C., 5th Cavalry Division.

Copies to :- Second Army "Q".
 1st, 2nd, 3rd & 4th Cavalry Divisions "Q".
 Usual Billeting List Distribution.
 O.C., 5th Cavalry Battalion (attached Canadian Corps).

WAR DIARY or INTELLIGENCE SUMMARY

Army Form C. 2118.

Place	Date	Hour	Summary of Events and Information	Remarks and references to Appendices
FRESSIN.	2nd		Casualties to 12 noon.- 6th Dragoons (att'd R.H.Gds) wounded 1 O.R.	
	4th		Casualties to 12 noon.- R.C.Dragoons killed 1 O.R., wounded 2 O.Rs.	
	6th		Casualties to 12 noon.- R.H.Guards wounded 8 O.Rs. 2nd Dragoons wounded 2 O.Rs. 7th D.Guards wounded 1 O.R.	
	7th		Orders received for the Division to move SOUTH.	
	9th		Casualties to 12 noon.- R.C. Dragoons killed 1 O.R. (accidentally). Ambala and Sec'bed Cav Bdes moved to the OUTREBOIS Area. Canadian Cav Bde and Divisional Troops moved into the area evacuated by Ambala and Sec'bed Bdes. Divisional Report Centre closed at FRESSIN at 11 a.m. and opened at OCCOCHES same hour.	
OCCOCHES.	10th		Canadian Cav Bde and Divisional Troops moved to OUTREBOIS Area. Ambala and Sec'bed Cav Bdes moved to the CONTAY Area. II Anzac Corps Mounted Troops handed over to G.H.Q. Troops. Railhead to CANDAS.	
QUERRIEU.	11th		Divisional Report Centre closed at OCCOCHES at 11 a.m. and opened at QUERRIEU same hour. Canadian Cav Bde and Divnl. Troops moved to CONTAY Area.	
		P.M.	Ambala and Sec'bed Cav Bdes moved to SUZANNE Area. Railhead to CORBIE.	
BOUVINCOURT	12th		Divisional Report Centre closed at QUERRIEU at 3 p.m. and opened at BOUVINCOURT same hour. Canadian Cav Bde and Divnl. Troops moved to SUZANNE Area.	
		P.M.	Ambala and Sec'bed Cav Bdes arrived in BOUGLY Area. Railhead to LA FLAQUE.	
	13th		Canadian Cav Bde and Divnl Troops arrived in BOUGLY Area. Railhead to LA CHAPELLETTE.	

Army Form C. 2118.

WAR DIARY
or
INTELLIGENCE SUMMARY.
(Erase heading not required.)

Instructions regarding War Diaries and Intelligence Summaries are contained in F. S. Regs., Part II. and the Staff Manual respectively. Title pages will be prepared in manuscript.

Place	Date	Hour	Summary of Events and Information	Remarks and references to Appendices
	13th (ctd)		Ammunition drawn from QUINCONCE Railhead (XZ). For Regts. 9,000 Red Flares. For A.H.T.Coy. 1,680 N. 1" Green Very Lights. 450 1,320 NX. 540,000 rds S.A.A. 2,560 Red Flares.	
	14th		All Green Flares handed in. Location of Units at 12 noon to-day (Appendix "A").	
	18th		No. 4 Motor Machine Gun Battery joined. 5th Cavalry Pioneer Battalion disbanded, and all ranks of this Division who formed part of it rejoined by bus from YPRES - transport moving by road and will rejoin on 20th. Administrative Instructions issued for move forward to Operations commencing on "Z" day. (Appendix "B").	
	20th.		Division moved up for operations. Report centre closed at BOUNINGCOURT at 5.30 a.m. and opened at the Sugar Factory, FINS same hour. About 12 noon the report centre moved up to R.9.b. (N.E. of VILLERS PLOUICH). 2 Troops of Yorkshire Dragoons joined as Divisional Troops.	
	21st		Division still engaged in Operations. Report Centre remains at R.9.b. Railhead to YPRES. Casualties to 12 noon.- 7th D.Guards wounded 2/Lt.R.S. GILMAN. 1 O.R. 13th M.G. Sqdn wounded 3 O.Rs. F.G. Horse killed Capt. D.J. CAMPBELL. 6 O.Rs. Wounded Major W.J. SHARPE. Lieut.W.J. COWEN. " E.McI. HOLIDAY. 17 O.Rs. Missing 56 O.Rs. R.C.Dragoons killed 1 O.R.	

WAR DIARY
or
INTELLIGENCE SUMMARY.

(Erase heading not required.)

Army Form C. 2118.

Place	Date	Hour	Summary of Events and Information	Remarks and references to Appendices
	21st (ctd)		R.C. Dragoons wounded 2 O.Rs. L.S. Horse wounded Lieut-Colonel M. DOCHERTY, D.S.O. 1 O.R.	
	22nd		Division withdrawn to a concentration area about EQUANCOURT. Report Centre closed at R.9.b. and opened at EQUANCOURT, same hour. Expenditure of ammunition to 12 noon.- 76,000 rds S.A.A. Casualties to 12 noon.- R.C. Dragoons wounded 3 O.Rs. L.S. Horse wounded 7 O.Rs. Canadian M.G. Sqdn wounded 1 O.R. R.C.H.A. Brigade wounded 2 O.Rs. Total Horse casualties 21st and 22nd.- 172. 60 remounts arrived as reinforcements. Detachment 1/1st Yorkshire Dragoons rejoined their regiment to-day.	
	23rd		Division moved to the SUZANNE Area. Report Centre closed at EQUANCOURT at 11 a.m. and opened at SUZANNE same hour. No. 4 Motor Machine Gun Battery left the Division to-day for Cavalry Corps. A.H.T. Company handed in to QUINCONCE the ammunition drawn by that unit on the 13th instant. Light Section, Reserve Park temporarily detached to the 1st Tanks Brigade.	
	24th		Division ordered to be prepared to move at 1 hour's notice from 8 a.m. Railhead to LA FLAQUE.	
	25th		Casualties to 12 noon :- 20th.Horse - Wounded 1 ord (self-inflicted). Canadian Signal Troop - Missing 1 ord (believed wounded). C.A.M.C. att'd R.C.Dragoons - Captain W.T.E. MINTIE C.A.M.C. Billetting List issued showing location of units in the SUZANNE Area (Appendix "C").	

Army Form C. 2118.

WAR DIARY
INTELLIGENCE/SUMMARY
(Erase heading not required.)

Instructions regarding War Diaries and Intelligence Summaries are contained in F.S. Regs., Part II. and the Staff Manual respectively. Title pages will be prepared in manuscript.

Place	Date	Hour	Summary of Events and Information	Remarks and references to Appendices
SUZANNE	26th.		Orders received for the division to move EAST.	
	27th.		Division moved into the MONCHY LAGACHE Area. Report Center closed at SUZANNE at 10am and opened at MONCHY LAGACHE same hour.	
MONCHY LAGACHE	28th.		Billetting list issued showing location of units at 12 noon this date. (Appendix "B").	
	30th.	a.m.	Division received orders to move in N.E. direction. Fighting troops and "A" Echelon moved forward for operations.	
		p.m.	Advanced Report Centre established at E.5.a. (Sheet. 62c) about 2pm. Division engaged in operations in afternoon.	
			Casualties this date :- 20th. Horse wounded 4 ori.	
			7th. Dragoon Guards killed 1 orb.	
			wounded 3 orb.	
			34th. Horse killed 1 ori.	
			wounded 6 ori.	
			F.G. Horse wounded 1 orb.	
			R.C. Dragoon wounded 6 orb.	

In the field
10/12/17.

[signature]
Lieut-Colonel
A.A. and Q.M.G.
5th. Cavalry Division.

SECRET

"Appendix A"

LIST OF BIVOUACS - 5TH.CAVALRY DIVISION.

Reference Map Sheet 62c 1:40000

```
Divisional Headquarters..........BOUVINCOURT.
Field Cashier....................With Supply Column.
Signal Squadron..................BOUVINCOURT.
Field Squadron...................BIAS FARM (P.15.a.)
C.R.H.A..........................BOUVINCOURT.
Ammunition Column................ESTREES en CHAUSSEE.
Supply Column....................LA CHAPELLETTE - VILLERS CARBONNEL
                                 Road. Head ½ mile S.of LA CAPELLETTE.
Ammunition Park..................With Supply Column.
Sanitary Section.................With Supply Column.
A.H.T.Company....................Q.13.d.6.4.
Reserve Park. (Hdqrs and No.2
                    Section)FLAMICOURT.
         (No.1 Section).....Q.13.d.6.1.
Railhead (Supplies)..............LA CHAPELLETTE.
```

CANADIAN CAVALRY BRIGADE.

```
Brigade Headquarters.............BOUCLY.
R.C.Dragoons.....................BOUCLY.
L.S.Horse........................BOUCLY.
F.G.Horse........................BOUCLY Chau.
"A" Battery R.C.H.A..............CARTIGNY.
"B" Battery R.C.H.A.,and Hdqrs...HAMELET.
Canadian M.G.Squadron............ROISEL.
Canadian C.F.A...................ROISEL.
Canadian M.V.Section.............ROISEL.
```

SEC'BAD CAVALRY BRIGADE.

```
Brigade Headquarters.............VRAIGNES.
7 .Dragoon Guards................BOUVINCOURT.
20th.Deccan Horse................BEAUMETZ.
34th.Poona Horse.................HANCOURT.
"N" Battery R.H.A................BRUSLE.
No.13 M.G.Squadron...............VRAIGNES.
Sec'bad I.C.F.A..................ROISEL.
Sec'bad M.V.Section..............VRAIGNES.
```

AMBALA CAVALRY BRIGADE.

```
Brigade Headquarters.............CARTIGNY.
8th.Hussars......................CARTIGNY.
9th.Hodson's Horse...............BRUSLE.
18th.Lancers.....................BRUSLE.
No.14 M.G.Squadron...............BRUSLE.
Mhow.I.C.F.A.....................CARTIGNY.
Ambala M.V.Section...............BEAUMETZ.
```

No.Q/213/11.   Headquarters 5th.Cavalry Division,
                                         14th.November 1917.

To/
    Cavalry Corps "Q".

                        Forwarded.

                                         Lieut-Colonel
                                for G.O.C., 5th.Cavalry Division.
Copies to :-
        Third Army "Q".
        1st,2nd,3rd and 4th.Cavalry Divisions "Q".
        Usual Billetting List distribution.

Area Comm'd's CARTIGNY, TINCOURT, ROISEL and VRAIGNES.

VIIth Corps "Q"

SECRET.　　　　　　　(Appendix B)

Headquarters, 5th Cavalry Division.
17th November 1917.

ADMINISTRATIVE INSTRUCTIONS.

Reference to the move of the Division to the foward concentration area.

1. **HORSE RUGS 2nd BLANKETS SURPLUS STORES.**

    (a) When units leave their present camp, the following will be collected at unit dumps :-

    Horse Rugs & 2nd Blankets. — (Except B Echelons and such transport units that can carry their own.

    Stoves. — (Except in the camps at BOUCLY. These will be required for B Echelon and Dismounted Men).

    Baths.
    Tents & Trench Covers. — (Except those in the camps at BOUCLY.
    Other surplus Govt. stores.

    (b) The situation of each dump (which should be on a lorry road) will be reported to Divisional Hqrs by the evening of the 18th instant.
    (c) Horses will remain rugged up until the last moment and horse rugs will be collected by the Dismounted Men.
    (d) Horse rugs and blankets will be carefully folded and tents properly packed at the dumps.
    (e) 1 Dismounted man will be left in charge of each dump until it is taken over. The D.A.D.O.S. will arrange for these men to join the Dismounted Reinforcements at BOUCLY. The D.A.D.O.S. will remove all dumps to the Ordnance Dump at BOUVINCOURT. They should be ready for removal by 9 a.m. on "Z" day.
    (f) D.A.D.O.S. will arrange to keep separate the property of each unit at the BOUVINCOURT dump.
    (g) O.C., A.S.C. will place 20 lorries at the disposal of the D.A.D.O.S.

SUPPLIES.

Supplies will be delivered at 10 a.m. on "Z"-1 day as under :-

For men. Full day's rations for consumption on "Z" day. Unconsumed portion to be carried on man to the forward concentration area.
For horse. 4 lbs hay and 4 lbs oats for consumption before leaving the present area. The remaining 8 lbs hay and 8 lbs oats for "Z" day will be issued in the forward concentration area from dumps which have already been arranged.

RESERVE RATIONS.

2 days' reserve rations and 20 lbs reserve oats have been issued to all units for fighting troops and A Echelons. These should be loaded at once in accordance with Organisation Tables, Table "D", except that 12 lbs oats instead of 8 lbs will be carried in the two nosebags.
Two L.G.S. wagons for Sec'bad and Ambala Bdes, and 1 for Canadian Bde will be detailed from the Light Section of the Reserve Park to complete their requirements for the carriage of 8 lbs oats with

A Echelon................

"A" Echelon. O.C., A.S.C. will order these wagons to join forthwith.
Brigades and Divnl. Troops will report to Divisional Hqrs by the evening of the 18th instant that —

(a) Every officer and man is in possession of 2 Iron Rations.
(b) That the third Iron Ration and the 20 lbs oats are loaded as above.

4. **VERY LIGHTS. FLARES.** With reference to G.S.713/1, dated 16/11/17;

(a) The O.C., Ammunition Park will take over 450 Green, 1" Very Light cartridges and issue 50 to each Regiment.(4 per troop Canadian Regiments and 3 per troop other regiments).
(b) Red Flares have been issued to Regiments already. Brigades will report that Regiments are in possession of (a) and (b) by the evening of the 18th instant.

5. **MOTOR CARS. LORRIES.** 2 G.S. cars and 2 "Q" cars only will be taken to the forward area. All other Divisional and Brigade cars will join the Supply Column on "Z" day and remain attached to it until further orders. The lorries attached to the Signal Sqdn and Field Sqdn will also join the Supply Column.

No.Q/513/6.

To/
Brigades and Divnl. Troops.

[signature]
Lieut-Colonel,
A.A. & Q.M.G., 5th Cavalry Division.

Copies to:—
General Staff.
"A" Section.
Gas Officer.

(Appendix B)

SECRET.

Headquarters, 5th Cavalry Division.
17th November 1917.

CONCENTRATION ORDER OF B ECHELON AND DISMOUNTED REINFORCEMENTS.

Ref. Map. ST. QUENTIN.
Sheet No. 18 1/100,000.

1. When the Division has left this area the B Echelon and Dismounted Reinforcements of Brigades and Divisional Troops will concentrate at BOUCLY on "Z" day.

2. The move will be in accordance with the attached table. Dismounted parties will move in rear of the B Echelon wagons of their Units.

3. (a) Personnel and horses of B Echelons will occupy huts and stables of Lord Strathcona's Horse. Wagons will park in the Chateau grounds.
   (b) Dismounted Reinforcements will occupy huts of the R.C. Dragoons.

4. Os.C., B Echelons of Brigades and representatives of Divisional Troops will report to Captain F.H. WILKES, R.C. Dragoons at X roads BOUCLY at 2 p.m. on "Z" day, for allotment of accommodation.

5. Officers should bring their own mess kits.

6. The Heavy Section of the Reserve Park will also move to BOUCLY under separate orders.

7. Orders for the move of the A.H.T. Coy will be issued later.

No. Q/513/3/2.

To

Brigades and Divnl. Troops.

Lieut-Colonel,
A.A. & Q.M.G., 5th Cavalry Division.

Copies to :-
Major R.H.O'D. PATERSON, 34th Poona Horse.
Captain F.H. WILKES, R.C. Dragoons.
General Staff.
Gas Officer.
Field Cashier.

MARCH TABLE.

Ref. Map. ST. QUENTIN.
Sheet No. 18 1/100,000.

UNIT.	STARTING POINT & TIME.	ROUTE.
Divnl. Hqrs. Signal Sqdn. C.R.H.A. 7th D. Guards.	X roads in BOUVINCOURT at 2 p.m.	BEAUMETZ – HANCOURT – BOUCLY.
20th Horse. Ambala M.V. Section.	Junction of CARTIGNY-HANCOURT, BEAUMETZ-HANCOURT roads N. of B in BEAUMETZ, at 2 p.m.	BEAUMETZ – HANCOURT – BOUCLY.
Sec'bad Bde H.Q. 34th Horse. 13th M.G. Sqdn. Sec'bad M.V. Section.	Junction of BOUCLY-HANCOURT, CARTIGNY-HANCOURT roads immediately S. of C. in HANCOURT, at 1.30 p.m.	Via HANCOURT – BOUCLY Road.
Ambala Bde H.Q. 8th Hussars. "A" Bty R.C.H.A	At X roads BRUSLE-CATELET, CARTIGNY-HANCOURT Roads W. of C in CARTIGNY, at 1.30 p.m. 9th Horse, 18th Lrs, "N" Bty R.H.A. & 14th M.G. Sqdn will join in rear of "A" Bty R.C.H.A. at BRUSLE.	Via BRUSLE.
Field Sqdn.	BIAS. FARM.	Via CARTIGNY and BRUSLE.
"B" Battery R.C.H.A.	HAMELET	Via MARQUAIX and TINCOURT.
Canadian M.G. Squadron. Canadian M.V. Section.	ROISEL.	Via MARQUAIX and TINCOURT.

Issued as an enclosure to No. Q/513/e/2, dated 17/11/17.

(Appendix B)

SECRET.   Headquarters, 5th Cavalry Division.
                                          18th November 1917.

WATER ARRANGEMENTS IN FORWARD CONCENTRATION AREA.
Reference plan of Camp N.E. of FINS.

On "Z" day.

(a)
- W.P.1.   will be at the disposal of Canadian Cav Bde until Z+2 hours.
- W.P.2.   ---- do ----   Sec'bad Cav Bde until Z+2 hours.
- W.P.3.   ---- do ----   Ambala Cav Bde until Z+2 hours.

(b)
- W.P.2 & W.P.3.   ---- do ----   No.1 "A" Echelon group from Z+2 to Z+2½ hours.
- W.P.1.   ---- do ----   Divnl. Hdqrs. from Z+2 to Z+2½ hours.

(c) W.P.1.   ---- do ----   No.2 "A" Echelon group from Z+2½ to Z+3 hours.

(d) Remaining groups water after the above times at W.P.1 and W.P.2.

2. The A.P.M. will make the necessary police arrangements at the water points.

3. Each Brigade will send forward 1 officer and 6 men to supervise watering.

4. Each point is capable of watering 2,500 horses in 1 hour. Troughs must be used from both sides simultaneously.

5. Great care should be taken to prevent damage to the wire fences round the watering point.

                                              No. Q/513/W.

To/ Brigades and Divnl. Troops (Horsed).

              For information and necessary action.
                                       H.H. Combe
                                         Lieut-Colonel,
              A.A.& Q.M.G., 5th Cavalry Division.

Copies to :- General Staff.
              Lieut. G.R.H. BENNETT, Fort Garry Horse.
              Capt. & Qr.Mr. A. HIATT, 7th Dragoon Guards.

(Appendix C)

S E C R E T.

LIST OF BIVOUACS - 5TH CAVALRY DIVISION.

Divisional Headquarters............	SUZANNE.
Field Cashier......................	PROYART.
Signal Squadron....................	SUZANNE.
Field Squadron.....................	SUZANNE.
C.R.H.A............................	SUZANNE.
Ammunition Column..................	SUZANNE
Supply Column......................	PROYART.
Supply Col.,"A" Section............	PROYART.
Sanitary Section...................	PROYART.
A.H.T. Company.....................	BOUCLY.
Res.Park(H.Q.& No.2 Section).......	BOUCLY.
No. 1 Section............	(Detached).
Railhead(Supplies).................	LA FLAQUE.

CANADIAN CAVALRY BRIGADE.
Brigade Headquarters...............	SUZANNE.
R.C. Dragoons......................	Camp 17 (SUZANNE).
L.S. Horse.........................	CAPPY.
F.G. Horse.........................	BOIS OLIMPE.
R.C.H.A. Brigade...................	BOIS OLIMPÉ
Canadian M.G. Squadron.............	SUZANNE.
Canadian C.F.A.....................	CAPPY.
Canadian M.V. Section..............	SUZANNE.

SEC'BAD CAVALRY BRIGADE.
Brigade Headquarters...............	MERICOURT.
7th Dragoon Guards.................	FROISSY CAMP.
20th Horse.........................	MERICOURT.
34th Horse.........................	CHUIGNOLLES.
"N" Battery R.H.A..................	LA NEUVILLE les BRAY.
No.13 M.G. Squadron................	MARLY Camp.
Sec'bad I.C.F.A....................	CHUIGNOLLES.
Sec'bad M.V. Section...............	MERICOURT.

AMBALA CAVALRY BRIGADE.
Brigade Headquarters...............	BRAY.
8th Hussars........................	BRAY.
9th Horse..........................	ETINEHEM.
18th Lancers.......................	CHIPILLY.
No.14 M.G. Squadron................	BRAY.
Mhow I.C.H.A.......................	ETINEHEM.
Ambala M.V. Section................	BRAY.

No.Q/213/12.   Headquarters, 5th Cavalry Division.
                                              25th November 1917.

To/
    Cavalry Corps "Q".

                    For information.

                                                Lieut-Colonel,
                for G.O.C., 5th Cavalry Division.

Copies to :-
        Third Army "Q".
        1st, 2nd, 3rd and 4th Cavalry Divisions "Q".
        Usual Billeting List Distribution.

(Appendix I)

SECRET.

LIST OF BIVOUACS - 5TH CAVALRY DIVISION.

Reference Map Sheet 62c - 1/40,000.

```
Divisional Headquarters................ MONCHY LAGACHE.
Field Cashier.......................... ESTREES en CHAUSSEE.
Signal Squadron........................ MONCHY LAGACHE.
Field Squadron......................... 
C.R.H.A............................... MONCHY LAGACHE.
Ammunition Column...................... MONCHY LAGACHE.
Supply Column.......................... ESTREES en CHAUSSEE.
Sanitary Section....................... MONCHY LAGACHE.
A.H.T. Company......................... ESTREES en CHAUSSEE.
Reserve Park........................... MONCHY LAGACHE.
Railhead(Supplies)..................... BRIE.
```

CANADIAN CAVALRY BRIGADE.
```
Brigade Headquarters................... MERAUCOURT.
R.C. Dragoons.             )
L.S. Horse.                )
F.G. Horse.                )
"A" Battery R.C.H.A.       )...... MERAUCOURT - MONTECOURT Area.
"B" Battery R.C.H.A.       )
Canadian M.G. Sqdn.        )
Canadian C.F.A.            )
Canadian M.V. Section.     )
```

SEC'BAD CAVALRY BRIGADE.
```
Brigade Headquarters................... TREFCON.
7th Dragoon Guards.        )
20th Horse.                )
34th Horse.                )
"N" Battery R.H.A.         )............ TREFCON Area.
No.13 M.G. Squadron.       )
Sec'bad I.C.F.A.           )
Sec'bad M.V. Section.      )
```

AMBALA CAVALRY BRIGADE.
```
Brigade Headquarters................... TERTRY.
8th Hussars.               )
9th Horse.                 )
18th Lancers.              )............ TERTRY and CAULAINCOURT Area.
No.14 M.G. Squadron.       )
Mhow I.C.F.A.              )
Ambala M.V. Section.       )
```

No.Q/213/13.

Headquarters, 5th Cavalry Division.
28th November 1917.

To/
Cavalry Corps "Q".

Forwarded.

Lieut-Colonel,
for G.O.C., 5th Cavalry Division.

Copies to :-
Third Army "Q".
1st, 2nd, 3rd, 4th Cavalry Divisions "Q".
Usual Billeting List Distribution.

No. Qm 113

Hqrs. 5th Cavalry Division
1st January 1918

To
A.G. in India
Army Hqrs.
Simla

Herewith Administrative War Diary of 5th Cavalry Division for month of December 1917.

for G.O.C. 5th Cav. Divn.

WAR DIARY or **INTELLIGENCE SUMMARY**

Army Form C. 2118.

Place	Date	Hour	Summary of Events and Information	Remarks and references to Appendices
MONCHY LAGACHE.	1st		Division still engaged in operations. "B" Echelons and Ammunition Column (Malt Section), Heavy Section, Reserve Park and Dismounted Reinforcements moved into ATHIES Area. Railhead to BRIE. Casualties to 12 noon.— 9th Horse.- Killed Major A.I. FRASER, D.S.O. " F.ST.J.ATKINSON. 8 O.R.I. Wounded 2/Lt. J.R.K. MURPHY (slightly at duty). Capt. M. DUDDING. Ress. HARBANT SINGH. Jem. MIR ALAM KHAN. " SARDAR KHAN. 35 O.R.I.(includes 7 slightly at duty). Missing 6 O.R.I. R.C. Dragoons.- wounded Lt. V.B. CROTHERS. 4 O.R.B. L.S. Horse.- Killed Lt-Col. M. DOCHERTY, D.S.O. Lieut. R. YOUNG. 9 O.R.B. Wounded Major J.C. CLARKE. 34 O.R.B.(includes 4 slightly at duty). Missing 6 O.R.B. Canadian M.G. Sqdn.- Killed Lieut. A.L. WAUGH. 2 O.R.B. Wounded Lt. A. PIERSON. } slightly at Lt. T.D. MacNEIL. } duty. 2 O.R.B. R.C.H.A. Brigade.- Wounded Lt. M.H.S. PENHALE. Lt. J.T. CASSELS. Lt. J.L. LAWSON. 12 O.R.B.(includes 4 slightly at duty). 7th D. Guards.- Killed 2/Lt. G.L. REID. 3 O.R.B. Wounded 15 O.R.B.(includes 6 slightly at duty)	

Army Form C. 2118.

WAR DIARY
or
INTELLIGENCE SUMMARY.
(Erase heading not required.)

Instructions regarding War Diaries and Intelligence Summaries are contained in F.S. Regs., Part II. and the Staff Manual respectively. Title pages will be prepared in manuscript.

Place	Date	Hour	Summary of Events and Information	Remarks and references to Appendices

	1st (ctd)		20th Horse.- Wounded Capt. N.F.C. MULLOK, M.C. 1 O.R.B.(Interpreter).
			 8th Hussars.- Killed Major Hon. R.N.D. RYDER. 4 O.R.B.
			            Wounded Lt. T.G. WATSON.
			            29 O.R.B.(includes 1 Interpreter).
			            Missing 6 O.R.B.
			 18th Lancers.- Killed Lt-Col. E.C. CORBYN.
			            6 O.R.I.
			          Wounded Capt. G.G. ROYSTON.
			            Lt. W.B. BLETSOE.
			            Capt. R. DENING.
			            Jem. FATEH KHAN.
			            30 O.R.I.
			 "N" Battery R.H.A.- Wounded 6 O.R.B.(includes 1 since died of wounds and
			                              (1 slightly at duty).	

	2nd		Casualties to 12 noon.- R.C. Dragoons.- Wounded 3 O.R.B. No. 14 M.G. Sqdn.- Wounded Lt. C.S. KERNICK(since died of wounds). 20th Horse.- Killed 2 O.R.I. 34 Wounded 10 O.R.I. 34th Horse.- Wounded 7 O.R.I. 8th Hussars.- Wounded 1 O.R.B.(slightly at duty). 9th Horse.- Wounded Ress. HARDIT SINGH. Division engaged in operations. Report Centre closed at E.5.a. at 4 .p.m. and opened at HEUDICOURT same hour.	
	3rd		Report Centre closed at HEUDICOURT at 12 noon and opened at LONGAVESNES same hour. Railhead to LA CHAPELETTE. Division withdrawn from the line and concentrated in bivouacs about VILLERS FAUCON and ROISEL, with the exception of R.H.A. and R.C.H.A. Brigades and Field Sqdn, R.E.	

WAR DIARY
or
INTELLIGENCE SUMMARY

Army Form C. 2118.

Instructions regarding War Diaries and Intelligence Summaries are contained in F.S. Regs., Part II. and the Staff Manual respectively. Title pages will be prepared in manuscript.

Place	Date	Hour	Summary of Events and Information	Remarks and references to Appendices
	3rd (ctd).		400 Dismounted Men (200 from 4th Cavalry Division and 200 from 5th Cavalry Division) formed a working party and located near HEUDICOURT. Ambala Cavalry Brigade (Dismounted) and No.13 M.G. Squadron moved up into the support line.	
	4th.		"B" Echelons joined up.	
	5th.		Ambala Brigade and 13th M.G. Squadron relieved by Infantry and moved to their area near VILLERS FAUCON.	
	6th.		R.H.A. and R.C.H.A. Brigades and Field Squadron rejoined Division to-day also 200 Dismounted Reinforcements who have been working under C.R.E., Cavalry Corps.	
	7th.			
	8th.		17th Bde R.H.A. and R.C.H.A. Brigades moved into action after dusk this date. Sec'bed Cav Bde moved to an area about BUIRE and BRUSH. DEVISE OLD BRUSLE. Ambala Cav Bde moved to an area about CARTIGNY. Divisional Headquarters moved to MONCHY LAGACHE. Report Centre closed at LONGAVESNES at 2 p.m. and opened at MONCHY BAGACHE same hour. Owing to sudden thaw, all roads in VII Corps area closed to lorries and all M.T., unless on very special duty or carrying wounded, etc. All supplies of this Division drawn by Horse Transport.	
	9th		Supply Column placed under orders of Cavalry Corps. Roads still closed to M. Transport.	
	10th		Roads still closed to M. Transport. Field Squadron placed under orders of C.R.E., Cavalry Corps.	
	11th		No. 13, 14 and Canadian M.G. Squadrons moved to GOMMECOURT to form a mobile Reserve to VI Corps.	
	12th		Field Squadron moved to POEUILLY CAULAINCOURT. Dismounted party of 150 men formed to work under C.R.E., Cavalry Corps and located at POEUILLY.	

Army Form C. 2118.

WAR DIARY
or
INTELLIGENCE SUMMARY.
(Erase heading not required.)

Place	Date	Hour	Summary of Events and Information	Remarks and references to Appendices
	12th (ctd)		No.13, 14 and Canadian M.G. Squadrons are now administered by the 3rd, 40th and 34th Divisions respectively. Light Trench Mortar Batteries returned from Third Army School of Instruction to Personnel for form 3 Batteries, and are attached to this Division.	Appendix A
	13th		32 Horses arrived as Reinforcements. Billeting list issued showing location of units at 12 noon this date.	
	18th		Division came under orders of Fifth Army at 12 noon this date. 24 Horses arrived as Reinforcements.	
	19th		310 Horses, 36 Mules arrived as Reinforcements.	
	20th		No.13, 14 and Canadian M.G. Squadrons returned to the Division this day.	
	24th		Billeting list issued showing locations of units 12 noon this date. 2 - 3" Stokes Mortars arrived for Instructional purposes.	Appendix B.
	25th		Casualties to 12 noon.- 20th Horse wounded 2 O.R.I.	
	29th		8th Hussars moved to TERTRY Area.	

S E C R E T.

(Appendix A)

LIST OF BIVOUACS - 5TH CAVALRY DIVISION.

Reference Map Sheet 62c. 1/40,000.

Divisional Headquarters	MONCHY LAGACHE.
Field Cashier	with supply column.
Signal Squadron	MONCHY LAGACHE.
Field Squadron	CAULAINCOURT.
O.R.H.A.	R.14.b.4.9.
Ammunition Column	near FOURQUES.
Supply Column	LA CHAPELLETTE - ETERPIGNY ROAD.
Sanitary Section	FOURQUES.
A.H.T. Company	ESTREES en CHAUSSEE.
Reserve Park	FOURQUES.
Railhead Supplies	LA CHAPELLETTE.

CANADIAN CAVALRY BRIGADE.

Brigade Headquarters	ROISEL (K.16.a.3.5.)
R.C. Dragoons	)
L.S. Horse	) about ROISEL.
F.G. Horse	)
R.C.H.A. Bde.	In the Line.
R.C.H.A. Bde (wagon lines)	In valley between SOYECOURT & POEUILLY.
Canadian M.G. Sqd.	temporarily detached with VI. Corps
Canadian C.F.A.	)
Canadian M.V. Section	) about ROISEL.

SEC'BAD CAVALRY BRIGADE.

Brigade Headquarters	V.4.d.
7th Dragoon Guards	BUIRE.
20th Horse	N. of DEVISE.
34th Horse	N. of DEVISE.
"N" Battery R.H.A.	In the Line
"N" Battery R.H.A. (wagon lines)	In valley between SOYECOURT & POEUILLY.
No.13 M.G. Squadron	Detached with VI Corps.
Sec'bad I.C.F.A.	COURCELLES.
Sec'bad M.V. Section	V.4.d.

AMBALA CAVALRY BRIGADE.

Brigade Headquarters	CARTIGNY.
8th Hussars	CARTIGNY.
9th Horse	BRUSLE.
18th Lancers	BRUSLE.
No. 14 M.G. Squadron	detached with VI Corps.
Mhow I.C.F.A.	CARTIGNY
Ambala M.V. Section	BRUSLE.

===

No. Q/213/14.   Headquarters, 5th Cavalry Division.
                  13th December 1917.

To/
Cavalry Corps "Q".

Forwarded.

H.W. Cobbe
Lieut-Colonel,
for G.O.C., 5th Cavalry Division.

Copies to :-
Third Army "Q".
1st, 2nd, 3rd, 4th, Cavalry Divisions.
Usual Billeting List Distribution.
VII Corps "Q"
Area Commandant, ROISEL.

(Appendix "B")

SECRET

LIST OF BIVOUACS - 5th. CAVALRY DIVISION

Reference Map Sheet 62c 1:40000

Divisional Headquarters	MONCHY LAGACHE
Field Cashier	ESTREES en CHAUSSEE
Signal Squadron	MONCHY LAGACHE
Field Squadron	W.8.b.8.6.
C.R.H.A.	R.14.b.4.9.
Ammunition Column	MONCHY LAGACHE
Supply Column	LA CHAPELLETTE
Sanitary Section	MONCHY LAGACHE
A.H.T. Company	ESTREES en CHAUSSEE
Reserve Park	MONCHY LAGACHE
Railhead Supplies	LA CHAPELLETTE

CANADIAN CAVALRY BRIGADE

Brigade Headquarters	MEREAUCOURT
R.C. Dragoons	)
L.S. Horse	) MEREAUCOURT Area.
F.G. Horse	)
R.C.H.A. Brigade	In the line.
R.C.H.A. Bde (Wagon Lines)	Q.34.c.0.5.
Canadian M.G. Squadron	)
Canadian C.F.A.	) MEREAUCOURT Area.
Canadian M.V. Section	)

SEC'BAD CAVALRY BRIGADE

Brigade Headquarters	TREFCON
7th. Dragoon Guards	)
20th. Horse	) TREFCON Area.
34th. Horse	)
"H" Battery R.H.A.	In the line.
"N" Battery R.H.A. (Wagon Lines)	)
No.13 M.G. Squadron	)
Sec'bad I.C.F.A.	) TREFCON Area.
Sec'bad M.V. Section	)

AMBALA CAVALRY BRIGADE

Brigade Headquarters	TERTRY
8th. Hussars	CARTIGNY
9th. Horse	)
18th. Lancers	)
No.14 M.G. Squadron	) TERTRY Area.
Mhow I.C.F.A.	)
Ambala M.V. Section	)

No.Q/213/15   Headquarters 5th. Cavalry Division.
                                         24th. December 1917.

To/Cavalry Corps "Q".

                 Forwarded.   Nutting Major
                                        Lieut-Colonel
                 for G.O.C., 5th. Cavalry Division.

Copies to :-
         Fifth Army "Q"
         1st, 2nd, 3rd, and 4th Cavalry Divisions "Q".
         Usual Billetting List distribution.
         VII Corps "Q".

(878) Wt. W8811/M2754 (E. 1851) 25,000 Pads. 10/17. M. & B., Ltd.   **Army Form C348** (Pads)

MEMORANDUM.

From 5th Cavalry Divn   To A.G. in India
Date 1st Feby 1918   Hd qrs. Simla

Herewith Administrative War Diary of 5th Cavalry Divisional Hdqrs for month of January 1918.

[Signature], Major
for G.O.C. 5th Cavy Divn.

Army Form C. 2118.

WAR DIARY
or
INTELLIGENCE SUMMARY

(Erase heading not required.)

A & Q 5. CAN. DIV.

Instructions regarding War Diaries and Intelligence Summaries are contained in F.S. Regs., Part II. and the Staff Manual respectively. Title pages will be prepared in manuscript.

Place	Date	Hour	Summary of Events and Information	Remarks and references to Appendices
MONCHY LAGACHE	3rd		2 Sections, A.T. Company, R.E. Joined Field Squadron.	
	6th		Division received orders to take over the trenches on the 15th instant.	
	11th		Thaw Scheme comes into force at 12 midnight. Orders re taking over the trenches cancelled.	
	14th		Thaw restrictions removed.	
	15th		Pioneer Battalion consisting of 20 Officers and 600 men from 2nd Dismounted Division arrived and are bivouaced at THIMPSON. Thaw Scheme in operation from 6 p.m. this date.	
	16th		94 Horses and 26 mules joined Division this date.	
	22nd		Normal traffic resumed.	
	23rd		Orders received for the Division to take over a portion of the line.	
	25th/26th		Division commenced to relieve the 1st Dismounted Division in the trenches.	
	26th/27th		Relief of the 1st Dismounted Division completed.	
BOUVINCOURT	27th		5th Cavalry Divisional Report Centre closed at MONCHY LAGACHE at 10 a.m. and opened at BOUVINCOURT same hour.	
	28th		Mounted portion of the Division commenced moving back by Brigades into the DOMART Area. Move as follows :- 1st day into the area.- HARBONNIERES - GUILLAUCOURT - WIENCOURT - BAYONVILLERS - WARFUSEE ABANCOURT - LAMOTTE - MARCELCAVE. 2nd day..........	

Army Form C. 2118.

WAR DIARY
or
INTELLIGENCE SUMMARY.

(Erase heading not required.)

Instructions regarding War Diaries and Intelligence Summaries are contained in F. S. Regs., Part II. and the Staff Manual respectively. Title pages will be prepared in manuscript.

Place	Date	Hour	Summary of Events and Information	Remarks and references to Appendices
	28th (ctd)		2nd day into the area.- VIGNACOURT - FLESSELLES - HAVERNAS - WARGNIES - NAOURRS - BERTEAUCOURT.	
			3rd day into the DOMART Area.	
			Canadian Cav Bde, mounted portion commences its march on the 28th. Ambala Cav Bde, mounted portion. } 5th Cavalry Reserve Park. } commence their march on the 30th. 5th Cavalry A.H.T. Company.	
			Sec'bad Cav Bde, mounted portion commences its march on the 1st February.	
			Administrative Instructions attached................................ the details	Appendix 'A'.
	30th		A rear Headquarters is established at DOMART-en-PONTHIEU to administer in the Back Area.	

Lieut-Colonel,
A.A.& Q.M.G., 5th Cavalry Division.

SECRET.   (Appendix A)   No.Q/521/7.
                    Headquarters, 5th Cavalry Division.
                                26th January 1918.
To/
    Brigades and Divnl. Troops.

               ADMINISTRATIVE INSTRUCTIONS.
               Reference O.O. No.51 dated 26th instant.

SUPPLIES.- Supplies will be delivered in the new area on the 1st day of the move of each Brigade about 12 noon. Rendezvous - entrance to PROYART from South.   On the subsequent days' marches, in their new area, rendezvous to be notified later.

CARRIAGE OF 2ND BLANKETS.- O.C., A.S.C. will detail 1 lorry per regiment and 1 per Brigade Hdqrs for the carriage of 2nd blankets. The lorry allotted to Brigade Hdqrs will carry the 2nd blankets of the M.G. Sqdn. On arrival in the new area, lorries will concentrate at B.H.Qs and await orders.

CARRIAGE OF HORSE RUGS.- O.C., A.S.C. will arrange for the A.H.T. wagons to join regiments, etc., for the carriage of horse rugs :-

        Regiments..................... @ 3 ... 27
        M.G. Squadrons................ @ 1 ... 3   * to remain till
    *   Field Squadron................ @ 1 ... 1   unit marches.
        Divnl. Hqrs................... @ 1 ... 1
        Ammunition Column............. @ 1 ... 1
        Brigade Hdqrs................. @ 1 ... 3

                                               36
                                              ====

These wagons are not to be used for any other purpose.

SURPLUS GOVERNMENT STORES.- Surplus Government stores and tentage for which no authorised transport exists will be dumped in the place already notified by you to this office. A guard of 1 N.C.O. and 3 men will be left over each dump. This guard will also act as loading party and proceed with the lorry to the new area. This guard will be provided with 4 days' rations.
    Tentage, as shown in my Q/444 dated 4/7/17 will be carried on units' transport.

MARCHING OUT CERTIFICATES.- Units will render a marching out certificate to the Area Commandant of the area in which the unit is situated.

SANITATION.- Huts and stables, etc., will be left in a thoroughly clean and sanitary condition. An officer should be left behind to see that these orders are carried out. Also the Divnl. Sanitary Section will be employed in assisting units in cleaning up each Brigade Area after vacation.

BILLETING OF HORSES UNABLE TO PROCEED ON LINE OF MARCH.- The attention of all concerned is drawn to G.R.O. 3059 re care of sick horses on the line of march, which cancels all previous instructions on the subject.

ADMINISTRATION OF BACK DETAILS.- A Divnl. Rear Hdqrs will be opened at DOMART-en-PONTHIEU, with Capt. J.G.M. O'HARA, Worcester Yeomanry acting as A.A.& Q.M.G., time and date to be notified later. Brigades will also arrange to open a Rear Hdqrs at their respective Brigade Hdqrs (Back Details).

BILLETS.- A list of billets has been circulated to Brigades for guidance.

                                        Nutting   Major,
                                For A.A.& Q.M.G., 5th Cavalry Division.
Copies to :-   Secbad
        "G".   Os.C./Bde Back Details.   A.D.P.S.   Field Cashier.
                       Gas Officer.   "A"

PROPOSED BILLETING AREA - 5TH CAVALRY DIVISION.

Ref. Maps LENS 11, ABBEVILLE 14 and AMIENS 17.

Divisional Headquarters............	DOMART-en-PONTHIEU.
D.A.D.O.S.........................	-- do --
A.P.M.............................	-- do --
A.D.M.S...........................	-- do --
A.D.V.S...........................	-- do --
Divnl. Gas Officer................	-- do --
Divnl. Claims Officer.............	-- do --
Field Cashier.....................	-- do --
O.C., A.S.C.......................	-- do --
5th Signal Squadron...............	-- do --
5th Field Squadron................	
Hqrs Bde R.H.A..................	
Ammunition Column.................	
5th Cav Supply Column.............	HALLOY-les-PERNOIS.
Sanitary Section..................	DOMART-en-PONTHIEU.
A.H.T. Company....................	-- do --
No. 1 Sec. Reserve Park...........	FIENVILLERS.
No. 2 Sec. Reserve Park...........	MONTRELET.
Railhead..........................	CANDAS.
AMBALA CAV BDE H.Q................	LONGUET.
1 Cavalry Regiment................	AILLY-le-HAUT CLOCHER - FAMECHON - BUSSES-BUSSEL.
1 Cavalry Regiment................	VILLERS-sous-AILLY - BRUCAMPS - VAUCHELLES les DOMART - MOUFLERS - ERGNIES.
1 Cavalry Regiment................	LONG - L'ETOILE.
Battery R.H.A.................	
M.G. Squadron.....................	EPAGNE - EAUCOURT-sur-SOMME.
M.V. Section......................	COCQUEREL.
Cavalry Field Ambulance...........	YAUCOURT-BUSSUS.
CANADIAN CAV BDE H.Q..............	FRANSU.
1 Cavalry Regiment................	DOMLEGER - BEAUMETZ - PROUVILLE - LONGVILLERS - ARGENVILLE.
1 Cavalry Regiment................	RIBEAUCOURT.
1 Cavalry Regiment................	GORENFLOS - DOMQUEUR - LE PLOUY.
Battery R.H.A.................	
M.G. Squadron.....................	BERNEUIL - LANCHES - GORGES - ST. HILAIRE - LE PLOUY.
Cavalry Field Ambulance...........	
M.V. Section......................	FRANSU - BERNAVILLE.
SEC'BAD CAV BDE H.Q...............	BELLOY-sur-SOMME.
2 Cavalry Regiment................	LA CHAUSSEE - TIRANCOURT - ARGOEUVRES - ST.SAUVEUR - BERTEAUCOURT-les-DAMES - ST.OUEN - BETHENCOURT-ST.OUEN.
1 Cavalry Regiment................	VIGNACOURT - HAVERNAS - NAOURS - WARGNIES.
Battery R.H.A.................	
M.G. Squadron.....................	FLESSELLES.
Cavalry Field Ambulance...........	BELLOY-sur-SOMME.
M.V. Section......................	-- do --

N.B. Places underlined denote headquarters of units.
CANAPLES, HALLOY-les-PERNOIS, PERNOIS, FIEFFES, FRANQUEVILLE, out of bounds for horses.

25/1/18.

DIVISIONAL ORDERS
By
Major-General H.J.M. MACANDREW, C.B., D.S.O.,
Commanding 5th Cavalry Division.

Part II.   15th January 1918.

1710.- COMMAND.

Major-General H.J.M. MACANDREW, C.B., D.S.O., having rejoined from leave, assumed command of the Division with effect from 14/1/18.

1711.- PROMOTIONS - INDIAN OFFICERS.

The following promotions are made :-

18th Lancers.- No.1863 Kot Dafadar MUHAMMAD ASHRAF KHAN to be Jemadar with effect from 7/10/17, vice Jemadar SHER BAHADUR KHAN, evacuated sick.

20th Horse.- No.219 Kot Dafadar JHANDA SINGH to be Jemadar with effect from 25/8/17, to complete to establishment.

No.3610 Kot Dafadar MAHFUZ ALI KHAN to be Jemadar with effect from 25/8/17, to complete to establishment.

34th Horse.- No.3329 Dafadar UMED SINGH to be Jemadar with effect from 16/10/17 vice Jemadar KALYAN SINGH, classified "P.B".

1712.- PROMOTIONS - INDIAN OFFICERS - CORRIGENDUM.

34th Horse.- In Divisional Order No.1704 dated 8/1/18, date of promotion to Risaldar-Major of Risaldar HAMIR SINGH, should be amended to read 14/10/17.

20th Horse.- In Divisional Order No.1695 of 27/12/17 for "No.226 Kot Dafadar LAHRI to be Jemadar with effect from 11/10/17 vice Jemadar GANGA BISHAN promoted" read "No.226 Kot Dafadar LAHRI to be Jemadar with effect from 25/8/17 to complete establishment" and for "No.425 Kot Dafadar ABDUL RAZAK KHAN to be Jemadar with effect from 12/10/17, vice Jemadar SHAIKH MUHI-UD-DIN, promoted" read " No.425 Kot Dafadar ABDUL RAZAK KHAN to be Jemadar with effect from 25/8/17 to complete establishment".

1713.- APPOINTMENTS REGIMENTAL - CORRIGENDUM.

20th Horse.- In Divisional Order No.1678 of 12/12/17 read " Lieut. W.W. BARROW is appointed officiating Quartermaster from 20/7/17, vice Captain F.B.N. TINLEY, M.C. vacated on promotion".

1714.- PROMOTIONS.

The undermentioned N.C.O. is promoted Acting Sergeant with pay, to fill establishment whilst employed as a Divisional Gas N.C.O. with 5th Cavalry Division, with effect from 15/11/17.

No.106084 Corporal W.E. WRIGHT, R.E., Gas Services.

(Authority.- Adv. G.H.Q. OB/26, dated 23/10/17).

1715.- BOUNDS.

The Divisional Ammunition Column camp, VRAIGNES is placed out of bounds to Indian troops owing to outbreak of mumps in that camp.

1716...........

1716.- COMMISSIONS.

Applications for Temporary commissions in the Supply Branch of the Army Service Corps can now be submitted. Candidates must not be under 35 years of age.
(Authority.- Q.M.G., G.H.Q. C/ASV/1847, dated 8/1/18).

1717.- O R D E R S.

The attention of all Canadian units is drawn to G.R.O.2977.

1718.- O R D E R S.

The attention of all concerned is drawn to the following Routine Orders :-

G.R.O. 3122.	ACCIDENTS - DAMAGE TO LEVEL CROSSINGS.
G.R.O. 3147.	MAPS.
C.C.R.O. 666.	PATHWAYS IN HUTTED CAMPS.
5/Army R.O.1844.	HUTS - TARRING OF ROOFS.

Nulting Major,
for A.A. & Q.M.G., 5th Cavalry Division.

N O T I C E.

LOST from the Indian Camp at VILLERS CARBONNEL about 3.30 p.m. on the afternoon of 2nd instant - a bicycle, No.34248 or 34218.
(Information to.- O.C., Indian Cavalry Pioneer Battalion).

DIVISIONAL ORDERS

By

Major-General H.J.M. MACANDREW, C.B., D.S.O.,
Commanding 5th Cavalry Division.

Part II.   23rd January 1918.

1720.- HONOURS AND REWARDS.

The Divisional Commander has much pleasure in notifying the following Honours and Rewards, which have been awarded in the NEW YEAR's HONOURS GAZETTE :-

COMPANION OF THE ORDER OF ST. MICHAEL AND ST. GEORGE.

Brigadier-General The Rt.Hon. J.E.B. SEELY, C.B., D.S.O.,
         Commanding Canadian Cavalry Brigade.

TO BE BREVET MAJOR.

Captain F.S. COLLINS, R.E., late O.C., 5th Field Squadron.

THE DISTINGUISHED SERVICE ORDER.

Lieut-Colonel W.H.P. ELKINS, late O.C., R.C.H.A. Brigade.
Lieut-Colonel A.N. FLEMING, I.M.S., O.C., Sec'bad I.C.F.A.
Lieut-Colonel R.R.B. JACKSON, A.S.C., O.C., A.S.C.
Major D.J. MACDONALD, Lord Strathcona's Horse.

MILITARY CROSS.

Captain H.K. BARNES, R.H.A., O.C., 17th Bde R.H.A. Ammn. Column.
Captain F.S. ANDERSON, R.H.A., late "N" Battery R.H.A
Lieut. F.A. FARQUHARSON, I.A.R., late 5th Field Squadron.

DISTINGUISHED CONDUCT MEDAL.

No.37712 B.S.M. F. FARLIE, R.H.A., 17th Bde R.H.A. Ammn Column.
    133 Farrier Q.M.S. W.A. CHINERY, R.H.A., "N" Battery R.H.A.

MERITORIOUS SERVICE MEDAL.

No. 50954 S.Q.M.S. H.A. DRAY, M.G.C., 14th Squadron M.G.C.
    9771 S.Q.M.S.(A/S.S.M) W. SILVESTER, 5th Field Squadron.
    A/862 Armourer Q.M.S. W.H. GOODWIN, A.O.C., Hqrs 5th Cav Divn.
    32018 Cpl.(A/Sgt) C.P. JAMES, R.E., 5th Signal Squadron.

INDIAN DISTINGUISHED SERVICE MEDAL.

Risaldar TEK SINGH, 9th Horse.
Jemadar SARDAR KHAN, 9th Horse.
Jemadar HABIB GUL, 9th Horse.
No.2588 Dafadar ABDUL SATAR KHAN, 9th Horse.
    2762 L/Dafadar NAWAB ALI KHAN, 9th Horse.
    2726 Sowar SARAIN SINGH, 9th Horse.
Jemadar ALAM SHER KHAN, 18th Lancers.
Jemadar KHUDA BAKSH KHAN, 18th Lancers.
Jemadar ADALAT KHAN, 18th Lancers.
No.1937 Dafadar ALLA DITTA KHAN, 18th Lancers.
    2411 Sowar MOHAMMAD JAN, 18th Lancers.
Risaldar KERSHED MOHAMMAD KHAN, 20th Horse.
No.670 Dafadar RAM SARUP, 20th Horse.
    3125 L/Dafadar NIADAR SINGH, 20th Horse.
    3461 Sowar(A/L/Dafadar) AUTAR SINGH, 20th Horse.
    1108 Sowar(A/L/Dafadar) MIR RONAQ ALI, 20th Horse.

P.T.O..............

Ressaidar BALWANT SINGH, 34th Horse.
Jemadar TAJ MOHAMMAD KHAN, 34th Horse.
Jemadar ANNO KHAN, 34th Horse.
No.2947 Dafadar SHER BAHADUR KHAN, 34th Horse.

1721.- APPOINTMENTS - REGIMENTAL.

18th Lancers.- Major V.A.S. KEIGHLY, M.V.O. to be officiating Commandant from 2/12/17, vice Lt-Col. E.C. CORBYN, killed in action.
Major C.H. MARSH, D.S.O. to be officiating 2nd-in-Command from 2/12/17, vice Major V.A.S. KEIGHLY, M.V.O.
Major C.G. RISLEY, D.S.O. to be officiating Squadron Commander from 2/12/17.
Captain A.H. BROOKE to be officiating Squadron Commander from 2/12/17, vice Major A.M. MILLS, D.S.O., transferred to England(Sick).

1722.- PROMOTIONS - INDIAN OFFICERS.

The following promotions are made :-
9th Horse.- Jemadar GANDHARAB SINGH to be Ressaidar, vice Ressaidar HARBANT SINGH, wounded, with effect from 1/12/17.
Jemadar MEWA SINGH to be Ressaidar vice Ressaidar SARDAR KHAN, wounded, with effect from 2/12/17.
No.1193 Kot Dafadar DAYA RAM, 16th Cav., attached, to be Jemadar vice Jemadar HARBANT SINGH, promoted, with effect from 1/12/17.
No.2588 Kot Dafadar ABDUL SATAR to be Jemadar, vice Jemadar MEWA SINGH, promoted, with effect from 2/12/17.
No. 600 Dafadar(Head Salutri) JETHA SINGH, 22nd Sam Browne's Cavalry, attached, to be Jemadar vice Jemadar FOJA SINGH, evacuated sick, with effect from 25/11/17.
18th Lancers.- No.1648 Kot Dafadar MIRZA KHAN to be Jemadar with effect from 2/12/17, vice Jemadar FATEH ALI KHAN, wounded and evacuated.

1723.- COMMISSIONS - ROYAL ARTILLERY.

For the present condidates below the rank of Corporal may be despatched to England for admission to Royal Artillery Officer Cadet Units, providing they are considered qualified in other respects for appointment to temporary, or Territorial Force Commissions in the Royal Artillery.
(Authority.- M.S., G.H.Q. 510/12535)

1724.- MARKING OF 4-GALLON PETROL TINS CONTAINING M.B.O.

In future the 4-gallon Petrol Tins containing M.B.O. will not have these letters on the can as at present; the sole difference will be the red marks.
The cases will be stencilled M.B.O. as heretofore.

1725.- RETURN - TROOPS UNDER CANVAS.

Reference Cav Corps R.O. 685; the return mentioned should reach this Headquarters on the 9th of each month.

1726.- O R D E R S.

The attention of all concerned is drawn to the following Routine Orders:-

C.C.R.O. 668. PRECAUTIONS AGAINST TRENCH FEET.
5/Army R.O.1849. DEMARKATION BETWEEN BRITISH AND FRENCH AREAS.
/Army R.O.1836 ELECTRIC LIGHTING SETS.
G.R.O. 3184. GERMAN TRENCH MORTARS & MACHINE GUNS FOR INSTRUCTIONAL PURPOSES.

Major,
for A.A.& Q.M.G., 5th Cavalry Division.

Army Form C. 2118.

WAR DIARY
of
INTELLIGENCE SUMMARY. 5th Cavalry Division
(Erase heading not required.)

A.A. & Q.M.G.

Instructions regarding War Diaries and Intelligence Summaries are contained in F.S. Regs., Part II. and the Staff Manual respectively. Title pages will be prepared in manuscript.

February 1915

Place	Date	Hour	Summary of Events and Information	Remarks and references to Appendices
DOMART	Feb 1st	11—	Billeting list showing location of Units at 12 noon this date	Appendix A
	"	11—	5th Cavalry Division Supply Column — Appendix A	
	"	8—	5th Cavalry Division locates KONTRE — HTS-CORPS-SAINTS	
	"	9—	Railhead of 5th Cavalry Division moved from CANDAS to KONTRE	
	"	10—	Orders issued for Right Section Heavy Park to move to Forward area	
	"	11—	Right Section Heavy Park arr. at LA CHAPELETTE	
	"	12—	Heavy arms Motor Lorries No. 1 arr.	Appendix B
	"	12½	Drawing of wire Instruction to relief of Musicants Heavy — Appendix C	
	"	13—	5th Cavalry Heavy Park received to forward Heavy Section to SBR 7th Dragoon Guards arrived from Cres	
	"	14—	H.Q. and one Sqn. 7th Dragoon Guards arrived from Cres SALICOURT to ans ARGŒUVES to Frequent	
	"	15	Orders issued for Headquarters, then to march to PONT-DE-MFTZ DECOURT	Appendix D
	"	16	HQ 5th Cavalry Division (less established at PONT DE MFTZ Heavy Sqn 5th Cavalry Heavy Part billets at GUINGUNE Right Section " " " " KRZETTMAZ Fifth Army Order No. 5/2/15	Appendix W
PONT-DE-MFTZ				

Place	Date	Hour	Summary of Events and Information	Remarks and references to Appendices
PONT-DE-METZ	Feb.	17th	5th Division relieved by 1st Newcastle Division. The supported unit crosses to the Back Area this date. Location as under:-	
			Headquarters Hotels - PONT-DE-METZ	
			9th Hodgson Horse - MOUFFLERS, VAUCHELLES, 1st - DOMART, 1ETO1
			9th Lancers - LONG	DRUCAMPS-VILLERS-SOUS
			18th M.G. Squadron - FRESNE FAUCOURT	AMY
			1st M.G. Squadron -	
			13th M.G. Squadron - FLIXECOURT	
			On completion of relief the following units recuperate in the Forward Area -	
			Canadian Brigade	
			Brigade Headquarters	VRAIGNES
			Fort Newcastle Rgt.	
			M.G. Squadron	VERMAND
			2 Newcastle Rgt.	VERMAND
			SECOND BDE	
			1st Dragoon Guards	VERMAND
			AMB M.G. Bgt.	
			5th Hussars	VERMAND

Army Form C. 2118.

WAR DIARY
or
INTELLIGENCE SUMMARY.
(Erase heading not required.)

Place	Date	Hour	Summary of Events and Information	Remarks and references to Appendices
PONT-DE-METZ	10th	18"	Party of 175 all ranks of 1st Dragoon Guards Moved back from 11th Car Bde for work under 258 Lt Tunnelling Coy of XIX Corps	
	"	20"	8th Hussars Advanced Party proceeded taking 50 horses for Coys under XIX Corps. 50 men of 8th Hussars at Fourier Area relieves by mounted parties from Back Area	
	"	21st	Canadian Cav Bde HQ has moved to THIEFAUCOURT. No men of 1st Dragoon Guards in Fourier Area relieved by mounted parties from Back Area	
	"	22nd	Canadian CFA moved to VERMAND. When CFA moved to Back Area and are located at YAUCOURT-BUSSUS.	
	"	23"	Party as detailed on Q5018/A/3 and Q5018/A/4 entrained for TARANTO - Appendix "F" Cav Corps Administrative Instruction N° 2	"Fi" "G"
			Cav Corps N° Q3494 P.A. forwarded for guidance	"F"
	24"		Party as detailed Q5018/A/15 and Q5018/A/14 entrained for TARANTO 13th Australian Light Horse marched from this Area to 4th Army Area - FROHEN-LE-GRAND	

WAR DIARY
or
INTELLIGENCE SUMMARY.

Army Form C. 2118.

Place	Date	Hour	Summary of Events and Information	Remarks and references to Appendices
PORT-SE-MITZ	Feb. 25th		Cav. Corps Q.3494 for embarkation at Taranto on 10th March. Appendix "K". Cav. Corps Administrative Instructions No. 5. Cav. Corps Instructions regarding N.T. Vehicles proceeding overseas.	"M"
	" "		Units as detailed in "C" Car. Adm. Q.53/1/1 moves to rest areas for embarkment. G.R.153/1/01	F
	" "		3rd Cavalry Ammunition Park rejoined 5th Cav. Supply Column. Theo. out	
	Feb. 27th		Parties of Group "A" as detailed in Q.53/1/17/3 — M6 — M9 — M9 entrained for Marseilles. Yorkshire Dragoon moves of M6/M7 — Appendix "A". Area being commenced by Ambala Bde.	M.M. #
	" "		1st M.G. Sqn moved to Tomani.	
	Feb. 28th		Moves of units took place as details in Q.53/1/9/3 Party's in details in Q.153/1/9/h entrained for Taranto Party in details in Q.53/1/14/1 entrained for Mars(eilles). Canadian Light Dragoons moves to this camp and out. 1/1st M.G. Sqn at Moufffaks Camp.	
			Orders for embarkment of party for Taranto on 1st March. Q.53/1/19/m Hurbata Corps appendix.	"O"
			Alterations in group "A" G.53/1/21/m	P

SECRET.

LIST OF BILLETS - 5TH CAVALRY DIVISION.
Ref. Map. LENS 11, ABBEVILLE 14, & AMIENS 17.

Divisional Headquarters	PONT de METZ.
Field Cashier	LONGPRE-les-Corps-Saints.
Signal Squadron	PONT de METZ.
Field Squadron	Forward Area.
C.R.H.A.	-do-
Ammunition Column	-do-
Supply Column	LONGPRE-les-Corps-Saints.
Sanitary Section	DOMART-en-PONTHIEU.
A.H.T. Company	ST. LEGER-les-DOMART.
Reserve Park. (Heavy)	QUINCONCE.
(Light)	V.12.C.1.3.
Railhead Supplies	LONGPRE-les-Corps-Saints

CANADIAN CAVALRY BRIGADE.

Brigade Headquarters	RIBEAUCOURT.
R.C.Dragoons	FRANSU - LE PLOUY - DOMQUEUR
L.S.Horse	CRAMONT.- LE MENAGE LES MASURES - MESNIL - DOMQUEUR - LONGVILLERS.
F.G. Horse	DOMLEGER - AGENVILLE - BEAUMETZ - PROUVILLE.
R.C.H.A. Brigade	Forward Area.
Canadian M.G. Squadron	BERNEUIL - ST HILAIRE.
Canadian C.F.A.	DOMART-en-PONTHIEU.
Canadian M.V. Section	CORENFLOS.

SEC'BAD CAVALRY BRIGADE.

Brigade Headquarters	BELLOY-sur-SOMME.
7th Dragoon Guards	ARGOEUVES - PICQUIGNY. LA CHAUSSEE - TIRAUCOURT.
20th Horse	BETHENCOURT - ST QUEN. BERTEAUCOURT-les-DAMES.
34th Horse	HAVERNAS - WARGNIES - NAOURS - VIGNACOURT.
"N" Battery R.H.A.	Forward Area.
13th Squadron M.G.C.	FLESSELLES.
Sec'bad I.C.F.A.	VIGNACOURT.
Sec'bad M.V. Section	BELLOY-sur-SOMME.

AMBALA CAVALRY BRIGADE.

Brigade Headquarters	LONGUET.
8th Hussars	AILLY - le-HAUT CLOCHER AILLY - BUIGNY-L'ABBE - YAUCOURT.
9th Horse	MOUFLERS - VAUCHELLES-les DOMART - L'ETOILE - BRUCAMP - VILLERS-sous-AILLY.
18th Lancers	LONG.
14th Squadron M.G.C	EPAGNE - EAUCOURT.
Mhow I.C.F.A	YAUCOURT. BUSSUS.
Ambala M.V. Section	LONG.

No. Q/213/16

Headquarters, 5th Cavalry Division.
6th March 1918.

To/
Cavalry Corps "Q"

Forwarded.

Captain,
for G.O.C., 5th Cavalry Division.

S E C R E T.   Appx B   Copy No. 6

Dismounted Divisions Order No. 7.

Dated 12th February 1918.

1. The 4th Dismounted Division will be relieved on the nights 13th/14th and 14th/15th inst, by the 72nd Infantry Brigade, 24th Division.

The 5th Dismounted Division will be relieved on the nights 15th/16th and 16th/17th by the 1st Cavalry Division.

On relief, 4th Dismounted Division will entrain at ROISEL and detrain at CALUA, 5th Dismounted Division will entrain at ROISEL and detrain at LONGPRE.

Orders for entrainment will be issued by A.A.& Q.M.G. Dismounted Divisions.

2. The following dismounted units, on completion of relief, will move as under :-

6th Dragoons.)	
17th Lancers.)	Huts at MONTIGNY FARM
1/1st Yorkshire Dragoons)	
7th Dragoon Guards.)	
8th Hussars.)	Tents at VERMAND.
Canadian Brigade (less	
M.G. Squadron.)	Huts at VERMAND.

Accommodation will be arranged by Cavalry Corps."O"

3. Reliefs and moves of M.G. Squadrons will be as follows :-

10 and 12th M.G. Squadrons, on relief by 24th Division will move under orders of 4th Dismounted Division.

11th M.G. Squadron will remain in its present position and come under the orders of the 24th Division until further orders.

On night of 13th/14th inst.

14th M.G. Squadron will be relieved by 1st M.G. Squadron and will then move to TADENCOURT and come under the orders of Ambala Brigade.

On the 16th inst.

2nd M.G. Squadron moves to JEANCOURT and occupies 1st M.G. Squadrons present camp.
7th, 9th and 15th M.G. Squadrons and Canadian M.G. Squadron, remain in their present positions.

4. The Cavalry T.M. Battery will be relieved on the night of 14th/15th inst., and will be accommodated at BEAUMETZ.
On relief they will come under orders of Cavalry Corps.
"O" Dismounted Divisions will provide lorry transport for personnel and stores.

5. Command of Centre Sector will pass to G.O.C., 24th Division at 10 a.m. on 15th inst.

6........

Dismounted Divisions Order No. 7. (contd).

6. Major-General Macandrew and Staff will be relieved by Major-General Mullins and Staff in Command of Dismounted Divisions. Command will pass at 10 a.m. on 17th inst.

7. There will be no change in artillery arrangements.

8. All other details of reliefs in Centre Sector will be arranged direct between 4th Dismounted Division and 72nd Infantry Brigade, and in Right Sector between 5th Dismounted Division and 1st Cavalry Division.

9. Transport (less that of units mentioned in para. 2. and of 11th, 13th and Canadian M.G. Squadrons) will move as follows.

On 14th inst.	4th Cavalry Division.	To PROYART Area.	via Main VERMAND VILLERS-BRETTONEUX Road.
On 15th inst.	5th Cavalry Division.	-do-	-do-

Any transport required by 4th Dismounted Division on the night of 14th/15th., and by the 5th Dismounted Division on the night 16th/17th., in connection with relief, will be supplied on application to "Q" Dismounted Divisions.

10. All Defence Schemes, Maps, Aeroplane Photos, etc., etc. will be handed over to incoming units and receipts given.

11. A.D.M.S. Dismounted Divisions will make the necessary arrangements for the reliefs of Medical personnel.
12. Completion of reliefs will be reported to H.Q. Dismtd. Divs.
13. ACKNOWLEDGE. (4th and 5th Dismounted Divisions by wire).

(sd) T. HODGSON.

Lt.Col. G.S.,
Dismounted Divisions.

Issued to :-

Copy No.		Copy No.		
1.	5th Dismounted Division.	13	Cavalry Corps.	
2.	4th Dismounted Division.	14	24th Division.	
3.	Cavalry Divn'l Artillery.	15	61st Division.	
4.	C.R.E., Dismounted Divisions	16	72nd Infantry Brigade.	
5.	M.G.C. do.	17	1st Cavalry Division.	
6.	A.A.& Q.M.G. do.			
7.	A.D.M.S. do.	19	3rd Cavalry Division.	
8.	D.A.D.O.S. do.	20	4th do.	(rear)
9.	A.P.M. do.	21	5th do.	(rear)
10.	Gas Officer. do.	22	5th do.	
11.	Signals. do.	23 - 25	War Diary.	
12.	Camp Commandant do.	26 & 27	Office.	

Appendix 'C'

SECRET. No. Q/641.

To:
    4th Dismounted Division.
    5th Dismounted Division.
    S.S.O. Dismounted Divisions.

Reference Dismounted Divisional Order No. 7. dated 12th February 1918.

Reference para 1. ENTRAINMENT.

Train accommodation from the line to ROISEL on the Light Railway for the 4th Dismounted Division on the nights of 13th/14th and 14th/15th has been arranged, as detailed in this office No. Q/638 dated 12th instant.

The 5th Dismounted Division will forward as soon as possible a statement of their requirements on the Light Railway, giving the following particulars :-

    Places at which trains are required.
    Times   " " " " "
    Numbers of Officers and Other ranks for which accommodation is required in each train and name of units.

The timings of the trains on the broad gauge from ROISEL will be notified as soon as received from the Cavalry Corps. It is probable that a train will leave ROISEL each morning at 8.0 a.m. i.e.

    for 4th Dismtd.Div.at 8.0 a.m. on mornings 14th & 15th.
    " 5th Dismtd.Div. " 8.0 a.m. "   "   16th & 17th.

Reference para 2. - ACCOMMODATION.

Application for accommodation for the 6th Dragoons, 17th Lancers and 1/1st Yorkshire Dragoons at MONTIGNY FARM should be made by 4th Dismounted Division to the Area Commandant HERVILLY - by 5th Dismounted Division/for the 7th Dragoon Guards, 8th Hussars and Canadian Brigade at VERMAND to the Area Commandant VENDELLES.

/for accommodation

A Camp of 120 tents is being arranged by the Cavalry Corps at ROISEL for the accommodation of units from the line awaiting entrainment on the broad guage railway for the nights of 13th/14th, 14th/15th, 15th/16th and 16th/17th. This camp will be in the vicinity of the Railway Station. The 4th and 5th Dismounted Divisions will arrange to take over this camp from the Area Commandant ROISEL on the afternoon of the day their relief commences.

Reference para 4.

The 4th Dismounted Division will inform this office as soon as possible as to the number of lorries required for the move of the Cavalry T.M.Battery to BEAUMETZ and giving details as to time and place these lorries will be met.

P. T. O.

Application for accommodation at BEAUMETZ will be made to the Area Commandant VRAIGNES.

Reference para 9. - TRANSPORT.

(a)   The transport of the following units will remain in the Forward Area for duty with their respective units :-

        Canadian Cav.Brigade,
        8th Hussars,
        7th Dragoon Guards,   } at VERMAND.
        13th M.G.Squadron.

        6th (Innis) Dragoons,
        17th Lancers,
        1/1st Yorkshire Dragoons,   } at MONTIGNY FARM.
        11th M.G.Squadron.

(b).   The detachments of 1st and 4th Reserve Parks will remain at MONTIGNY FARM till completion of relief of 4th Dismounted Division, rejoining their respective units on 15th instant. The 4th Reserve Park is at LA CHAPELLETTE.

(c).   The detachments of the 3rd and 5th Reserve Parks will remain at VERMAND until the completion of relief of the 5th Dismounted Division; rejoining their respective units on the 17th instant. The 5th Reserve Park is at LA CHAPELLETTE.

(d).   The remainder of the transport of the 4th Dismounted Division and parties to move by road will march to the PROYART Area on the 14th instant rejoining their units in the Back Area on the 15th instant.

      The remainder of the transport and parties to move by road of the 5th Dismounted Division will march to the PROYART Area on the 15th instant; rejoining their units in Back Area on the 16th.

      4th and 5th Dismounted Divisions will wire the strength of parties for whom accommodation is required in the PROYART Area as soon as possible.

(e).   The road party of the Dismounted Divisional H.Q. will march with the 5th Dismounted Division transport on the 15th instant under the B.T.O. 5th Dismounted Division.

(f).   Application for additional transport required by Dismounted Divisions in connection with their relief will be forwarded to this office as soon as possible.

Reference para 11. - MEDICAL.

The A.D.M.S. will notify this office by 6.0 p.m. to-night the date and number for which accommodation is required in the PROYART Area, also details as to train accommodation required.

SUPPLIES.

The S.S.O. will arrange the following issues of rations :-

(a).   For parties proceeding by rail - 2 days at ROISEL.

(b).......

(b). For parties proceeding by road - 2 days plus the unexpended portion.

Parties remaining in the forward area will continue to be rationed by the S.S.O. Dismounted Divisions.

Indian Reserve Rations in strong points etc, will be withdrawn to their respective Refilling Points under arrangements made by 4th and 5th Dismounted Divisions. In the cases in which this has not already been done, Indian Reserve Rations will be replaced by British Reserve Rations.

Receipts for Reserve Rations handed over to incoming will be forwarded to this office

M.P.Raymond
Captain,
D.A.A.&.Q.M.G. Dismounted Divisions.

H.Q. Dismtd.Divns,
13th February 1918.

Copies to :-

Cavalry Corps "Q".
4th Cavalry Division. "Q".
5th Cavalry Division. "Q".
A.D.M.S. Dismtd.Divns.
"Q" Dismtd.Divns.
D.A.D.O.S.
Area Commdt. HERVILLY.
"   "   VENDELLES.
"   "   ROISEL.
"   "   BEAUMETZ.

No. A/7959.

Headquarters, 5th Cavalry Division.
15th February 1918.

To/
Brigades.
A.S.C.
D.A.D.O.S.
A.P.M.
Canadian F.A.
Sanitary Section.
A.D.V.S.

5th Cavalry Division Rear Headquarters will march from DOMART to PONT de METZ on the 16th instant.

1. All spare horses and transport will form up in the square at 8.45 a.m., ready to march at 9 a.m. Head of the Column facing towards BERNEUIL.

2. They will march by the route DOMART, VIGNACOURT, ST VAST, ST. SAVEUR, AILLY-sur-SOMME, DREUIL, SAVEUSE, PONT de METZ.

3. The Police will march under the orders of the A.P.M.

4. O.C., A.S.C., will detail a lorry to be at the offices at 9 a.m.

5. The Ambala Signal Troop will march to H.Q. Ambala Brigade under the N.C.O. in charge.

6. The French Mission will march independently.

7. The Ordnance will move under orders of the D.A.D.O.S.

8. The Sanitary Section will remain at DOMART under the orders of O.C., 7th Canadian Field Ambulance.

(sd) G. O'HARA,
Captain,
A/D.A.A.& Q.M.G., 5th Cavalry Division.

SECRET.   No Q-531/R/3.

Headquarters, 5th Cavalry Division.

21st February 1918.

To

Sec'bad Cavalry Brigade.
Ambala Cavalry Brigade.
O.C., A.S.C.
A.D.M.S.
Camp Commandant.
Field Squadron.
Signal Squadron.
17th Bde R.H.A.

Reference para 1 of Cavalry Corps No C.R/6 dated 21-2-18 forwarded with my Q-531/R/2 of date.

---

1. The composition of parties will be as follows :-
   (a) 23rd February :-

	B.O's.	I.O's.	I.O.R's.	Remarks.
Comdg. Officer	1(a)	-	-	(a) Field Officer of Sec'bad Bde.
Adjutant.	1(b)	1(c)	-	(b) From Sec'bad Bde.
				(c) From 9th Horse.
Quarter Master.	1(d)	-	-	(d) From Ambala Bde.
From Regts.	9(f)	12(e)	-	(e) 2 from 18th Lan.
				6 from 34th Horse.
				4 from 20th Horse.
				(f) 3 from 9th Horse & 2 from each of other I.C.Regts.
Medical Officer.	1(h)	1(g)(h)		(g) Sub-Asst. Surgeon.
				(h) Detailed by A.D.M.S.
Pioneer Battn.	4	4		

TOTAL 35 Officers.

Pioneer Battn.	-	-	379(i)	(i) Includes 13 fols.
4 Regts @ 50 each.	-	-	200	
Medical.	-	-	138(k)	(k) detailed by ADMS from Mhow, Sec'bad & Fd. Ambs & San. Sec.

TOTAL 717 O.R's.

(b) 24th February:-

	B.O's.	O.R.B's.	Remarks.
B.Gen. BEATTY.	1.	-	
A.D.C.	1.	-	
Major NUTTING.	1.	-	
Capt WHEATLEY.	1.	-	
Major CLEGG.	1.	-	
ASC Officer. A.S.C	1.	-	
Clerks details	-	2.	
Provost.	-	2(m)	(m) Detailed by A.P.M.
Signal operators.	-	2(n)	(n) Detailed by O.C. Sigs.
D.R's.	-	3(n)	
Batmen.	-	6(o)	(o) For above officers.

Above will form Advanced Cavalry Divisional Staff

British Officers.	24(p)	-	(p) 6 from each I.C. Regt.
Batmen for above.	-	4(q)	(q) 1 from each I.C. Regt.
A.S.C. personnel.	-	30(r)	(r) Detailed by O.C., A.S.C.
A.S.C. details.	+	32(s)	(s) Detailed by O.C., A.S.C. from 4th Cav. Sup. Column.

2. The O.C., A.S.C. will arrange for three lorries to at the H.Qrs of each of the Ind.Cav.Regts at 10 am on 23rd Feb and also in consultation with A.D.M.S. for sufficient lorries for the Medical details for the conveyance of parties and kits to the station.

On the 24th Feb the O.C., A.S.C. will arrange for one lorry to be at the H.Qrs of each of the Sec'bad and Ambala Bdes for the conveyance of details and baggage to the station.

Lieut. Col.
A.A and Q.M.G., 5th Cavalry Division.

SECRET.   No Q.531/R/4.

Headquarters, 5th Cavalry Division,
22nd February 1918.

To

Sec'bad Cavalry Brigade.
Ambala Cavalry Brigade.
O.C., A.S.C.
A.D.M.S.
Camp Commandant.
Field Squadron.
Signal Squadron.
17th Bde R.H.A.
A.P.M.

The following amendments are made to this office No Q531/R/3 of 21st February.:-

Para 1(a):-
　　Erase entries opposite "From Regts" and substitute the following :-

```
                    B.O's.   I.O's.
"From Regts.        8(f)  n 13(e)  (e) 1 from 9th Horse
                                       2 from 18th Lancers.
                                       6 from 34th Horse.
                                       4 from 20th Horse.
                                   (f) 2 from each Regt.
```

Para 1(b) is reconstructed as follows :-

```
                    B.O's.   I.O's.   O.R's
(b) Maj.Nutting.      1.
    Capt Wheatley.    1.
    Maj.Clegg.        1.
    A.S.C.officer
      i/cASC details           1.
    Clerk.            -                  1.
    Provost.          -                  2(m)  (m)Detailed by A.P.M.
    Signal Operators- -                  2(n)  (n)Detailed by Sigs.
    D.R's(with Motor Bikes)              3(n)
    Batmen.           -                  4(o)  (o)For above officers.
```

Above will form advanced Cavalry Divisional Staff.

```
Ind.Cav.Regts.   25(p)          (30(q) (p) 7 from 9th Horse
                                ( 4(r)    6 from each of
                                              other Regts.
                                     (q)15 from Ambala and
                                           15 from SEC'BAD.
                                     (r)Br Batmen-1 from
                                            each Cav.Regt.
14th M.G.Sqdn.    1.              9
A.S.C.personnel.-                30(s) (s)Detailed by O.C.,
                                            A.S.C.
```

2, OC ASC will arrange for 1 lorry to be at the H.Q. of each Cav Regt and 1 lorry to be at M G Sqdn (14th) at 10 am on 24th for personnel and baggage.

　　　　　　　　　　　　　　　　Lieut.Colonel.
　　　　　　　　　A.A and Q.M.G., 5th Cavalry Division.

SECRET.   No Q-531/R/6.

                            Headquarters, 5th Cavalry Division.
                            23rd February 1918.

To

    Secbad Cavalry Bde.   (4)
    Ambala Cavalry Bde.   (4)
    17th Bde R.H.A.   (1)
    5th Field Squadron.   (1)
    5th Signal Squadron. (1)
    O.C.A.S.C.   (2)
    A.D.M.S.   (1)
    A.D.V.S.   (1)
    D.A.D.O.S.   (1)

Appendix "F"

    Cav. Corps "Q", Roar No C&R./12 dated 22-2-18, forwarded for guidance with reference to my No Q-531/11 of 22-2-18.

                                    [signature]
                                    Lieut. Colonel,
                            A.A and Q.M.G., 5th Cavalry Division.

SECRET.   No Q-531/11.
                    Headquarters, 5th Cavalry Division.
                    22nd February 1918.

To
  ✗ Sec'bad Cavalry Brigade.
  ✗ Ambala Cavalry Brigade.
  ✗ A.D.M.S.
  ✗ O.C., A.S.C.
  ✗ D.A.D.O.S.
  ✗ A.D.V.S.
  ✗ A.P.M.
  ✗ Camp Commandant.
  ✗ 5th Field Squadron.
  ✗ 5th Signal Squadron.
  ✗ 17th Bde. R.H.A.
    Cavalry Corps. "Q" Rear.
    4th Cavalry Division.

Appendix "F"

           Reference move of Division Eastwards (Overseas)
           ----

1. Troops will commence entraining for MARSEILLES on the 25th Feb.
    The entraining station will be either LONGUEAU or
SALEUX.   4 trains will leave daily.

2. Sialkot Cavalry Brigade will entrain first and will be followed
by the Indian Regiments and other details of the Ambala Brigade. The
latter will probably commence entraining on the 27th Feb.

3. Units will move to billets S.W. of AMIENS on receipt of orders,
as follows:-

	Area	Date	Remarks
(a) 9th Horse.	PROUZEL - PLACHY BUYON - BUYON - NAMPTY - NEUVILLE sous LOEUILLY.	25th Feb.	At present occupied by 6th Cavalry.
(b) 18th Lancers.	SAISSEVAL - BRIQUEMESNIL - CLAIRY SAULCHOIX - GUIGNEMICOURT - BOVELLES.	26th Feb.	At present occupied by 17th Lancers.
(c) 14th M.G. Squadron.	RUMIGNY ~~To be notified later.~~	27th ~~26th~~ Feb.	
(d) Mhow Cav. Fd. Amb. & Ind. details Amb. M.V. Section	RUMIGNY ~~-ditto-~~ attached to & in Area of 18th Lancers.	26th Feb.	
(e) 34th Horse.	BOUGAINVILLE - REVELLES - PISSY - SEUX.	To be notified later.	At present occupied by 19th Lancers.
(f) 20th Horse.	SAINS en AMIENOIS - GUYENCOURT - REMIENCOURT - COTTENCHY.	ditto.	At present occupied by Yorkshire Dragoons.
(g) Sec'bad Bde Headquarters.	CREUSE.	ditto.	At present occupied by Sialkot Bde. H.Q.
(h) Sec. Cav. Fd. Ambulance.	To be notified later.	ditto.	
(i) Sec. Mob. Vet. Section.	Ditto.	Ditto.	

4. On receipt of orders, the 7th D.G's and 13th M.G.Sqdn. will move
to billets nearer LONGPRE.   These will be notified later.

5. Attention is directed to my Q-531/b dated 29-1-18. (Unmarked ✗)

                                        H H Cobbe
                                        Lieut. Colonel.
                              A.A and Q.M.G., 5th Cavalry Division.

SECRET.   No.Q.531/Q/1.

                        Headquarters, 5th Cavalry Division,
                                    24th February, 1918.

To/
        Sec'bad Cavalry Brigade.

                                                approve
                                                  "F"

        Reference my Q.531/11 of 22.2.18.

        Erase sub-para.3 (f) and enter :-

Unit.	Area.	Date.	Remarks.
(f) 20th Horse	SAISSEVAL – BRIQUEMESNIL – CLAIRY SAULCHOIX – BOVELLES.	To be notified later.	On vacation of area by 18th Lancers

                                (sd.)   H.H. COBBE
                                            Lt-Colonel,
                            A.A.& Q.M.G., 5th Cavalry Division.

Copies to :-
            A.D.M.S.
            O.C. A.S.C.
            D.A.D.O.S.
            A.D.V.S.
            4th Cavalry Division.
            Cavalry Corps "Q" Rear.

Appendix "F1"

SECRET.   No. CR/12.

To,
    Brigades & Divisional Units.

ADMINISTRATIVE INSTRUCTIONS NO. 2.

In continuation of No. CR/6 of 21/2/18.

1.   Entrainment of Group 2, will begin on 25th February, and will proceed at the rate of 4 trains a day.
        Order of Units proceeding will be as follows, as far as is known at present.

        Sialkot Brigade.
        Indian Units of Ambala Brigade.
        Lucknow Brigade.

2.   Group 2 will be under the orders of Brigadier-General L.L. MAXWELL. C.M.G. Commanding Sialkot Cavalry Brigade.
        Group 3 will probably be under Command of Brigadier-General GREGORY. Commanding Sec'bad Brigade.

3.   The 17th Lancers will move from its present billeting area on 26/2/18 to LONG, when it will come under the administration of the Ambala Cavalry Brigade. The area vacated by the 17th Lancers is at the disposal of 5th Cavalry Division from 12 noon on 26th instant.

4.   The areas of Sialkot Brigade as regiments and units entrain are placed at the disposal of 5th Cavalry Division.

5.   Composition of each train in Group 1, will probably be one coach at 20 Officers, 30 covered trucks at 25 to 30 O.Rs. or 8 animals, 17 flat trucks.
        In reckoning accommodation a limbered G.S. Wagon is taken at 2, two-wheeled vehicles; 1 G.S. Wagon and a half limber can go on a flat truck as a rule, but apparently all flat trucks are not big enough.

6.   30 lorries will go on the first day; the wheels must be removed from these; and they will not include any workshop or store lorries.

7.   Lieut MACPHERSON, 6th Cavalry, will go ahead with the A.D.V.S. 5th Cavalry Division and act as Staff Officer, and will meet troops of Group 2 as they arrive at MARSEILLES.

                                        G. Maitland
H.Q. 4th Cav.Div.   Lieutenant-Colonel,
22/2/18.   A.A.&.Q.M.G. Cavalry Corps (Rear). "Q"

Copy to Cavalry Corps "
        5th Cavalry Division. 20 copies.

Appendix "G"

SECRET.

Cav.Corps G.3494/A.I. 22.2.18

Cavalry Corps 'Q' Rear. (10).
4th Cavalry Division.
5th Cavalry Division.

1. The attention of all units entraining is called to G.R.O. 3189 para. 7.

2. The Indian Cavalry Pioneer Battalion left Forward Area this morning for SALEUX.

3. The Base, B.E.F. ITALY will collect the special issue of Winter Clothing, such as fur coats, &c, at TARANTO.

4. G.S. Wagons with Cavalry Field Ambulances for carriage of blankets will be returned to the Auxiliary (Horse) Co. of their Division.

5. Auxiliary (Horse) Cos. of the 4th & 5th Cavalry Divisions are being withdrawn to work under the direct orders of Fifth Army.

6. In addition to the numbers already given, 226 Officers & 1360 O.Rs. will probably sail from TARANTO on 10th April.

7. Lorries will have to be loaded at LONGEAU Station, as there are no facilities at SALEUX. It will be necessary to either take the superstructures off, or remove the wheels of the lorries, otherwise they will not pass through the French tunnels.

8. All completely British Units go on Part VII A. ,W.E.; Indian Units on Part XVII W.E.

[signature]

Lieut-Colonel,
for D.A. & Q.M.G. Cavalry Corps.

22.2.18.

Copy to/'G'   A.D.Signals.
       A.D.C.   D.D.R.
       C.R.E.   Chem.Advr.
       L.S.& T. D.D.M.S.
       A.D.O.S. D.D.V.S.
       C.M.G.O. D.A.D.P.S.
       'A'

No Q 531/12./23-2-18

Forwarded for guidance.

[signature] Lt Col
A.D.Q.M.G. 5th Cav Dn

Appendix A

S E C R E T.   No.G.531/R/7.

Headquarters, 5th Cavalry Division,
25th February, 1918.

To:/
    Sec'bad Cavalry Brigade (5)   O.C., A.S.C. (2)
    Ambala Cavalry Brigade (5)   A.D.V.S. (1)
    17th Brigade R.H.A. (1)   D.A.D.O.S. (1)
    5th Field Squadron. (1)   Camp Commandant. (1)
    5th Signal Squadron. (1)   "G". (1)
    A.D.M.S. (3)   "A" (1)
    4th Cavalry Division (1)   War Diary (3)
    Cavalry Corps Rear (1)

1. Group "A" will embark at MARSEILLES on March 4th.

2. The following will form Group "A" and detailed orders for entrainment which, for 5th Cavalry Division units, will be on 27th and 28th inst., will be issued later :- The 9th Hodson's Horse will be the first unit to entrain :-

	Officers	O.R.	Animals	4 Wheel	2 Wheel	Ambles.	Cars.
4th Cavalry Divn.	71	1249	1824	23	79	7	2
	1	55	67	9	11	7	--
Total.	72	1304	1891	32	90	14	2
Surplus to be found by 4th Cavalry Divn.		225					
Total 4th Cav. Divn.	72	1529	1891	32	90	14	2
5th Cavalry Divn.							
9th Hodson's Horse	24	450	671	6	14	--	--
18th Lancers	18	355	435	6	14	--	--
Ambala M.V.S.	1	14	24	1	2	--	--
Mhow C.F.A.	1	50	67	9	9	7	2
Sec'bad C.F.A.	--	34	67	8	9	--	--
20th Deccan Horse	1-I.O.	45	--	--	--	--	--
34th Poona Horse	1-I.O.	45	--	--	--	--	--
Total 5th Cav. Divn.	46	993	1314	29	48	7	2
Grand Total.	118	2522	3205	61	128	21	4

4-wheeled, 110.   2-wheeled 100.

3. Entraining Station will be SALEUX.

4. Each train will carry 3 days' rations and forage in bulk for the journey.

5. Personnel will entrain fully equipped and clothed.

6. A table showing HALTES REPAS will be issued to the O.C. train at the entraining station.

7. Orders for the disposal of personnel and horses of the units concerned which do not accompany this group will be issued later.

Lt-Colonel,
A.A.& Q.M.G., 5th Cavalry Division.

Appendix H.

SECRET.   No Q-531/R/8.

Headquarters, 5th Cavalry Division.
26-2-18.

To
9th Hodsons Horse.

9th Hodson's Horse will commence entraining at SALEUX on the 27th as follows :-

(a) <u>No 9 Train.</u> - 1 coach, 31 covers and 8 flats.

B.O's.	I.O's.	O.R's.	Animals.	4 wheeled vehicles.	2 wheeled Vehicles
2.	3.	150.	180.	6.	14.

Commence entraining at 7-30 -hours.
Train leaves at 10-30-hours.

(b) <u>No 10 Train:-</u>   1 coach, 40 covers.

B.O's.	I.O's.	O.R's.	Animals.	4 wheeled vehicles.	2 wheeled vehicles
2.	3.	150.	246.	-------	-------

Commence entraining at 16-30-hours.
Train leaves at 19-30-hours.

O.C. 9th Horse will detail an officer to command each train and also a British or Indian Officer as QuarterMaster and Adjutant.

2.   3 days rations in bulk will be taken over by the Q.Mr. at the station

3.   A.D.M.S. will make necessary Medical arrangements for each train.

4.   2nd and 3rd blankets will be taken over by D.A.D.O.S. before departure from Billets.

5.   An Officer of the Divnl. Staff will meet the O.C. Train at the Station at 7-30 a.m., and 16-30 hours respectively.

6.   No 11 Train will leave SALEUX at about 7-30 a.m., on the 28th. Entraining will commence at 4-30-hours. Further details as regards composition will be sent on the 27th.

Lieut. Colonel.
A.A and Q.M.G., 5th Cavalry Division.

Copy to :-
Ambala Cavalry Brigade.
Sec'bad Cavalry Brigade.
A.D.M.S.
O.C., A.S.C.
D.A.D.O.S.
4th Cavalry Division.
Cav. Corps "Q" Rear.
"A".
"G".
Liaison Officer.
Camp Commandant.

SECRET.
No. Q.531/R/9.

Appendix H2

Headquarters, 5th Cavalry Division,
27th February, 1918.

To/
    O.C.,
        9th Hodson's Horse.

In continuation of this office Q.531/R/8 dated 26th inst.

1. Ref. para.6.

The following is the detail for No.11 Train:-

    No.11 Train - 1 Coach, 40 Covers.

B.O's.	I.O's.	O.R's.	Animals.	Vehicles.
2	3	150	180	Nil.

Commence entraining at 5.30 hours.

Train leaves at 8.30 hours.

2. Orders regarding the remainder of the Regiment will follow.

3. Acknowledge by bearer.

                                                  Lt-Colonel,

                A.A.& Q.M.G., 5th Cavalry Division.

Copies to :-
    Sec'bad Cavalry Brigade.
    A.D.M.S.
    O.C. A.S.C.
    D.A.D.O.S.
    4th Cavalry Division.
    Cavalry Corps "Q" Rear.
    "A".
    "G".
    Liaison Officer.
    Camp Commandant.

Appendix I

SECRET

No. G.531/Q/3.

Headquarters, 5th Cavalry Division,
26th February, 1918.

To/
    Sec'bad Cavalry Brigade.   A.D.M.S.
    Ambala Cavalry Brigade.   O.C., A.S.C.
    17th Brigade, R.H.A.   D.A.D.O.S.
    5th Field Squadron.   A.D.V.S.
    5th Signal Squadron.   A.P.M.
    4th Cavalry Division.   Camp Commandant.
    Cavalry Corps "Q", Rear.   Brig-General C.H. RANKIN.

1. The following moves will take place on the 28th February :-

   (a) <u>7th Dragoon Guards</u>.- To billets in LONGPRE.

   ROUTE.- BELLOY SUR SOMME - ETOILE - CONDE FOLIE.
   To be clear of CONDE FOLIE at 1 p.m.

   (b) <u>13th M.G. Squadron</u>.- To billets in COCQUEREL.

   O.C., A.S.C. will detail 9 lorries to be at FLESSELLES at
       9 a.m. to take dismounted personnel.

   (c) <u>Sec'bad Cav. Bde. H.Q.</u>- and <u>Sec'bad Mob. Vet. Sect.</u> to CREUSE

   TIME and ROUTE optional.

   (d) <u>20th Horse</u>.- To area SAINS EN AMIENNOIS - GUYNCOURT -
           REMIENCOURT - COTTENCHY.

   ROUTE.- VIGNACOURT - ST VAST EN CHAUSSEE - AMIENS.
   STARTING POINT.- VIGNACOURT - 10.15 a.m.

   (e) <u>34th Horse</u>.- To area BOUGAINVILLE - REVELLES - PISSY - SEUX.

   ROUTE.- VIGNACOURT - PICQUIGNY.
   To be clear of VIGNACOURT at 10 a.m.

   (f) <u>5th Cavalry Sanitary Section</u>.- To SALOUEL.

2. On completion of move 7th Dragoon Guards and 13th M.G. Squadron will come under orders of G.O.C., Ambala Cavalry Brigade.

Lt-Colonel,
A.A.&Q.M.G., 5th Cavalry Division.

SECRET.　　　No Q-531/R/11.

Headquarters, 5th Cavalry Division.
27th February 1918.

To
  9th Horse.
  18th Lancers.
  A.D.M.S.
  O.C.A.S.C.
  D.A.D.O.S.
  Sec'bad Field Ambulance.
  Ambala Cavalry Brigade.
  Sec'bad Cavalry Brigade.
  French Mission.
  Camp Commandant.
  "A" & "G".
  Signal Squadron.
  A.D.V.S.4th Cav.Divn.
  Capt LEE, Sanitary Section.
  4th Cav.Divn."Q".
  Cav.Corps,"Q" Rear.

Appendix "J"

The following personnel from this Division will entrain at SALEUX Railhead for TARANTO on the 28th February :-

	B.O's.	I.O's.	O.R.B.	O.R's.I.
5th Cavalry Sanitary Section.	1.	-	1.	22.
9th Hodsons Horse.	2.	2.	-	91.
Sec'bad Fd.Ambulance.	-	-	1.	25.
Total.	3.	2.	2.	138.

The O.C., A.S.C. will detail the following transport :-
  5 Lorries for 9th Horse at PROUZEL at 12 noon.
  1 lorry for Sanitary Section at SALOUEL at 12 noon.

2. All personnel will be at the Station to commence entraining at 13-30-hours. Train will leave at 16-20-hours.

3. Each man will be in possession of the iron ration and the unexpended portion of the day's ration.
  11 days rations will be taken over in bulk by the O.C.Train from the R.S.O.

4. Captain LEE, I.M.S., will be in Medical Charge of the train.

5. The D.A.D.O.S. will arrange to take over the 2nd and 3rd blankets.

6. The 4th Cav.Divn is detailing a Field Officer to Command the Train.

7. Details of other units will entrain for TARANTO on March 1st.

H.E.Cochran Lieut. for
A.A and Q.M.G., 5th Cavalry Division.

Appendix K

SECRET.   No. QA/707.

[Stamp: 5TH CAVALRY DIVISION No. QS21/R/10 Date 27-2-18]

To,
Brigades and Divisional Units.

ADMINISTRATIVE INSTRUCTIONS. No. 3.

Reference 6925/1/11 . (Q.A.1). dated 21/2/18, (4th Cavalry Division No. C/8795).

1. The party shown under "A" to sail from MARSEILLES on 4th March will proceed under Command of Brigadier-General L.L.MAXWELL, C.M.G. Captain F.GWATKIN, Staff Captain Sialkot Brigade, will go with him as his Staff Officer. General MAXWELL will arrive at MARSEILLES in a few days.

2. Party shown under "B" will consist chiefly of Lucknow Brigade and will be under Command of a Lieutenant-Col. of that Brigade.

3. Party "C" will be Commanded by Brigadier-General C.L.GREGORY, who will take Captain SIMPSON as his Staff Officer.

4. Party "D" will be under Command of a Lieut-Col, of Mhow Brigade.

5. Brigadier-General GREGORY will assume Command of the Division on this arrival at MARSEILLES, until he embarks on March 20th. The senior Officer remaining will take over from him.

6. Divisional Headquarters will sail partly from TARANTO on 10th March and partly from MARSEILLES on 10th. {Sailing

7. Lieut R.S.MACPHERSON, 6th Cavalry has proceeded to MARSEILLES as Staff Officer to the Division.
When Major G.B.HOWELL arrives at MARSEILLES he will assume the duties of Staff Officer to the Division, assisted by Lieut MACPHERSON.
These Officers will remain at MARSEILLES until the last party sails on April 11th.
Similarly the A.D.V.S. 4th Cavalry Division (Major HOLDNESS) and a Supply Officer (Captain SHORT), are remaining at MARSEILLES till April 11th.

The duties of the above Officers are to meet the Troops as they arrive and perform such administrative duties, as are necessary in connection with all troops of the Division proceeding to EGYPT.

G R Maitland
Lieutenant-Colonel,
A.A.& Q.M.G. 4th Cavalry Division.

H.Q. 4th Cav.Div.
25/2/18.

Copy to, Cavalry Corps "Q".
5th Cavalry Division.
Lieut MACPHERSON. (3 copies).

SECRET. QMG. 6925/1/21 (Q.A.1)

Appendix "L"

Cav. Corps Q.3494 - 24.2.18.

Fifth Army.
G.O.C., L. of C. Area.

In continuation of my 6925/1/5 (Q.A.1) dated 20/2/1918:

1. Personnel to embark from TARANTO on March 10th will be made up as shewn in Appendix "A" attached hereto.

2. Personnel will entrain in accordance with Appendix "B" attached hereto.

3. Personnel will entrain fully equipped and clothed as laid down in my 6925 (Q.A.3) dated 24th January, 1918.

4. Rations will be placed on trains as shewn in column 7 of Appendix "B".

5. A table showing Haltes Repas on the journey to TARANTO will be handed to the O.C. each train at the Station under arrangements to be made by the D.G.T.

6. A telegram will be sent to this office by the formations shewn in Column 8 giving the strengths of officers and other ranks entrained each day, British and Native personnel being shewn separately, and the number of days rations placed on each train.

7. Acknowledge.

G.H.Q.
23rd February, 1918.

(sgd) R.S. MAY.
M.G.
for Quartermaster General.

Copy to/ zzzz Cav. Corps   Cav. Corps (Rear).

2.

Cavalry Corps 'Q' Rear.

For action.

24.2.18.

Copy to/4th Cav.Div.Q.   G.O.C.R.A.   D.A.D.R.T. PERONNE.
     5th Cav.Div.Q.   D.D.M.S.   "A"
     'G'   D.D.V.S.
     A.D.S.&.T.   D.D.R.
     A.D.O.S.   Chem.Advr.
     C.R.E.   C.M.G.O.
     A.D.C.   D.A.D.P.S.
     A.P.M.   A.D.Signals.

Lieut-Colonel
for D.A. & Q.M.G. Cavalry Corps.

Appendix 1

APPENDIX "A".

Detail of Units that will embark at TARANTO on 10th March, 1918.

	Officers.	Other Ranks.
Personnel from Units of Indian Cavalry Divisions.	226	1350
No. 11 Indian Field Veterinary Section	1	76
No. 19 Indian Field Veterinary Section	-	85
No. 20 Indian Field Veterinary Section	1	64
No. 21 Indian Field Veterinary Section	-	71
No. 22 Indian Field Veterinary Section	1	51
No. 23 Indian Field Veterinary Section	-	74
Reinforcements for Indian Cavalry from MARSEILLES	16	490
	245	2260

APPENDIX "B".

1	2	3	4	5	6	7	8	9	10	11
Date of Entrainment.	Entraining Station.	U N I T.	No. of Trains	Strength Offrs O.Rs		No. of days rations to be put on train	Arrangements to be made by	Traffic with	Destination.	REMARKS.
26th Feby.	ROUEN	No. 21) No. 22) Indian Field No. 23) Veterinary No. 20) Sections. (part)	1	∅ 1	240	2	G.O.C. L. of C. Area.	Traffic ROUEN.	SALEUX.	∅ Draft conducting Officer, who will return on completion. G.O.C. Cavalry Corps will arrange for this party to be accommodated at SALEUX for night 26/27 and 27/28 and to move to TARANTO on 28th as shown below.
28th Feby.	SALEUX	No. 21) No. 22) Indian Field No. 23) Veterinary No. 20) Sections. (part) Personnel from Indian Cavalry Units.	1	113	240) 560)	11	Fifth Army	Traffic PERONNE	TARANTO.	Will sail from TARANTO on March 10th
1st March	SALEUX	Personnel from Indian Cavalry Units	1	113	600	10	Fifth Army	Traffic PERONNE	TARANTO	Will sail from TARANTO on March 10th.
3rd March	MARSEILLES	No. 11) Indian No. 19) Field Veterinary part No.20) Sections. Reinforcements.	1	4 16	180) 480)	8	G.O.C. L. of C. Area	Traffic MAR- SEILLES	TARANTO	Will sail from TARANTO on March 10th

Appendix M

S E C R E T.   Cav.Corps G.3494 - 25.2.18.

Cavalry Corps 'Q' Rear.
4th Cavalry Division.
5th Cavalry Division.

Reference my G.3494/Q.I. dated 22.2.18, para. 6, for "10th April" read 10th March.

2.   Under instructions from War Office no mechanical transport other than the following makes will be embarked :-

VAUXHALL, SUNBEAM, TALBOT, FORD, and TRIUMPH.

D. Transport is arranging the necessary exchanges. The 30 lorries detailed in para. 6 of Q.M.G. 6925/1/11 (Q.a.1) of 21.2.18 (issued under Cav.Corps G.3494 - 22.2.18) for transport work at MARSEILLES are not affected.

(Authority :- G.H.Q. wire O.A.1/240 d. 24.2.18).

                                        J. H. Callander Capt.
                                        for Lieut-Colonel,
25.2.18.   for D.A.& Q.M.G Cavalry Corps.

         Copy to/A.D.S.& T.   A.D.Signals.
                'G'   D.D.R.
                A.D.C.   Chem.Advr.
                C.R.E.   D.D.M.S.
                A.D.O.S.   D.D.V.S.
                C.M.G.O.   D.A.D.P.S.
                               A.P.M.

SECRET.   No Q-531/R/13.
　　　　　　　　　　　　　　Headquarters, 5th Cavalry Division.
　　　　　　　　　　　　　　28th February 1918.

Appendix "O"

To /
　　18th Lancers.
　　20th Horse.
　　34th Horse.
　　Sec'bad Field Ambulance.
　　Sec'bad Bde.
　　Sec'bad Signal Troop.
　　Sec'bad Mobile Vet.Section.
　　O.C.,A.S.C.
　　14th M.G.Squadron.
　　D.A.D.O.S.
　　Major Jarvis, 20th Deccan Horse.
　　Capt Hassard, Sec.Field Amb.

1.　The following personnel will entrain for TARANTO on the 1st March :-

	B.O's.	I.O's.	O.R.B.	O.R.I.	Remarks.
18th Lancers.	@	3.	%	98.	
20th Horse.	@	5.	%	93.	@ All B.O's present,
34th Horse	@	4.	%	110.	except C.O., & 4 others
Sec'bad Fd.Ambulance.	1.	-	1.		
Sec'bad Bde H.Qrs.	-	-	14.	3.	% Includes any British
Sec'bad Mob.Vet.Sec.	-	-	-	5.	Batmen & Followers
O.C.,A.S.C.	-	-	4.	-	taken.
14th M.G.Sqdn.	2.	-	9.	-	
D.A.D.O.S.	-	-	16.	-	
Sec'bad Signal Troop.	-	-	4.	-	
Total.		12.	48.	305.	

Div HQrs　　　　　　　　　　　　　　-　　　1　- # included in 305 ORS

2.　Regiments will report today to Divisional Headquarters the names of officers going and remaining.
　　Regiments will also report at the same time the number of Officers expected to rejoin from leave with dates of rejoining.

3.　Major Jarvis, 20th Horse will command the train. Sec'bad Bde will detail an Adjutant & Q.Mr. for the train.

4.　　　Captain Hassard, Sec.Fd.Amb. will be in Medical charge of train.

5.　Commence entraining at 13-hours.
　　Train leaves at 16-20-hours.

6.　10 days rations will be taken over in bulk by the Q.Mr.
　　Each man will be in possession of Iron Ration and the unexpended portion of the day's ration.

7.　Nominal Roll, in duplicate, of each party is required at the station at time of entraining.

8.　The D.A.D.O.S. will arrange to take over the 2nd and 3rd blankets.

9.　The O.C.,A.S.C. will detail the following transport :-
　　5 lorries for 18th Lancers H.Qrs, at 11 a.m.,
　　5 lorries for 20th Horse H.Qrs at 11 a.m.,
　　6 lorries for Poona Horse H.Qrs at 11 a.m.,
　　2 lorries at Sec'bad Bde H.Qrs for details of Bde H.Q.,)
　　　　　　　　　　　　　　　　　　　　　M.Vet.Section　　) at 11 a.m.,
　　　　　　　　　　　　　　　　　　　　　Signal Troop.　　)

1 lorry at 14th M.G. Sqdn HQ at 11 am.

　　　　　　　　　　　　　　　　　　　　　　　　Lieut.Colonel.

A.A. and Q.M.G., 5th Cavalry Division.

Appendix "P"

SECRET.   Q-531/R/14.

Headquarters, 5th Cavalry Division.

28th February 1918.

To

Sec'bad Cav. Bde.
Ambala Cav. Bde.
5th Signal Squadron.
A.D.M.S.
O.C., A.S.C.
D.A.D.O.S.
Camp Commandant.
4th Cavalry Division. Q
Cavalry Corps Q Rear.

Reference my No Q-531/R/7 dated 25th February 1918.

The following alterations are made in the details going to MARSEILLES in Group A :-

		Officers.	O.R.I.	Animals.	4 Whd.V.	2 W.V.
For	"18th Lancers	18.	355.	485	6	14.
Read	"18th Lancers	11.	309.	485.	6.	14.

2. The Poona and Deccan Horse will not be required to send any personnel with this group.

3. About 3 officers, 121 O.R's and followers and 186 animals of the 18th Lancers will remain to go with group "B".

Lieut. Colonel.

A.A and Q.M.G., 5th Cavalry Division.

War Diary Q   *Appendix N*

SECRET & URGENT.   Fifth Army No. Q/2/71.
                              6925 /(Q.A.1).

D.D.S.& T.
Fifth Army.
No. C/303.
8/2/18.

Fifth Army.

Reference G.H.Q. letter O.B/2160 dated 20/1/18.

The horses, transport and equipment of units to be broken up, as enumerated in Appendix II of the above quoted letter (except the 4 British Cavalry Regiments, 4th and 5th Cavalry Reserve Parks and Mechanical transport, for which separate instructions will be issued later) will be disposed of as follows :-

1. RIDING AND PACK HORSES.

(a). As many as are required will be transferred, under instructions which will be issued by D.Remounts, to make good deficiencies in establishments of units ordered to be transferred to EGYPT, vide Appendix I of the above quoted letter, plus 10% spares.

(b). The remainder will be absorbed as far as possible, in filling existing vacancies in 1st, 2nd and 3rd Cavalry Divisions and units of the 4th and 5th Cavalry Divisions which are not under immediate orders to proceed to EGYPT or to be broken up, under instructions which will be issued by the Director of Remounts.

(c). Any riding and pack animals which cannot be absorbed under para (b), will be disposed of under instructions which will be issued by the Director of Remounts.

(d). The transfer of animals mentioned in para (a) will be carried out as soon as possible to enable horses so transferred to be clipped. This clipping must be completed not less than 10 days before entrainment.

(e). Picketing gear and saddlery will be transferred with animals disposed of under paras. (a), (b), and (c) and (d) if required.

2. REGIMENTAL TRANSPORT of units to be broken up, as enumerated in Appendix II of the above quoted letter, except the 4 British Cavalry Regiments, 4th and 5th Cavalry Reserve Parks, and the 4th and 5th Cavalry Auxiliary Horse Transport Companies, will be despatched to the Advanced Horse Transport Depot ABBEVILLE as complete turns-outs under arrangements to be made by Fifth Army with G.O.C. L. of C. Area as soon as the breaking up of the Units to which they belong is completed.

On arrival at the Advanced Horse Transport Depot these turns-out will be disposed of under arrangements to be made by the Director of Transport.

3. The 4th and 5th Cavalry Auxiliary Horse Transport Companies will be despatched as complete units to the ABBEVILLE Area under arrangements to be made by Fifth Army with G.O.C. L. of C. Area.

On arrival....

On arrival in the ABBEVILLE Area these units will be broken up at at the Advanced Horse Transport Depot, under arrangements to be made by the Director of Transport.

4. Surplus saddlery and Harness other than that despatched with complete turns-out to the A.H.T.Depot ABBEVILLE, will be evacuated to the Ordnance Base Depot HAVRE, under arrangements to be made by Fifth Army.

5. Equipment will be collected, checked and returned to the Ordnance Depot at the Base.

6. The personnel will retain their arms, accoutrements, full scale of clothing, steel helmets, box respirators and blankets.

7. Ammunition will be returned to Ammunition Railheads.

8. Reserves of small box respirators and containers will be examined by Chemical Advisers or Divisional Gas Officers, who will decide which may be regarded as "unused" and fit for re-issue. The cases containing these will be clearly stencilled "unused" before they are returned to the Base.

9. The Horse Transport and Supply Officers of A.S.C. units which are to be broken up will be instructed to report as soon as their services can be dispensed with to the A.S.C. Base Depot (Horse Transport and Supply) HAVRE.

10. When the breaking up of the units enumerated in Appendix II of the above quoted letter is completed, a statement will be rendered to this office by Fifth Army showing how horses, vehicles, stores, saddlery and harness have been disposed of.

11. All animals of units ordered to be transferred to EGYPT will be malleined immediately these units have been completed to establishment plus 10%

G.H.Q.
6/2/18.

(Signed) R.S.MAY. Major-General,
for Quartermaster General.

Cavalry Corps.
D.D.S.&.T.
D.D.O.S.
D.D.R.

For necessary action. Report required by para 10 should be forwarded to this office.

A.H.Q.
7th Feb:1918.

(Signed) A.G.NICOL SMITH. Major,
for Major-General.
D.A.&.Q.M.G. Fifth Army.

SECRET & URGENT.

No. Q/531/6.

Headquarters, 5th Cavalry Division.
12th February 1918.

To,
Ambala Cavalry Brigade.
Sec'bad Cavalry Brigade.   A.D.M.S.
17th Brigade R.H.A.
5th Field Squadron.
5th Signal Squadron.
O.C., A.S.C.
D.A.D.O.S.
A.D.V.S.
"A"
"Q"

For guidance.

2.   Before any horses are transferred to units proceeding to EGYPT to complete establishment, or for other reasons, they must be malleined in the unit which they are leaving and NOT after joining their new unit.

Lieutenant-Colonel.
A.A.&.Q.M.G. 5th Cavalry Division.

No. QM.158

Headquarters 5th Cavy Divn
1st March 1917

To A.G. in India
　　Army Headquarters
　　　Simla.

Herewith war diary (Administrative) of the 5th Cavalry Division for the month of February 1917.

[signature] Lieut. Col.
for G.O.C. 5th Cavy Divn.

WAR DIARY or INTELLIGENCE SUMMARY.

Army Form C. 2118.

Place	Date	Hour	Summary of Events and Information	Remarks and references to Appendices
DOMART	Feb.	4th	Billeting list showing locations of Units at 12 noon this date	APPENDIX "A"
"	"	8th	5th Cavalry Division Supply Column locates KOMPRÉ-LES-CORPS-SAINTS.	
"	"	9th	Railheads of 5th Cavalry Division moves from CANDAS to LONGPRÉ	
"	"	11th	Orders received for Right Section Reserve Park to move to Fourth Army area.	
"	"	12th	Right Section Reserve Park locates at LA CHAPELETTE.	
"	"	12th	Reinforcement Division Order No. 7 issued.	APPENDIX "B"
"	"	13th	Administrative Instructions to relief of Divisions.	APPENDIX "C"
"	"	13th	Heavy Section 5th Cavalry Reserve Park moved to Fourgon area	
"	"	14th	H.Q. and one Squadron 7th Dragoon Guards moved from ST. SAUFLIEU and ARGOEUVES to TREQUIGNY.	
"	"	15th	Orders issued for Headquarters Rear to march from DOMART to PONT-DE-METZ	APPENDIX "D"
PONT-DE-METZ	"	16th	H.Q. 5th Cavalry Division (Rear) established at PONT-DE-METZ Heavy Section 5th Cavalry Reserve Park establishing at QUIMCOSE Right Section 5th Cavalry Reserve Park now locates at ESTRÉE-EN-CHAUSSÉE	Appendix "D" Appendix "H"

Fifth Army No. S/2/71

Army Form C. 2118.

WAR DIARY
or
INTELLIGENCE SUMMARY.
(Erase heading not required.)

Place	Date	Hour	Summary of Events and Information	Remarks and references to Appendices

PONT-DE-METZ	Feb.	17th	5th Dismounted Division relieves by 1st Dismounted Division. The regimental units located to the Back Area this date. Locations as under:-
			 Headquarters details - PONT-DE-METZ
			 1st Hodson Horse - MOUFLERS, VADCHELLES-LES-DOMART, L'ETOILE
			 9th Lancers - LONG
			 18th M.G. Squadron - FRAGNE. FAUCOURT.
			 14th M.G. Squadron - FLIXECOURT
			 13th M.G. Squadron
			 On completion of relief the following Units remained in the Forward Area:-
			    Canadian Brigade
			    Brigade Headquarters - VRAIGNES
			    Fur Mounted Rif.
			    M.G. Squadron - VERMAND
			    2 Dismounted Rif.
			    Sec'bad Bde
			    7th Dragoon Guards - VERMAND
			    Ambala Bde
			    8th Hussars - VERMAND
				DOMART. L'ETOILE, BRUCAMPS. VILLERS-SOUS-AILLY.

WAR DIARY
or
INTELLIGENCE SUMMARY.

Army Form C. 2118.

Place	Date	Hour	Summary of Events and Information	Remarks and references to Appendices
PONT-DE-METZ	Feb.	18th	Party of 178 all ranks of 7th Dragoon Guards relieved party from 4th Cav. Div. for work under 258th Tunnelling Coy of HEAVILY.	
"		20th	8th Hussars fatigue party proceeded to 1 MONS for work under XIX Corps. 50 men of 8th Hussars in Forward Area relieved by similar number from Back Area.	
"		21st	Canadian Cav. Bde. H.Q. Rear moved to RIBEAUCOURT. 40 men of 7th Dragoon Guards in Forward Area relieved by similar number from Back Area.	
"		22nd	Canadian C.F.A. moved to VERMAND. Now C.F.A. moved to Back Area and are treated at VAUCOURT-BUSSUS.	"G" "F"
"		23rd	Party as detailed in Q/631/A/3 and Q/631/A/4 entrained for TARANTO. Administrative Instructions No. 2 Cav. Corps No. Q 3494/A/ forwarded for guidance.	"F" "G"
"		24th	Party as detailed in Q/631/A/5 and Q/631/A/4 entrained for TARANTO. 13th Australian Light Horse marched from this Area to H- Army Area - FROHEN-LE-GRAND.	"F"

Army Form C. 2118.

WAR DIARY
or
INTELLIGENCE SUMMARY.
(Erase heading not required.)

Instructions regarding War Diaries and Intelligence Summaries are contained in F. S. Regs., Part II. and the Staff Manual respectively. Title pages will be prepared in manuscript.

Place	Date	Hour	Summary of Events and Information	Remarks and references to Appendices
PONT-DÉ-METZ	Feb. 25th		Cav. Corps Q.3494 for embarkation at TARANTO on 10th March Approxy	"K" "K" 27.
			Cav. Corps Administrative Instructions No 5.	
			Cav. Corps Instructions regarding M.T. Vehicles proceeding overseas.	"F"
	Feb. 26th		Visits as details in 5th Cav. Div. Q.53/1/1 & as amended by Q.53/1/21 moves to new areas for entrainment	
			5th Cavalry Ammunition Park reported 5th Cav. Supply Column this date.	"H, H₁"
	Feb. 27th		Parties of Group "A"	
			Parties as details in Q.53/1/7/3. M/8. M/9 entrained for MARSEILLES	
			Yorkshire Dragoons arrived at ALBERT - AIRAINES area being administered by Aubelei Bce.	
			14th M.G. Sqdn moved to ROMIANY	
	Feb. 28th		Moves & emts took place as details in Q.53/1/1	"I"
			Party as details in Q.53/1/R/1 entrained for TARANTO	"J"
			Party as details in Q.53/1/M/9/ entrained for MARSEILLES	"M₂"
			6th Inniskilling Dragoons moved to this area and are billeted in MOUFLERS Comm.	
			Orders for embarkation of party for TARANTO on 1st March.	"O"
			Alterations in Group "A" — Q.53/1/R/14 — un-letters "F"	"T"

SECRET.

App. A

LIST OF BILLETS - 5TH CAVALRY DIVISION.
Ref. Map. LENS 11, ABBEVILLE 12, & AMIENS 17.

Divisional Headquarters................	PONT de METZ.
Field Cashier.........................	LONGPRE-les-Corps-Saints.
Signal Squadron.......................	PONT de METZ.
Field Squadron........................	Forward Area.
C.R.H.A..............................	-do-
Ammunition Column.....................	-do-
Supply Column.........................	LONGPRE-les-Corps-Saints.
Sanitary Section......................	DOMART-en-PONTHIEU.
A.M.T. Company........................	ST. LEGER-les-DOMART.
Reserve Park. (Heavy).................	QUINCONCE.
(Light).................	V.I.H.C.1.3.
Railhead Supplies.....................	LONGPRE-les-Corps-Saints

CANADIAN CAVALRY BRIGADE.
Brigade Headquarters..................	RIBEAUCOURT.
R.C.Dragoons..........................	FRANSU - LE PLOUY - DOMQUEUR
L.S.Horse............................	CRAMONT.- LE MESNIL LES MASURES - MESNIL - DOMQUEUR - LONGVILLERS.
F.G. Horse............................	DOMLEGER - AGENVILLE - BEAUMETZ - PROUVILLE.
R.C.H.A. Brigade......................	Forward Area.
Canadian M.G. Squadron................	BERNEUIL - ST HILAIRE.
Canadian C.F.A........................	DOMART-en-PONTHIEU.
Canadian M.V. Section.................	COMDEFLOS.

SEC'BAD CAVALRY BRIGADE.
Brigade Headquarters..................	BELLOY-sur-SOMME.
7th Dragoon Guards....................	ARGOEUVES - PICQUIGNY. LA CHAUSSEE - TIRAUCOURT.
20th Horse............................	BETHENCOURT - ST OUEN. BENTEAUCOURT-les-DAMES.
34th Horse............................	HAVERNAS - MARCHIES - LAOURS - VIGNACOURT.
"N" Battery R.H.A.....................	Forward Area.
13th Squadron M.G.C...................	FLESSELLES.
Sec'bad I.C.F.A.......................	VIGNACOURT.
Sec'bad M.V. Section..................	BELLOY-sur-SOMME.

AMBALA CAVALRY BRIGADE.
Brigade Headquarters..................	LONGUET.
8th Hussars...........................	AILLY - le-HAUT CLOCHER AILLY - BUIGNEY-L'ABBE - YAUCOURT.
9th Horse.............................	MOUFLERS - VAUCHELLES-les DOMART - L'ETOILE - BRUCAMP - VILLERS-sous-AILLY.
18th Lancers..........................	LONG.
14th Squadron M.G.C...................	BRUNE - EAUCOURT.
Khos I.C.F.A..........................	YAUCOURT. BUSSUS.
Ambala M.V. Section...................	LONG.

No. G/213/16

Headquarters, 5th Cavalry Division.
5th March 1918.

To/
Cavalry Corps " ".

Forwarded.

Captain,
for G.O.C., 5th Cavalry Division.

SECRET.   appx B   Copy No. 6

Dismounted Divisions Order No. 7.

Dated 12th February 1918.

1. The 4th Dismounted Division will be relieved on the nights 13th/14th and 14th/15th inst. by the 72nd Infantry Brigade, 24th Division.

The 5th Dismounted Division will be relieved on the nights 15th/16th and 16th/17th by the 1st Cavalry Division.

On relief, 4th Dismounted Division will entrain at ROISEL and detrain at SALUX, 5th Dismounted Division will entrain at ROISEL and detrain at LONGPRE.
Orders for entrainment will be issued by A.A.& Q.M.G. Dismounted Divisions.

2. The following dismounted units, on completion of relief, will move as under :-

    6th Dragoons.   )
    17th Lancers.   )   Huts at MONTIGNY FARM
    1/1st Yorkshire Dragoons)

    7th Dragoon Guards.   )
    8th Hussars.   )   Tents at VERMAND.

    Canadian Brigade (less
    M.G. Squadron.)   ...   Huts at VERMAND.

Accommodation will be arranged by Cavalry Corps "Q"

3. Reliefs and moves of M.G. Squadrons will be as follows :-

10 and 12th M.G. Squadrons, on relief by 24th Division will move under orders of 4th Dismounted Division.

11th M.G. Squadron will remain in its present position and come under the orders of the 24th Division until further orders.

On night of 13th/14th inst.

14th M.G. Squadron will be relieved by 1st M.G. Squadron and will then move to VADENCOURT and come under the orders of Ambala Brigade.

On the 16th inst.

2nd M.G. Squadron moves to JEANCOURT and occupies 1st M.G. Squadrons present camp.
7th, 9th and 13th M.G. Squadrons and Canadian M.G. Squadron, remain in their present positions.

4. The Cavalry T.M. Battery will be relieved on the night of 14th/15th inst., and will be accommodated at BEAUMETZ.
On relief they will come under orders of Cavalry Corps.
"Q" Dismounted Divisions will provide lorry transport for personnel and stores.

5. Command of Centre Sector will pass to G.O.C., 24th Division at 10 a.m. on 15th inst.

                                          6........

Dismounted Divisions Order No. 7. (contd).

6. Major-General Macandrew and Staff will be relieved by Major-General Mullins and Staff in Command of Dismounted Divisions. Command will pass at 10 a.m. on 17th inst.

7. There will be no change in artillery arrangements.

8. All other details of reliefs in Centre Sector will be arranged direct between 4th Dismounted Division and 72nd Infantry Brigade, and in Right Sector between 5th Dismounted Division and 1st Cavalry Division.

9. Transport (less that of units mentioned in para. 2. and of 11th, 13th and Canadian M.G. Squadrons) will move as follows.

On 14th inst.	4th Cavalry Division.	To PROYART Area.	via Main VERMAND VILLERS-BRETTONEUX Road.
On 15th inst.	5th Cavalry Division.	-do-	-do-

Any transport required by 4th Dismounted Division on the night of 14th/15th., and by the 5th Dismounted Division on the night 16th/17th., in connection with relief, will be supplied on application to "Q" Dismounted Divisions.

10. All Defence Schemes, Maps, Aeroplane Photos, etc., etc. will be handed over to incoming units and receipts given.

11. A.D.M.S. Dismounted Divisions will make the necessary arrangements for the reliefs of Medical personnel.
12. Completion of reliefs will be reported to H.Q. Dismtd. Divs.
13. ACKNOWLEDGE. (4th and 5th Dismounted Divisions by wire).

(sd) M.T. HODGSON.

Lt.Col. G.S.,
Dismounted Divisions.

Issued to :-

Copy No.		Copy No.		
1.	5th Dismounted Division.	13	Cavalry Corps.	
2.	4th Dismounted Division.	14	24th Division.	
3.	Cavalry Divn'l Artillery.	15	61st Division.	
4.	C.R.E., Dismounted Divisions	16	72nd Infantry Brigade.	
5.	M.G.C. do.	17	1st Cavalry Division.	
6.	A.A.& Q.M.G. do.			
7.	A.D.M.S. do.	19	3rd Cavalry Division.	
8.	D.A.D.O.S. do.	20	4th do.	(rear)
9.	A.P.M. do.	21	5th do.	(rear)
10.	Gas Officer. do.	22	5th do.	"Q"
11.	Signals. do.	23 - 25	War Diary.	
12.	Camp Commandant do.	26 & 27	Office.	

SECRET.   No. Q/641.

Appx C

To/
    4th Dismounted Division.
    5th Dismounted Division.
    S.S.O. Dismounted Divisions.

    Reference Dismounted Divisional Order No. 7. dated 12th February 1918.

Reference para. 1. ENTRAINMENT.

    Train accommodation from the line to Roisel on the light Railway for the 4th Dismounted Division on the nights of 13th/14th and 14th/15th has been arranged, as detailed in this office No. Q/638 dated 12th instant.

    The 5th Dismounted Division will forward as soon as possible a statement of their requirements on the Light Railway, giving the following particulars :-

        Places at which trains are required.
        Times   "   "   "   "   "
        Numbers of Officers and Other Ranks for which accommodation is required in each train and name of units.

    The timing of the trains on the broad gauge from ROISEL will be notified as soon as received from the Cavalry Corps.   It is probable that a train will leave ROISEL each morning at 8.0 a.m. i.e.

        for 4th Dismtd Div at 8.0 a.m. on mornings 14th & 15th.
         " 5th   "   "   " 8.0 a.m. "   "   16th & 17th.

Reference para. 2. - ACCOMMODATION.

    Application for accommodation for the 6th Dragoons, 17th Lancers and 1/1st Yorkshire Dragoons at MONTIGNY FARM should be made by 4th Dismounted Division to the Area Commandant HERVILLY - by 5th Dismounted Division, for accommodation for the 7th Dragoon Guards, 8th Hussars and Canadian Brigade at VERMAND to the Area Commandant VENDELLES.

    A Camp of 120 tents is being arranged by the Cavalry Corps at ROISEL for the accommodation of Units from the line awaiting entrainment on the broad gauge railway for the nights of 13th/14th, 14th/15th, 15th/16th and 16th/17th.   This camp will be in the vicinity of the Railway Station.   The 4th and 5th Dismounted Divisions will arrange to take over this camp from the Area Commandant ROISEL on the afternoon of the day their relief commences.

Reference para. 4.

    The 4th Dismounted Division will inform this office as soon as possible as to the number of lorries required for the move of the Cavalry T.M. Battery to BEAUMETZ and giving details as to time and place these lorries will be met.

                                                    contd.

Application for accommodation at BEAUMETZ will be made to the Area Commandant VRAIGNES.

Reference para 9. - TRANSPORT.

(a) The transport of the following units will remain in the Forward Area for duty with their respective units :-

    Canadian Cav. Brigade.)
    8th Hussars.)
    7th Dragoon Guards.) at VERMAND.
    13th M.G. Squadron.)

    6th (Innis) Dragoons.)
    17th Lancers.)
    1/1st Yorkshire Dragoons.) at MONTIGNY FARM.
    11th M.G. Squadron.)

(b) The detachments of 1st and 4th Reserve Parks will remain at MONTIGNY FARM till completion of relief of 4th Dismounted Division, rejoining their respective units on 15th instant. The 4th Reserve Park is at LA CHAPELLETTE.

(c) The detachments of the 3rd and 5th Reserve Parks will remain at Vermand until the completion of reliefs of the 5th Dismounted Division rejoining their respective units on the 17th instant. The 3rd Reserve Park is at La Chapellette.

(d) The remainder of the transport of the 4th Dismounted Division and the parties to move by road will march to Proyart Area on the 14th inst. rejoining their units in the back area on the 15th inst.
    The remainder of the transport and parties to move by road of the 5th Dismounted Division will march to Proyart Area on the 15th inst; rejoining their units in back area on the 16th.
    4th & 5th Dismounted Divisions will wire the strength of parties for whom accommodation is required in the Proyart Area., as soon as possible.

(e) The road party of the Dismounted Divisional H.Q. will march with the 5th Dismounted Division transport on the 15th instant under the B.T.O., 5th Dismounted Division.

(f) Application for additional transport required by Dismounted Divisions in connection with their relief will be forwarded to this Office as soon as possible.

Reference para II - MEDICAL.

    The A.D.M.S. will notify this office by 6 p.m. to-night the date and number for which accommodation is required in the PROYART Area, also details as to train accommodation required.

SUPPLIES.

    The S.S.O will arrange the following issues of rations :-

(a) For parties proceeding by rail - 2 days at ROISEL

                                                            b........

(b) For parties proceeding by road - 2 days plus the unexpended portion

Parties remaining in the Forward Area will continue to be rationed by the S.S.O. Dismounted Divisions.

Indian Reserve Rations in strong points etc. will be withdrawn to their respective Refilling Points under arrangements made by 4th and 5th Dismounted Divisions. In the cases in which this has not already been done, Indian Reserve rations will be replaced by British Reserve Rations.

Receipts for reserve rations handed over to incoming units will be forwarded to this office.

H.Q. Dismtd Divs.
13th Feb. 1918.
               (sd) M.C. RAYMOND.
                                   Captain
      D.A.A.& Q.M.G., Dismounted Divisions.

Copies to :-

      Cavalry Corps "Q"
      4th Cavalry Division "Q"
      5th Cavalry Division "Q"
      A.D.M.S. Dismtd. Divs.
      "Q" Dismounted Divs.
      D.A.D.O.S.
      Area Commdt. HERVILLY.
         "   " VENDELLES.
         "   " OISEL.
         "   " BEAULET.

No. A/7959.

Headquarters, 5th Cavalry Division.
15th February 1918.

To/
Brigades.
A.S.C.
D.A.D.O.S.
A.P.M.
Canadian F.A.
Sanitary Section.
A.D.V.S.

5th Cavalry Division Rear Headquarters will march from DOMART to PONT de METZ on the 16th instant.

1. All spare horses and transport will form up in the square at 8.45 a.m., ready to march at 9 a.m. Head of the Column facing towards BERNEUIL.

2. They will march by the route DOMART, VIGNACOURT, ST VAST, ST. SAVEUR, AILLY-sur-SOMME, DREUIL, SAVEUSE, PONT de METZ.

3. The Police will march under the orders of the A.P.M.

4. O.C., A.S.C., will detail a lorry to be at the offices at 9 a.m.

5. The Ambala Signal Troop will march to H.Q. Ambala Brigade under the N.C.O. in charge.

6. The French Mission will march independently.

7. The Ordnance will move under orders of the D.A.D.O.S.

8. The Sanitary Section will remain at DOMART under the orders of O.C., 7th Canadian Field Ambulance.

(sd) G. O'HARA,
Captain,
A/D.A.A.& Q.M.G., 5th Cavalry Division.

War diary   Appendix "E"

SECRET.   No Q-531/R/3.

Headquarters, 5th Cavalry Division.

21st February 1918.

To

Sec'bad Cavalry Brigade.
Ambala Cavalry Brigade.
O.C., A.S.C.
A.D.M.S.
Camp Commandant.
Field Squadron.
Signal Squadron.
17th Bde R.H.A.

Reference para 1 of Cavalry Corps No C.R/6 dated 21-2-18 forwarded with my Q-531/R/2 of date.

---

1. The composition of parties will be as follows :-
(a) 23rd February:-

	B.O's.	I.O's.	I.O.R's.	Remarks.
Comdg. Officer	1(a)	–	–	(a) Field Officer of Sec'bad Bde.
Adjutant.	1(b)	1(c)	–	(b) From Sec'bad Bde.
				(c) From 9th Horse.
Quarter Master.	1(d)	–	–	(d) From Ambala Bde.
From Regts.	9(f)	12(e)	–	(e) 2 from 18th Lan.
				6 from 34th Horse.
				4 from 20th Horse.
				(f) 3 from 9th Horse & 2 from each of other I.C.Regts.
Medical Officer.	1(h)	1(g)(h)	–	(g) Sub-Asst. Surgeon.
				(h) Detailed by A.D.M.S.
Pioneer Battn.	4	4		

TOTAL 35 Officers.

Pioneer Battn.	–	–	379(i)	(i) Includes 13 fols.
4 Regts @ 50 each.	–	–	200	~~(j) Includes servants for above officers.~~
Medical.	–	–	138(k)	(k) detailed by ADMS from Mhow, Sec'bad & Fd. Ambs & San. Sec.

TOTAL 717 O.R's.

(b) 24th February:-

	B.O's.	O.R.B's.	Remarks.
B.Gen. BEATTY.	1.	-	
A.D.C.	1.	-	
Major NUTTING.	1.	-	
Capt WHEATLEY.	1.	-	
Major CLEGG.	1.	-	
A.S.C. Officer. A.S.C. details	1.	-	
Clerks	-	2.	
Provost.	-	2(m)	(m) Detailed by A.P.M.
Signal operators.	-	2(n)	(n) Detailed by O.C. Sigs.
D.R's.	-	3(n)	
Batmen.	-	6(o)	(o) For above officers.

Above will form Advanced Cavalry Divisional Staff

British Officers.	24(p)	-	(p) 6 from each I.C. Regt.
Batmen for above.	-	4(q)	(q) 1 from each I.C. Regt.
A.S.C. personnel.	-	30(r)	(r) Detailed by O.C., A.S.C.
A.S.C. details.	+	32(s)	(S) Detailed by O.C., A.S.C. from 4th Cav. Sup. Column.

2. The O.C., A.S.C. will arrange for three lorries to at the H.Qrs of each of the Ind.Cav.Regts at 10 am on 23rd Feb and also in consultation with A.D.M.S. for sufficient lorries for the Medical details for the conveyance of parties and kits to the station.

On the 24th Feb the O.C., A.S.C. will arrange for one lorry to be at the H.Qrs of each of the Sec'bad and Ambala Bdes for the conveyance of details and baggage to the station.

Lieut.Col.
A.A and Q.M.G., 5th Cavalry Division.

Appendix "E"

SECRET.   No.Q.531/R/4.

Headquarters, 5th Cavalry Division.
22nd February 1918.

To
  Sec'bad Cavalry Brigade.
  Ambala Cavalry Brigade.
  O.C., A.S.C.
  A.D.M.S.
  Camp Commandant.
  Field Squadron.
  Signal Squadron.
  17th Bde R.H.A.
  A.P.M.

The following amendments are made to this office No Q.531/R/3 of 21st February.:-

Para 1(a):-
    Erase entries opposite "From Regts" and substitute the following :-

	B.O's.	I.O's.	O.R's
"From Regts.	8(f) n	13(e)	(e) 1 from 9th Horse
			2 from 18th Lancers.
			6 from 34th Horse.
			4 from 20th Horse.
			(f) 2 from each Regt.

Para 1(b) is reconstructed as follows :-

	B.O's.	I.O's.	O.R's
(b) Maj.Nutting.	1.		
Capt Wheatley.	1.		
Maj.Clegg.	1.		
A.S.C.officer i/cASC details	1.		
Clerk.	-		1.
Provost.	-		2(m) (m)Detailed by A.P.M.
Signal Operators	-		2(n) (n)Detailed by Sigs.
D.R's(with Motor Bikes)			3(n)
Batmen.	-		4(o) (o)For above officers.

Above will form advanced Cavalry Divisional Staff.

Ind.Cav.Regts.	25(p)		(30(q) (p) 7 from 9th Horse
			(4(r) 6 from each of other Regts.
			(q)15 from Ambala and 15 from SEC'BAD.
			(r)Br Batmen-1 from each Cav.Regt.
14th M.G.Sqdn.	1.		9
A.S.C.personnel.-			30(s) (s)Detailed by O.C., A.S.C.

2, OC ASC will arrange for 1 lorry to be at the H.Q. of each Cav Regt and 1 lorry to be at M G Sqdn (14th) at 10 am on 24th for personnel and baggage.

J.W.Nobbs. Lieut.Colonel.
A.A and Q.M.G., 5th Cavalry Division.

SECRET.   No Q-531/R/6.

                    Headquarters, 5th Cavalry Division.
                         23rd February 1918.
To/

    Secbad Cavalry Bde.   (4)
    Ambala Cavalry Bde.   (4)
    17th Bde R.H.A.   (1)
    5th Field Squadron.   (1)
    5th Signal Squadron.   (1)
    O.C.A.S.C.   (2)
    A.D.M.S.   (1)
    A.D.V.S.   (1)
    D.A.D.O.S.   (1)

    Cav.Corps "Q", Rear No C.R./12 dated 22-2-18, forwarded for guidance with reference to my No Q-531/11 of 22-2-18.

                            Lieut. Colonel.

            A.A and Q.M.G., 5th Cavalry Division.

Appendix F1

SECRET.   No Q-531/11.
                            Headquarters, 5th Cavalry Division.
                            22nd February 1918.
To
 x Sec'bad Cavalry Brigade.
 x Ambala Cavalry Brigade.
 x A.D.M.S.
 x O.C., A.S.C.
 x D.A.D.O.S.
 x A.D.V.S.
 x A.P.M.
 x Camp Commandant.
 x 5th Field Squadron.
 x 5th Signal Squadron.
 x 17th Bde. R.H.A.
   Cavalry Corps. "Q" Rear.
   4th Cavalry Division.

Appendix "F"

Reference move of Division Eastwards (Overseas)

1. Troops will commence entraining for MARSEILLES on the 25th Feb. The entraining station will be either LONGUEAU or SALEUX. 4 trains will leave daily.

2. Sialkot Cavalry Brigade will entrain first and will be followed by the Indian Regiments and other details of the Ambala Brigade. The latter will probably commence entraining on the 27th Feb.

3. Units will move to billets S.W. of AMIENS on receipt of orders, as follows:-

	Area	Date	Remarks
(a) 9th Horse.	PROUZEL - PLACHY BUYON - BUYON - NAMPTY - NEUVILLE sous LOEUILLY.	26th Feb.	At present occupied by 6th Cavalry.
(b) 18th Lancers.	SAISSEVAL - BRIQUEMESNIL- CLAIRY SAULCHOIX- GUIGNEMICOURT-BOVELLES.	26th Feb.	At present occupied by 17th Lancers.
(c) 14th M.G. Squadron.	~~To be notified later.~~ RUMIGNY	~~26th~~ 27th Feb.	
(d) Mhow Cav.Fd. Amb. & Ind. details Amb. M.V. Section	~~ditto~~ RUMIGNY attached to & in Area of 18th Lancers.	26th Feb.	
(e) 34th Horse.	BOUGAINVILLE - REVELLES- PISSY - SEUX.	To be notified later.	At present occupied by 19th Lancers.
(f) 20th Horse.	SAINS en AMIENOIS- GUYENCOURT-REMIENCOURT- COTTENCHY.	ditto.	At present occupied by Yorkshire Dragoons.
(g) Sec'bad Bde Headquarters.	CREUSE.	ditto.	At present occupied by Sialkot Bde.H.Q.
(h) Sec.Cav.Fd. Ambulance.	To be notified later.	ditto.	
(i) Sec.Mob.Vet. Section.	Ditto.	Ditto.	

4. On receipt of orders, the 7th D.G's and 13th M.G. Sqdn. will move to billets nearer LONGPRE. These will be notified later.

5. Attention is directed to my Q-531/b dated 29-1-18. (those marked X)

                                        H.W. Cobbe
                                        Lieut. Colonel.
                            A.A and Q.M.G., 5th Cavalry Division.

SECRET.   No.Q.531/Q/1.

                                    Headquarters, 5th Cavalry Division,
                                         28th February, 1918.

To/
      Sec'bad Cavalry Brigade.

                                                    Appendix "F"

      Reference my Q.531/11 of 22.2.18.

      Erase sub-para.3 (f) and enter :-

Unit.	Area.	Date.	Remarks.
(f) 20th Horse	SAISSEVAL - BRIQUEMESNIL - GLAIRY SAULCHOIX - BOVELLES.	To be notified later.	On vacation of area by 18th Lancers

                              (sd.)   H.H. COBBE

                                      Lt-Colonel,

                          A.A.& Q.M.G., 5th Cavalry Division.

Copies to :-
            A.D.M.S.
            O.C. A.S.C.
            D.A.D.O.S.
            A.D.V.S.
            4th Cavalry Division.
            Cavalry Corps "Q" Rear.

SECRET.   No. CR/12.

Appendix "F"

To,
   Brigades & Divisional Units.

ADMINISTRATIVE INSTRUCTIONS NO. 2.

In continuation of No. CR/6 of 21/2/18.

1. Entrainment of Group 2, will begin on 25th February, and will proceed at the rate of 4 trains a day.
   Order of Units proceeding will be as follows, as far as is known at present.

   Sialkot Brigade.
   Indian Units of Ambala Brigade.
   Lucknow Brigade.

2. Group 2 will be under the orders of Brigadier-General L.L.MAXWELL, C.M.G. Commanding Sialkot Cavalry Brigade.
   Group 3 will probably be under Command of Brigadier-General GREGORY, Commanding Sec'bad Brigade.

3. The 17th Lancers will move from its present billeting area on 26/2/18 to LONG, when it will come under the administration of the Ambala Cavalry Brigade. The area vacated by the 17th Lancers is at the disposal of 5th Cavalry Division from 12 noon on 26th instant.

4. The areas of Sialkot Brigade as regiments and units entrain are placed at the disposal of 5th Cavalry Division.

5. Composition of each train in Group 1, will probably be one coach at 20 Officers, 30 covered trucks at 25 to 30 O.Rs. or 8 animals, 17 flat trucks.
   In reckoning accommodation a limbered G.S.Wagon is taken at 2, two-wheeled vehicles; 1 G.S.Wagon and a half limber can go on a flat truck as a rule, but apparently all flat trucks are not big enough.

6. 30 lorries will go on the first day; the wheels must be removed from these; and they will not include any workshop or store lorries.

7. Lieut MACPHERSON, 6th Cavalry, will go ahead with the A.D.V.S. 5th Cavalry Division and act as Staff Officer, and will meet troops of Group 2 as they arrive at MARSEILLES.

                                              G.Maitland

H.Q. 4th Cav.Div.   Lieutenant-Colonel,
22/2/18.   A.A.&.Q.M.G. Cavalry Corps (Rear). "Q"

Copy to Cavalry Corps " ".
   5th Cavalry Division. 20 copies.

Appendix "G"

S E C R E T.

Cav. Corps G.3494/A.I. 22.2.18

Cavalry Corps 'Q' Rear. (10).
4th Cavalry Division.
5th Cavalry Division.

1. The attention of all units entraining is called to G.R.O. 3189 para. 7.

2. The Indian Cavalry Pioneer Battalion left Forward Area this morning for SALEUX.

3. The Base, B.E.F. ITALY will collect the special issue of Winter Clothing, such as fur coats, &c, at TARANTO.

4. G.S. Wagons with Cavalry Field Ambulances for carriage of blankets will be returned to the Auxiliary (Horse) Co. of their Division.

5. Auxiliary (Horse) Cos. of the 4th & 5th Cavalry Divisions are being withdrawn to work under the direct orders of Fifth Army.

6. In addition to the numbers already given, 226 Officers & 1366 O.Rs. will probably sail from TARANTO on 10th April.

7. Lorries will have to be loaded at LONGEAU Station, as there are no facilities at SALEUX. It will be necessary to either take the superstructures off, or remove the wheels of the lorries, otherwise they will not pass through the French tunnels.

8. All completely British Units go on Part VII A. W.E.; Indian Units on Part XVII W.E.

Lieut-Colonel,
for D.A.& Q.M.G. Cavalry Corps.

22.2.18.

Copy to/ 'G'   A.D.Signals.
         A.D.C.   D.D.R.
         C.R.E.   Chem.Advr.
         A.S.& T.   D.D.M.S.
         A.D.O.S.   D.D.V.S.
         C.M.G.O.   E.A.D.P.S.
         'A'

Forwarded for guidance.

War diary Appendix H

SECRET.
No.G.531/R/7.

Headquarters, 5th Cavalry Division,
25th February, 1918.

To:/
Sec'bad Cavalry Brigade (5)   O.C., A.S.C. (2)
Ambala Cavalry Brigade (5)   A.D.V.S. (1)
17th Brigade R.H.A. (1)   D.A.D.O.S. (1)
5th Field Squadron. (1)   Camp Commandant. (1)
5th Signal Squadron. (1)   "G". (1)
A.D.M.S.(3)   "A" (1)
4th Cavalry Division (1)   War Diary (3)
Cavalry Corps Rear (1)

1. Group "A" will embark at MARSEILLES on March 4th.

2. The following will form Group "A" and detailed orders for entrainment which, for 5th Cavalry Division units, will be on 27th and 28th inst., will be issued later :- The 9th Hodson's Horse will be the first unit to entrain :-

	Officers	O.R.	Animals	4 Wheel	2 Wheel	Ambles.	Cars.
4th Cavalry Divn.	71	1249	1824	23	79	7	2
	1	55	67	9	11	7	-
Total.	72	1304	1891	32	90	14	2
Surplus to be found by 4th Cavalry Divn.		225					
Total 4th Cav. Divn.	72	1529	1891	32	90	14	2
5th Cavalry Divn.							
9th Hodson's Horse	24	450	671	6	14	-	-
18th Lancers	18	355	485	6	14	-	-
Ambala M.V.S.	1	14	24	1	2	-	-
Mhow C.F.A.	1	50	67	8	9	7	2
Sec'bad C.F.A.	-	34	67	8	9	-	-
20th Deccan Horse	1-J.O.	45	-	-	-	-	-
34th Poona Horse	1-J.O.	45	-	-	-	-	-
Total 5th Cav. Divn.	46	993	1314	29	48	7	2
Grand Total.	118	2522	3205	61	128	21	4

4-wheeled, 110.   2-wheeled 100.

3. Entraining Station will be SALEUX.

4. Each train will carry 3 days' rations and forage in bulk for the journey.

5. Personnel will entrain fully equipped and clothed.

6. A table showing HALTES REPAS will be issued to the O.C. train at the entraining station.

7. Orders for the disposal of personnel and horses of the units concerned which do not accompany this group will be issued later.

J.H.W. Cobbe
Lt-Colonel,
A.A.& Q.M.G., 5th Cavalry Division.

Appendix H1

SECRET. No Q-531/R/8.

Headquarters, 5th Cavalry Division.
26-2-18.

To
9th Hodsons Horse.

9th Hodson's Horse will commence entraining at SALEUX on the 27th as follows :-

(a) <u>No 9 Train.</u> - 1 coach, 31 covers and 8 flats.

B.O's.	I.O's.	O.R's.	Animals.	4 wheeled vehicles.	2 wheeled Vehicles
2.	3.	150.	180.	6.	14.

Commence entraining at 7-30 -hours.
Train leaves at 10-30-hours.

(b) <u>No 10 Train:</u>- 1 coach, 40 covers.

B.O's.	I.O's.	O.R's.	Animals.	4 wheeled vehicles.	2 wheeled vehicles
2.	3.	150.	246.	-------	-------

Commence entraining at 16-30-hours.
Train leaves at 19-30-hours.

O.C.9th Horse will detail an officer to command each train and also a British or Indian Officer as QuarterMaster and Adjutant.

2. 3 days rations in bulk will be taken over by the Q.Mr. at the station

3. A.D.M.S. will make necessary Medical arrangements for each train.

4. 2nd and 3rd blankets will be taken over by D.A.D.O.S. before departure from Billets.

5. An Officer of the Divnl.Staff will meet the O.C.Train at the Station at 7-30 a.m., and 16-30 hours respectively.

6. No 11 Train will leave SALEUX at about 7-30 a.m., on the 28th. Entraining will commence at 4-30-hours. Further details as regards composition will be sent on the 27th.

J.H.H.Cobbe
Lieut.Colonel.
A.A and Q.M.G., 5th Cavalry Division.

Copy to :-
Ambala Cavalry Brigade.
Sec'bad Cavalry Brigade.
A.D.M.S.
O.C., A.S.C.
D.A.D.O.S.
4th Cavalry Division.
Cav.Corps "G" Rear.
"A".
"G".
Liaison Officer.
Camp Commandant.

SECRET.
No. Q.531/R/9.

Headquarters, 5th Cavalry Division,
27th February, 1918.

To/
    O.C.,
        9th Hodson's Horse.

In continuation of this office Q.531/R/8 dated 26th inst.

1. <u>Ref. para.6.</u>

   The following is the detail for No.11 Train:-

   No.11 Train - 1 Coach, 40 Covers.

B.O's.	I.O's.	O.R's.	Animals.	Vehicles.
2	3	150	180	Nil.

   Commence entraining at 5.30 hours.

   Train leaves at 8.30 hours.

2. Orders regarding the remainder of the Regiment will follow.

3. Acknowledge by bearer.

                              Lt-Colonel,

A.A.& Q.M.G., 5th Cavalry Division.

Copies to :-
    Sec'bad Cavalry Brigade.
    A.D.M.S.
    O.C. A.S.C.
    D.A.D.O.S.
    4th Cavalry Division.
    Cavalry Corps "Q" Rear.
    "A".
    "G".
    Liaison Officer.
    Camp Commandant.

Appendix "I"

SECRET

No.G.531/Q/3.

Headquarters, 5th Cavalry Division,
26th February, 1918.

To/

Sec'bad Cavalry Brigade.	A.D.M.S.
Ambala Cavalry Brigade.	O.C., A.S.C.
17th Brigade, R.H.A.	D.A.D.O.S.
5th Field Squadron.	A.D.V.S.
5th Signal Squadron.	A.P.M.
4th Cavalry Division.	Camp Commandant.
Cavalry Corps "Q", Rear.	Brig-General C.H. RANKIN.

1. The following moves will take place on the 28th February :-

   (a) <u>7th Dragoon Guards.</u>- To billets in LONGPRE.

   ROUTE.- BELLOY SUR SOMME - ETOILE - CONDE FOLIE.
   To be clear of CONDE FOLIE at 1 p.m.

   (b) <u>13th M.G. Squadron.</u>- To billets in COCQUEREL.

   <u>O.C. A.S.C.</u> will detail 9 lorries to be at FLESSELLES at
   9 a.m. to take dismounted personnel.

   (c) <u>Sec'bad Cav. Bde. H.Q.</u>- and <u>Sec'bad Mob. Vet. Sect.</u> to CREUSE

   TIME and ROUTE optional.

   (d) <u>20th Horse.</u>- To area SAINS EN AMIENOIS - GUYNCOURT -
                                REMIENCOURT - COTTENCHY.

   ROUTE.- VIGNACOURT - ST VAST EN CHAUSSEE - AMIENS.
   STARTING POINT.- VIGNACOURT - 10.15 a.m.

   (e) <u>34th Horse.</u>- To area BOUGAINVILLE - REVELLES - PISSY - SEUX.

   ROUTE.- VIGNACOURT - PICQUIGNY.
   To be clear of VIGNACOURT at 10 a.m.

   (f) <u>5th Cavalry Sanitary Section.</u>- To SALOUEL.

2. On completion of move 7th Dragoon Guards and 13th M.G. Squadron
will come under orders of G.O.C., Ambala Cavalry Brigade.

Lt-Colonel,
A.A.&.Q.M.G., 5th Cavalry Division.

SECRET.   No Q-531/R/11.

Headquarters, 5th Cavalry Division.
27th February 1918.

Appendix "J"

To
  9th Horse.
  18th Lancers.
  A.D.M.S.
  O.C.A.S.C.
  D.A.D.O.S.
  Sec'bad Field Ambulance.
  Ambala Cavalry Brigade.
  Sec'bad Cavalry Brigade.
  French Mission.
  Camp Commandant.
  "A" & "G".
  Signal Squadron.
  A.D.V.S. 4th Cav. Divn.
  Capt LEE, Sanitary Section.
  4th Cav.Divn. "Q".
  Cav.Corps, "Q" Rear.

The following personnel from this Division will entrain at SALEUX Railhead for TARANTO on the 28th February :-

	B.O's.	I.O's.	O.R.B.	O.R's.I.
5th Cavalry Sanitary Section.	1.	-	1.	22.
9th Hodsons Horse.	2.	2.	-	91.
Sec'bad Fd. Ambulance.	-	-	1.	25.
Total.	3.	2.	2.	138.

The O.C., A.S.C. will detail the following transport :-
    5 Lorries for 9th Horse at PROUZEL at 12 noon.
    1 lorry for Sanitary Section at SALOUEL at 12 noon.

2. All personnel will be at the Station to commence entraining at 13-30-hours. Train will leave at 16-20-hours.

3. Each man will be in possession of the iron ration and the unexpended portion of the day's ration.
    11 days rations will be taken over in bulk by the O.C.Train from the R.S.O.

4. Captain LEE, I.M.S., will be in Medical Charge of the train.

5. The D.A.D.O.S. will arrange to take over the 2nd and 3rd blankets.

6. The 4th Cav.Divn is detailing a Field Officer to Command the Train.

7. Details of other units will entrain for TARANTO on March 1st.

H.E. Cochran
Lieut. for
A.A and Q.M.G., 5th Cavalry Division.

Appendix "K"

SECRET.　　　　　　　　　　　　　　No. QA/707.

To,
Brigades and Divisional Units.

ADMINISTRATIVE INSTRUCTIONS. No. 3.

Reference 6925/1/11 (Q.A.1). dated 21/2/18.
~~(4th Cavalry Division No. C/8795).~~

1. The party shown under "A" to sail from MARSEILLES on 4th March will proceed under Command of Brigadier-General L.L.MAXWELL, C.M.G. Captain F.GWATKIN, Staff Captain Sialkot Brigade, will go with him as his Staff Officer. General MAXWELL will arrive at MARSEILLES in a few days.

2. Party shown under "B" will consist chiefly of Lucknow Brigade and will be under Command of a Lieutenant-Col. of that Brigade.

3. Party "C" will be Commanded by Brigadier-General C.L.GREGORY, who will take Captain SIMPSON as his Staff Officer.

4. Party "D" will be under Command of a Lieut-Col, of Mhow Brigade.

5. Brigadier-General GREGORY will assume Command of the Division on his arrival at MARSEILLES, until he embarks on March 20th. The senior Officer remaining will take over from him.

6. Divisional Headquarters will sail partly from (Sailing) TARANTO on 10th March and partly from MARSEILLES on 10th.

7. Lieut R.S.MACPHERSON, 6th Cavalry has proceeded to MARSEILLES as Staff Officer to the Division.
　　When Major G.B.HOWELL arrives at MARSEILLES he will assume the duties of Staff Officer to the Division, assisted by Lieut MACPHERSON.
　　These Officers will remain at MARSEILLES until the last party sails on April 11th.
　　Similarly the A.D.V.S. 4th Cavalry Division (Major HOLDNESS) and a Supply Officer (Captain SHORT), are remaining at MARSEILLES till April 11th.

　　The duties of the above Officers are to meet the Troops as they arrive and perform such administrative duties, as are necessary in connection with all troops of the Division proceeding to EGYPT.

　　　　　　　　　　　　　　　　　GRMaitland
H.Q. 4th Cav.Div.　　　　　　　　　　Lieutenant-Colonel,
25/2/18.　　　　　　　　　　A.A.& Q.M.G. 4th Cavalry Division.

Copy to, Cavalry Corps "Q".
　　　　5th Cavalry Division,
　　　　Lieut MACPHERSON. (3 copies).

SECRET.   QMG. 6925/1/21 (Q.A.1)

Cav.Corps Q.3494 - 24.2.18.

Fifth Army.
G.O.C., L. of C. Area.

In continuation of my 6925/1/5 (Q.A.1) dated 20/2/1918:

1. Personnel to embark from TARANTO on March 10th will be made up as shewn in Appendix "A" attached hereto.

2. Personnel will entrain in accordance with Appendix "B" attached hereto.

3. Personnel will entrain fully equipped and clothed as laid down in my 6925 (Q.A.3) dated 24th January, 1918.

4. Rations will be placed on trains as shewn in column 7 of Appendix "B".

5. A table showing Haltes Repas on the journey to TARANTO will be handed to the O.C. each train at the Station under arrangements to be made by the D.G.T.

6. A telegram will be sent to this office by the formations shown in Column 8 giving the strengths of officers and other ranks entrained each day, British and Native personnel being shown separately, and the number of days rations placed on each train.

7. Acknowledge.

(sgd) R.S. MAY.
G.H.Q.   M.G.
23rd February, 1918.   for Quartermaster General.

Copy to/ **** Cav. Corps   Cav.Corps (Rear).

2.

Cavalry Corps 'Q' Rear.

For action.

24.2.18.
                                                    Lieut.Colonel
                                            for D.A.& Q.M.G. Cavalry Corps.

Copy to/ 4th Cav.Div.   G.O.C.R.A.   D.A.D.R.T. PERONNE.
         5th Cav.Div.   D.D.M.S.
         'G'   D.D.V.S.
         A.D.S.&.T.   D.D.R.
         A.D.O.S.   Chem.Advr.
         C.R.E.   C.M.G.O.
         A.D.C.   D.A.D.P.S.
         A.P.M.   A.D.Signals.

Appendix

APPENDIX "A".

Detail of Units that will embark at TARANTO on 10th March, 1918.

	Officers.	Other Ranks.
Personnel from Units of Indian Cavalry Divisions.	226	1350
No. 11 Indian Field Veterinary Section ...	1	76
No. 19 Indian Field Veterinary Section ...	-	85
No. 20 Indian Field Veterinary Section ...	1	64
No. 21 Indian Field Veterinary Section ...	-	71
No. 22 Indian Field Veterinary Section ...	1	51
No. 23 Indian Field Veterinary Section ...	-	74
Reinforcements for Indian Cavalry from MARSEILLES	16	490
	245	2260

APPENDIX "B".

1	2	3	4	5	6	7	8	9	10	11
Date of Entrainment.	Entraining Station.	U N I T.	No. of Trains	Strength Offrs. O.Rs		No. of days rations to be put on train	arrangements to be made by	Traffic with	Destination.	REMARKS.
26th Feby.	ROUEN.	No. 21) Indian Field No. 22) Veterinary No. 23) Sections. No. 20) (part)	1	∅ 1	240	2	G.O.C. L. of C. Area.	Traffic ROUEN.	SALEUX.	∅ Draft conducting Officer who will return on completion. G.O.C. Cavalry Corps will arrange for this party to be accommodated at SALEUX for night 26/27 and 27/28 and to move to TARANTO on 28th as shown below.
28th Feby.	SALEUX	No. 21) Indian Field No. 22) Veterinary No. 23) Sections. No. 20) (part)	1		240)	11	Fifth Army	Traffic PERONNE	TARANTO	Will sail from TARANTO on March 10th
		Personnel from Indian Cavalry Units.		113	560)					
1st March	SALEUX	Personnel from Indian Cavalry Units	1	113	600	10	Fifth Army	Traffic PERONNE	TARANTO	Will sail from TARANTO on March 10th.
3rd March	MARSEILLES	No. 11) Indian No. 19) Field Veter- part No.20) inary Sections. Reinforcements.	1	4	180) 490)	8	G.O.C. L. of C. Area	Traffic MARSEILLES	TARANTO	Will sail from TARANTO on March 10th

Appendix "M"

S E C R E T.   Cav.Corps G.3494 - 25.2.18.

Cavalry Corps "A" Rear.
4th Cavalry Division.
5th Cavalry Division.

Reference my G.3494/A.1. dated 23.2.18, para. 6, for "10th April" read 10th March.

2.   Under instructions from War Office no mechanical transport other than the following makes will be embarked :-

VAUXHALL, SUNBEAM, TALBOT, FORD, and TRIUMPH.

D. Transport is arranging the necessary exchanges. The 30 lorries detailed in para. 6 of A.G. 6925/1/11 (A.1) of 21.2.18 (issued under Cav.Corps G.3494 - 22.2.18) for transport work at MARSEILLES are not affected.

(Authority:- G.H.Q. wire O.A.1/240 d. 24.2.18).

25.2.18.

[signed] A. Hallander Capt.
for Lieut-Colonel,
for D.A.& Q.M.G Cavalry Corps.

Copy to/A.D.S.& T.   A.D.Signals.
'G'   D.D.R.
A.D.C.   Chem.Advr.
C.R.E.   D.D.M.S.
A.D.O.S.   D.D.V.S.
C.H.G.O.   D.A.D.P.S.
'I'   A.P.M.

SECRET.   No Q-531/R/13.

Appendix "O"

Headquarters, 5th Cavalry Division.
28th February 1918.

To/

18th Lancers.
20th Horse.
34th Horse.
Sec'bad Field Ambulance.
Sec'bad Bde.
Sec'bad Signal Troop.
Sec'bad Mobile Vet.Section.
O.C.A.S.C.
14th M.G.Squadron.
D.A.D.O.S.
Major Jarvis, 20th Deccan Horse.
Capt Hassard, Sec.Field Amb.

----

1. The following personnel will entrain for TARANTO on the 1st March:-

	B.O's.	I.O's.	O.R.B.	O.R.I.	Remarks.
18th Lancers.	@	3.	%	93. 93	
20th Horse.	@	5.	%	93.	@ All B.O's present,
34th Horse	@	4.	%	110.	except C.O., & 4 others
Sec'bad Fd.Ambulance.	1.	-	1.		
Sec'bad Bde H.Qrs.	-	-	14.	3.	% Includes any British
Sec'bad Mob.Vet.Sec.	-	-	-	5.	Batmen & Followers
O.C.,A.S.C.	-	-	4.	-	taken.
14th M.G.Sqdn.	2.	-	9.	-	
D.A.D.O.S.	-	-	16.	-	
Sec'bad Signal Troop.	-	-	4.	-	
Total.	@	12.	48	305.	
Div HQrs	-	-	1	-	# included in 305 ORB

2. Regiments will report today to Divisional Headquarters the names of officers going and remaining.
   Regiments will also report at the same time the number of Officers expected to rejoin from leave with dates of rejoining.

3. Major Jarvis, 20th Horse will command the train. Sec'bad Bde will detail an Adjutant & Q.Mr. for the train.

(a)

4. Captain Hassard, Sec.Fd.Amb. will be in Medical charge of train.

5. Commence entraining at 13-hours.
   Train leaves at 16-20-hours.

6. 10 days rations will be taken over in bulk by the Q.Mr.
   Each man will be in possession of Iron Ration and the unexpended portion of the day's ration.

7. Nominal Roll, in duplicate, of each party is required at the station at time of entraining.

8. The D.A.D.O.S. will arrange to take over the 2nd and 3rd blankets.

9. The O.C., A.S.C. will detail the following transport :-
   5 lorries for 18th Lancers H.Qrs. at 11 a.m.,
   5 lorries for 20th Horse H.Qrs at 11 a.m.,
   6 lorries for Poona Horse H.Qrs at 11 a.m.,
   2 lorries at Sec'bad Bde H.Qrs for details of Bde H.Q.,)
                                    M.Vet.Section   ) at 11 a.m.,
                                    Signal Troop.   )

1 lorry at 14th M.G. Sqdn HQ at 11 am.

H M Cobbe
Lieut.Colonel.

A.A and Q.M.G., 5th Cavalry Division.

Appendix "P"

SECRET.   Q-531/R/14.

Headquarters, 5th Cavalry Division.

28th February 1918.

To

    Sec'bad Cav.Bde.
    Ambala Cav.Bde.
    5th Signal Squadron.
    A.D.M.S.
    O.C.,A.S.C.
    D.A.D.O.S.
    Camp Commandant.
    4th Cavalry Division.Q
    Cavalry Corps Q Rear.

Reference my No Q-531/R/7 dated 25th February 1918.

The following alterations are made in the details going to MARSEILLES in Group A :-

	Officers.	O.R.I.	Animals.	4 Whd.V.	2 W.V.
For "18th Lancers	18.	355.	485	6	14.
Read "18th Lancers	11.	309.	485.	6.	14.

2. The Poona and Deccan Horse will not be required to send any personnel with this group.

3. About 3 officers, 121 O.R's and followers and 186 animals of the 18th Lancers will remain to go with group "B".

Lieut.Colonel.
A.A and Q.M.G.,5th Cavalry Division.

SECRET & URGENT. Fifth Army No. O/2/71.
6925/(Q.A.1).

O.O.S.A.T.
Fifth Army.
No. O/303.
6/2/18.

Fifth Army.

Reference G.H.Q. letter O.B/2160 dated 26/1/18.

The horses, transport and equipment of units to be broken up, as enumerated in Appendix II of the above quoted letter (except the 4 British Cavalry Regiments, 4th and 5th Cavalry Reserve Parks and Mechanical transport, for which separate instructions will be issued later) will be disposed of as follows :-

1. **RIDING AND PACK HORSES.**

(a). As many as are required will be transferred, under instructions which will be issued by D.Remounts, to make good deficiencies in establishments of units ordered to be transferred to EGYPT, vide Appendix I of the above quoted letter, plus 10% spares.

(b). The remainder will be absorbed as far as possible, in filling existing vacancies in 1st, 2nd and 3rd Cavalry Divisions and units of the 4th and 5th Cavalry Divisions which are not under immediate orders to proceed to EGYPT or to be broken up, under instructions which will be issued by the Director of Remounts.

(c). Any riding and pack animals which cannot be absorbed under para (b), will be disposed of under instructions which will be issued by the Director of Remounts.

(d). The transfer of animals mentioned in para (a) will be carried out as soon as possible to enable horses so transferred to be clipped. This clipping must be completed not less than 10 days before entrainment.

(e). Picketing gear and saddlery will be transferred with animals disposed of under paras. (a), (b), and (c) and (d) if required.

2. REGIMENTAL TRANSPORT of units to be broken up, as enumerated in Appendix II of the above quoted letter, except the 4 British Cavalry Regiments, 4th and 5th Cavalry Reserve Parks, and the 4th and 5th Cavalry Auxiliary Horse Transport Companies, will be despatched to the Advanced Horse Transport Depot ABBEVILLE as complete turn-outs under arrangements to be made by Fifth Army with G.O.C. L. of C. Area as soon as the breaking up of the Units to which they belong is completed.

On arrival at the Advanced Horse Transport Depot these turn-outs will be disposed of under arrangements to be made by the Director of Transport.

3. The 4th and 5th Cavalry Auxiliary Horse Transport Companies will be despatched as complete units to the ABBEVILLE Area under arrangements to be made by Fifth Army with G.O.C. L. of C. Area.

On arrival....

On arrival in the ABBEVILLE Area these units will be broken up at at the Advanced Horse Transport Depot, under arrangements to be made by the Director of Transport.

4. <u>Surplus saddlery and Harness</u> other than that despatched with complete turns-out to the A.H.T.Depot ABBEVILLE, will be evacuated to the Ordnance Base Depot HAVRE, under arrangements to be made by Fifth Army.

5. Equipment will be collected, checked and returned to the Ordnance Depot at the Base.

6. The personnel will retain their arms, accoutrements, full scale of clothing, steel helmets, box respirators and blankets.

7. Ammunition will be returned to Ammunition Railheads.

8. Reserves of small box respirators and containers will be examined by Chemical Advisers or Divisional Gas Officers, who will decide which may be regarded as "unused" and fit for re-issue. The cases containing these will be clearly stencilled "unused" before they are returned to the Base.

9. The Horse Transport and Supply Officers of A.S.C. units which are to be broken up will be instructed to report as soon as their services can be dispensed with to the A.S.C. Base Depot (Horse Transport and Supply) HAVRE.

10. When the breaking up of the units enumerated in Appendix II of the above quoted letter is completed, a statement will be rendered to this office by Fifth Army showing how horses, vehicles, stores, saddlery and harness have been disposed of.

11. All animals of units ordered to be transferred to EGYPT will be malleined immediately these units have been completed to establishment plus 10%

G.H.Q.   (Signed) R.S.MAY. Major-General,
6/2/18.   for Quartermaster General.

Cavalry Corps.
D.D.S.&T.
D.D.O.S.
D.D.R.

For necessary action. Report required by para 10 should be forwarded to this office.

                                  (Signed) A.G.NICOL SMITH. Major,
                                        for Major-General.
A.H.Q.   D.A.&Q.M.G. Fifth Army.
7th Feb:1918.

SECRET & URGENT.

No. Q/531/6.

Headquarters, 5th Cavalry Division.
12th February 1918.

To,

Ambala Cavalry Brigade.
Sec'bad Cavalry Brigade.   A.D.M.S.
17th Brigade R.H.A.
5th Field Squadron.
5th Signal Squadron.
O.C., A.S.C.
D.A.D.O.S.
A.D.V.S.
"A".
"Q"

For guidance.

2.   Before any horses are transferred to units proceeding to EGYPT to complete establishment, or for other reasons, they must be malleined in the unit which they are leaving and NOT after joining their new unit.

[signature]

Lieutenant-Colonel.
A.A.&.Q.M.G. 5th Cavalry Division.

Hdqrs. 5th Cavalry Divn.
No. 0/496
30/4/18

To
A.G. in India
Army Hdqrs
Simla

Herewith Administrative War Diary of 5th Cavalry Division for March 1918.

H. Nutrie Major
D.A.A. & Q.M.G.
5th Cavy Divn.

WAR DIARY
or
INTELLIGENCE SUMMARY.

Headquarters (Reds from 2/48tms)
7th S. Carly Bde

Place	Date	Hour	Summary of Events and Information	Remarks and references to Appendices
PONT-DE-METZ	March 1st		Orders for the entrainment of Group "A" continued - O.53.1/19/15	"A"
"	2nd		Parties as detailed in Appendix "A" entrained for MARSEILLES	B
"	"		Preliminary details of Group "B" issued - O/53/1/R/16.	C
"	3rd		Appendix B cancelled and O-53/1/R/17 substituted	
"	"		following additional articles of clothing authorised for British personnel proceeding overseas. Orders received that this is to be drawn from Cavalry Caps "O" (Rear) Wolseley Helmet - 1 per man	
			Pagri - "	
			Chin Strap - "	
			Khaki drill suits - "	
"	5th		Orders for entrainment of certain details of Group "B" on the 7th March O-53/R/18	D
"	7th		Parties as detailed in O.53/R/18 entrained for MARSEILLES	
"	8th		Orders for entrainment of remaining details issued - O.53/R/19.	E
"	9th		Cavalier Car Boc. left this area to join 111 Can. Division	

Army Form C. 2118.

WAR DIARY
or
INTELLIGENCE SUMMARY.
(Erase heading not required.)

Instructions regarding War Diaries and Intelligence Summaries are contained in F. S. Regs., Part II. and the Staff Manual respectively. Title pages will be prepared in manuscript.

Place	Date	Hour	Summary of Events and Information	Remarks and references to Appendices
PONT DE METZ	March 9th		7th D.G's marched from LONGPRE area to join III Cavalry Division. 8th Hussars marched from LONGPRE area to join 9th Cav Bde I Cav. Division.	
"	"	15H	Mate's and twos issued for entrainment of details of 5th Cav Bde. D-53/R/20	
"	"	19H	Parties as in Appendix J. detained for MARSEILLES.	
"	"	20H	Parties as in Appendix J. entrained for MARSEILLES. Divisional Report Centre closes at PONT DE METZ and opens in FIGT on arrival	

See War Diary Advanced Divisional Hqrs.

Hubert Major
for A.A. & Q.M.G. Cavalry

SECRET.   Appendix 'A' War Diary
                    No Q-531/R/15.

                                Headquarters, 5th Cavalry Division.
                                         1st March 1918.
To
    18th Lancers.
    Sec'bad Cavalry Brigade.
    O.C., A.S.C.
    A.D.M.S.
    D.A.D.O.S.
    Camp Commandant.
    French Mission.
    4th Cavalry Divn.Q.
    Cavalry Corps, Q.Rear.
    Sec'bad Field Ambulance.
    ----

1. Group "A" will continue entraining on the 2nd March as follows:-
    Entraining Station SALEUX.

    (a) <u>No 12 Train</u> :- 1 Coach, 35 Covers and 12 Flats.

	B.O's.	I.O's.	O.R's & Fols.	Animals.	4-Wheels	2-Whls.	Motor Amb.
18th Lancers.	2.	4.	140.	232.	6.	14.	-
Sec.Field Amb.	-	-	8.	-	-	-	4.

            Commence Entraining 23-30-hours, on 1st March.
            Train leaves 2-30-hours, 2nd March.

    (b) <u>No 13 Train.</u> :- 1 Coach and 47 Covers.

	B.O's.	I.O's.	O.R's & Fols:	Animals.
18th Lancers.	2.	3.	159.	253.

            Commence Entraining at 5-30-hours on 2nd March.
            Train Leaves at 8-30-hours on 2nd March.

    (c) <u>No 14 Train</u> :- 1 Coach, 22 Covers and 18 Flats.

	B.O's.	O.R's.	Animals.	4-Wheels.	2-Wheels.	Motor Amblce.	Box Cars.
@ Capt.COLLET.AVC. @ Ambala Mob.V.Sec.	1.	16.	24.	1.	2.	-	-
5th San.Sec.	-	2.	-	-	-	-	2.
(O.C., A.S.C) Remainder from 4th Cav.Dn-Mhow Vet.Sec., Amb.C. Fd.Amblce.	1.	57.	67.	9.	11.	7.	

            Commence Entraining at 8-30-hours on 2nd March.
            Train leaves at 11-30-hours on 2nd March.

    (d) <u>No 15 Train</u> :- 1 Coach, 23 Covers and 24 Flats.

	B.O's.	O.R's.	Animals.	4-Wheels.	2-Wheels.	Motor Ambs.	Box Car.	Motor Car.
Sec.Fd.Amb.	1.	34.	67.	8.	9.	-	-	-
Mhow Fd.Amb.	-	50.	67.	8.	9.	7.	-	-
Signal Sqdn.	-	1.	-	-	-	-	1.	-
Divnl.H.Q.	-	2.	-	-	-	-	-	2.

            Commence Entraining at 15-30-hours on 2nd March.
            Train Leaves at 20-30-hours on 2nd March.

                                              <u>Para 2.</u>-------

Continued :-

2. O.C.18th Lancers will detail officers to command Nos 12 & 13 Trains.
Capt COLLET,A.V.C.will command No 14 train and the officer detailed by Sec.Field Ambulance will command No 15 train.

3. The remainder of the 18th Lancers will go to Marseilles with Group "B".

O.C.,18th Lancers will hand to the Divisional Staff Officer at the station a statement showing the exact number of officers (Br.& Ind),O.R's and animals which are remaining behind.

The O.R's 18th Lancers detailed for the D.A.C's in Franck (vide my A.8250 of 28th Feb:) will remain. Orders for their disposal will be issued on the 2nd.March.

4. O.C.Trains will take over three days iron rations in bulk.
Each man will be in possession of the iron ration and the unexpended portion of the day's ration.

5. A.D.M.S.will make necessary Medical arrangements.

6. 2nd and 3rd blankets will be taken over by D.A.D.O.S.

7. An officer of the Divisional Staff will meet the O.C.Trains at the station at entraining times.

8. O.C.Trains will obtain from the R.T.O,a table showing Haltes Repas on the journey.

H W Cole
Lieut.Colonel.
A.A and Q.M.G.5th Cav.Division.

Copy to Ambala Mot Vet Section
Mhow Cav F A Amb.
Signal Sqdn

War diary

No. CR/46.

To,
Mhow Brigade,   O.C. Det. Sialkot Bde. at BACOUEL.
Lucknow Brigade.   O.C. Ind.Vet.Sect. at BACOUEL.
A.D.M.S.   A.D.V.S.
O.C., A.S.C.

---

1. Following will be at SALEUX Station at 1.0 p.m. to-morrow 23th instant to entrain for TARANTO.

		BO.	IO.	BOR.	IOR.	
Dethmt.	6th Cavalry.	1	2	–	97	) BACOUEL.
"	19th Lancers.	–	1	–	52	)
"	2nd Lancers.	2	2	–	50	
	38th C.I.Horse.	–	6	–	81	
	Sialkot C.F.A.	–	1	1	27	
	Ambala C.F.A.	–	–	–	8	
	Lucknow C.F.A.	1	2	6	75	
	Jodhpur C.F.A.	–	–	–	20	
	5th Cavalry Div.	3	2	2	138	
	Total.	7	16	9	548	

2. A.D.M.S. will be responsible for the arrival of Lucknow C.F.A. and details Ambala and Sialkot C.F.A. and Lucknow Brigade for Jodhpur C.F.A.

3. The nominal roll in duplicate of each party is required at the Station at time of entraining (4th Cav.Div. only).

4. O.C., A.S.C. will detail lorries as follows :-

    H.Q. 38th C.I.Horse.   5 lorries at 11.0 a.m.
    H.Q. 2nd Lrs.   3   "   " 11.0 a.m.
    Maire at BACOUEL
    (for Ind.Vet Secs).   8   "   " 10.30 a.m.
    Maire at BACOUEL
    (for Sialkot Bde
    details).   1   "   " 10.30 a.m.

5. The 5th Cavalry Division are detailing O.C. train and Mhow Brigade an Adjutant and Q.M.

G.R.Maitland
Lieut-Colonel,
A.A.&Q.M.G. Cavalry Corps "Q" (Rear).

27/2/18.

SECRET.   No. Q-531/R/16.

War Diary Appendix 'B'

Headquarters, 5th Cavalry Division.
2nd March 1918.

To

Sec'bad Cavalry Brigade.
18th Lancers.
Camp Commandant.
5th Signal Squadron.
O.C., A.S.C.
Sec'bad Mob.Vet.Section.
A.D.M.S.
D.A.D.O.S.
B.T.O., Sec'bad Cavalry Brigade.
French Mission.
A.D.V.S., 4th Cavalry Division.
4th Cavalry Division, "Q".
Cavalry Corps, "Q", Rear.

Group "B", sailing from MARSEILLES on the 10th March 1918.
---

1. The details of the 5th Cavalry Division included in this Group will be:-

	B.O's.	I.O's.	O.R.B.	O.R.I.	Animals.	2-Whls.	4-Whls.	Motors.
(a) (Div.H.Q.	-	-	22.	7.	50.	2.	2.	2.
(5th Sig.Sq.	2.	-	22.	3.	24.	3.	-	1.
(Hqrs.A.S.C.	1.	-	15.	4.	15.	3.	1.	-
(b) 18th Lancers.	1.	4.	1.	130.	181.	-	-	-
(c) Sec'bad M.V.S.	-	-	-	3.	6.	2.	1.	-
34th Poona Hse.	-	1	-	32.	64.	14.	6.	-
20th Horse.	-	-	-	12.	24.	-	6.	-

Sec'bad Bde H.Q. 1 (The Brigade Transport Officer, who will be in charge of (c))

The remainder of the group will consist of details from 4th Cav.Divn.

2. Group "B" will commence entraining early on the 3rd March. The details of this Division will probably entrain on the 4th March.

H.E. Cochrane, Lieut.Colonel.
A.A and Q.M.G., 5th Cavalry Division.

War Diary Appendix 'B'

SECRET.   No Q-531/R/17.

Headquarters, 5th Cavalry Division.
3rd March 1918.

To

Sec'bad Cavalry Brigade.
18th Lancers Detachment.
Camp Commandant.
5th Signal Squadron.
O.C., A.S.C.
Sec'bad Mob.Vet.Sec.
A.D.M.S.
D.A.D.O.S.
B.T.O., Sec'bad Cav.Bde.
French Mission.
A.D.V.S., 4th Cavalry Division.
4th Cavalry Division.Q.
Cavalry Corps Q, Rear.

----

1. This office No Q-531/R/16 dated 2nd March 1918 is cancelled and the following substituted.:-

2. The details of the 5th Cavalry Division included in Group "B", sailing from MARSEILLES on March 10th 1918, will be :-

	B.O.	I.O.	O.R.B.	O.R.I.	Animals.	2-Whls.	4-Whls.	Box Car.	Motor Car.	Bike
(a) (Div.H.Q.	-	-	22.	7.	50.	2.	2.	-	3.	-
(Sig.Sqdn.	2.	-	23.	3.	24.	3.	-	1.	-	5.
(H.Q.A.S.C.	1.	-	15.	4.	15.	3.	1.	-	-	-
(b) 18th Lancrs.	2.	4.	1.	130.	186.	-	-	-	-	-
(c) 34th Horse.	2.	4.	-	200.	306.	13.	6.	-	-	-
(d) 20th Horse.	-	-	-	30.	62.	13.	6.	-	-	-
Sec.Mob.V.Sec.	-	-	3.	-	6.	2.	1.	-	-	-
Sec.Sig.Troop	-	-	2.	-	4.	2.	-	-	-	-
Sec.Bde.H.Q. 1(@)	-	-	8.	-	11.	5.	1.	-	-	-

(@) The B.T.O., who will be in charge of (d).

Remainder of this group will consist of details from 4th Cavalry Division

3. This will leave one water cart with the detachment of Poona Horse and one with the Deccan Horse. They will accompany them with Group "C".

4. Group "B" will probably commence entraining early on 5th March. The details of this Division will probably entrain on the 6th March (night) or early morning of 7th March.

Lieut.Colonel.
A.A and Q.M.G., 5th Cavalry Division.

Appendix 'D'

SECRET.   No Q-531/R/18.
                                    Headquarters, 5th Cavalry Division.
To   5th March 1918.

  Sec'bad Cavalry Brigade.
  18th Lancers Detachment.
  Camp Commandant.
  5th Signal Squadron.
  O.C., A.S.C.
  Sec'bad Mob.Vet.Sec.
  A.D.M.S.
  D.A.D.O.S.
  D.A.D.O.S., 4th Cav.Divn.
  B.T.O., Sec.Cav.Bde.
  French Mission.
  A.D.V.S., 4th Cavalry Division.
  4th Cavalry Division."Q".
  Cavalry Corps,"Q",Rear.

1. The details of the 5th Cavalry Division proceeding with Group B, will entrain for Marseilles on the 7th March as follows :-

	B.O.	I.O.	O.R.B.	O.R.I.	Animals.	4-Whs.	2-Whs.	Motor Car.	Box Car.
(a) 4th Cav.San.Sec.	1.	-	15	1.	-	-	-	-	2.
20th Horse.	1.	-	-	30.	62.	6.	13.	-	-
Sec.Bde.H.Q.	1(@)-		8	-	11.	1.	5.	-	-
Sec.Sig.Trp.	-	-	1.	-	2.	-	2.	-	-
Sec.M.V.Sec.	-	-	3.	-	6.	1.	2.	-	-
5th Cav.Dn.Hqrs.	-	-	17.	9.	48.	2.	2.	2.	-

(@) The B.T.O.

(a) in No 25 Train - 1 coach, 30 covers and 17 flats.
    Commence entraining 5-30-hours on 7th March.
    Train leaves 8-30-hours on 7th March.

(b) No 26 Train - 1 coach, 35 covers and 12 flats.

	B.O.	I.O.	O.R.B.	O.R.I.	Animals.	4-Whs.	2-Whs.	Motor Car.	Box Car.
34th Horse.	2.	2.	-	112.	166.	6.	13.	-	-
H.Q., A.S.C.	-	-	19	-	15.	1.	3.	-	-
Sig.Sqdn.	1.	-	16.	-	24.	-	3.	-	1.
Div.Hqrs.	-	-	1.	-	-	-	-	1.	-

Commence entraining 8-30-hours on 7th March.
Train leaves 11-30-hours on 7th March.

(c) No 27 Train.- 1 coach and 47 covers.

	B.O.	I.O.	O.R.B.	O.R.I.	Animals.	4-Whls.	2-Whls.
34th Horse.	2.	2.	-	88.	140.	-	-
18th Lancers.	2.	4.	1.	130.	186.	-	-

Commence entraining 17-30-hours on 7th March.
Train leaves at 20-30-hours on 7th March.

2. Sec'bad Cav.Bde will detail officers to command Nos.25 & 26 Trains. Major Howell, 18th Lancers will command No 27 Train.

3. The remainder of Divisional Hqrs. and Sec'bad Cav.Bde will go to Marseilles with Group "C".
    Sec'bad Cav.Bde., Camp Commandant, A.D.M.S., A.D.V.S., and D.A.D.O.S. will send to Div.Hqrs by 6 p.m., on 6th March the exact number of Officers (Br and Ind), O.R's and animals which will remain for group "C".

4. O's.C.Trains will take over 3 days iron rations in bulk at the station. Each man will be in possession of the iron ration and the unexpended portion of the days ration.

5.   A.D.M.S. will make necessary Medical Arrangements.

6.   2nd and 3rd Blankets will be taken over by D.A.D.O.S.

7.   An officer of the Divisional Staff will meet O's.C.Trains at the station at entraining times.

8.   O's.C.Trains will obtain from the R.T.O. a table showing Haltes Repas on the journey.

H.E. Cochran
Lieut for
A.A and Q.M.G., 5th Cavalry Division.

Appendix 'C'

SECRET.　　　　　　　No.Q-531/R/19.

　　　　　　　　　　　　　　　　Headquarters, 5th Cavalry Division.
To　　　　　　　　　　　　　　　　8th March 1918.

　　Sec'bad Cavalry Brigade.
　　Sec'bad C.Field Amb.
　　Camp Commandant.
　　5th Signal Squadron.
　　"X", Sound Ranging Section.
　　Sec'bad M.V.Section.
　　A.D.M.S.
　　D.A.D.O.S.
　　D.A.D.O.S., 4th Cav.Divn.
　　French Mission.
　　A.D.V.S., 4th Cavalry Division.
　　4th Cav.Divn., Q.
　　Cavalry Corps, Q, Rear.

1.　The remaining details of the 5th Cavalry Division will entrain as follows :-
　　Entraining station SALEUX. Dates and times will be notified later.

(a) Train No 28.- 1 coach, 47 covers.

	B.O.	I.O.	O.R.B.	O.R.I.	Animals.	2-whl.	4-whl.	Motor Cars.	Motor Ambs.
34th Horse.	8.	4.	2.	170.	320.	-	-	-	-

(b) Train No 29.- 1 coach, 6 flats, 41 covers.

	B.O.	I.O.	O.R.B.	O.R.I.	Animals.	2-whl.	4-whl.	Motor Cars.	Motor Ambs.
34th Horse.	1.	1.	-	31.	46.	1.	-	-	-
Sec.Bde.H.Q.	4.	1.	28.	7.	33.	-	-	2.	-
Sec.C.Fd.Amb.	1.	-	11.	23.	-	-	-	-	5.
20th Horse.	2.	3.	1.	89.	184.	1.	-	-	-

(c) Train No 30. 1 coach 47 covers.

	B.O.	I.O.	O.R.B.	O.R.I.	Animals.	2-whl.	4-whl.	Motor Cars.	Motor Ambs.
20th Horse.	5.	4.	2.	208.	312.	-	-	-	-

(d) Train No 31.- 1 coach, 17 flats, 30 covers.

	B.O.	I.O.	O.R.B.	O.R.I.	Animals.	2-whl.	4-whl.	Motor Cars.	Motor Ambs.
20th Horse.	3.	2.	2.	110.	118.	-	-	-	-
Divnl.H.Q.	2.	-	24.	2.	-	-	-	4.	-
5th Sig.Sqdn.	2.	-	20.	-	-	-	-	-	-
Sec.Sig.Troop.	1.	-	16.	1.	15.	-	-	-	-
2nd Lancers.	1.	-	-	32.	56.	14.	4.	-	-
X Sound Rg.Sec.	-	-	3.	-	-	-	-	3.	-

(e) Train No 32.- 1 coach, 47 covers.

	B.O.	I.O.	O.R.B.	O.R.I.	Animals.	2-whl.	4-whl.	Motor Cars.	Motor Ambs.
Sec.M.V.Sec.	1.	-	10.	6.	18.	-	-	-	-
2nd Lancers.	10.	-	-	170.	297.	-	-	-	-

2.　Sec'bad Cavalry Brigade will detail officers to command Trains Nos 28, 29, 30 and 31.

　　　　　　　　　　　　　　　　　　　　W.E.Cochran
　　　　　　　　　　　　　　　　　　　　　　Lieut.for
　　　　　　　　　　　　　　　　A.A and Q.M.G., 5th Cavalry Division.

SECRET.

Appendix

No. Q-531/R/20.

Headquarters, 5th Cavalry Division.

15th March 1918.

To,
Sec'bad Cavalry Brigade.
Sec'bad C.Field Amb.
Camp Commandant.
5th Signal Squadron.
"X" Sound Ranging Section.
Sec'bad M.V.Section.
A.D.M.S.
D.A.D.O.S.
D.A.D.O.S., 4th Cav.Divn.
French Mission.
A.D.V.S., 4th Cavalry Divn.
4th Cav.Divn. "Q"
Cavalry Corps, "Q", Rear.

Reference this office No.Q-531/R/19, dated 8th March 1918.

1. The remaining details of the 5th Cavalry Division will entrain on the dates and times as specified below :-

   (a) Train No.28. 1 coach, 47 covers.
       Train leaves 8.30 hours on 19th March.
       Commence entraining 5.30 hours on 19th March.

   (b) Train No.29. 1 coach, 6 flats, 41 covers.
       Train leaves 11-30 hours on 19th March.
       Commence entraining 8.30 hours on 19th March.

   (c) Train No.30. 1 coach, 47 covers.
       Train leaves 20-30 hours on 19th March.
       Commence entraining 17-30 hours on 19th March.

   (d) Train No.31. 1 coach, 17 flats, 30 covers.
       Train leaves 8-30 hours on 20th March.
       Commence entraining 5-30 hours on 20th March.

2. Lieut-Colonel A.N.FLEMING, I.M.S. will be in command of Train No.29. Sec'bad Cavalry Brigade will detail officers to command trains No.28, 30, 31, and 32.

3. O's.C. Trains will take over 3 days iron rations in bulk at the Station.
   Each man will be in possession of the iron ration and the unexpended portion of the day's ration.

4. A.D.M.S. will make necessary Medical arrangements.

5. 2nd and 3rd blankets will be taken over by D.A.D.O.S.

6. An officer of the Divisional Staff will meet O.C. Trains at the Station at entraining times.

7. O'sC Trains

7. O's.C. Trains will obtain from the R.T.O. a table showing Haltes Repas on the journey.

8. O.C., A.S.C. will furnish lorries as follows :-

34th Poona Horse. 2 Lorries at PISSY at 8.0.p.m. on 18th instant.

20th Deccan Horse. 3 Lorries at PREUZEL at 8.0.p.m. on 18th instant.

Divl. Headquarters. 1 Lorry at 8.0.p.m. on 19th instant.

H.E Cochran
Lieut,
for A.A. & Q.M.G. 5th Cavalry Division.

Appendix A

SECRET.   No G-531/R/15.

                Headquarters, 5th Cavalry Division.
                        1st March 1918.
To /
    18th Lancers.
    Sec'bad Cavalry Brigade.
    O.C., A.S.C.
    A.D.M.S.
    D.A.D.O.S.
    Camp Commandant.
    French Mission.
    4th Cavalry Divn.Q.
    Cavalry Corps, Q.Rear.
    Sec'bad Field Ambulance.
    ----

1. Group "A" will continue entraining on the 2nd March as follows:-
    Entraining Station SALEUX.

    (a) No 12 Train :-   1 Coach, 35 Covers and 12 Flats.

	B.O's.	I.O's.	O.R's & Fols.	Animals.	4-Wheels	2-Whls.	Motor Amb.
18th Lancers.	2.	4.	140.	232.	6.	14.	-
Sec. Field Amb.	-	-	8.	-	-	-	4.

        Commence Entraining 23-30-hours, on 1st March.
        Train leaves 2-30-hours, 2nd March.

    (b) No 13 Train. :- 1 Coach and 47 Covers.

	B.O's.	I.O's.	O.R's & Fols:	Animals.
18th Lancers.	2.	3.	159.	253.

        Commence Entraining at 5-30-hours on 2nd March.
        Train Leaves at 8-30-hours on 2nd March.

    (c) No 14 Train :- 1 Coach, 22 Covers and 18 Flats.

	B.O's.	O.R's.	Animals.	4-Wheels.	2-Wheels.	Motor Amblce.	Box Cars.
Capt. COLLET. AVC. @							
Mob.V.Sec.	1.	16.	24.	1.	2.	-	-
5th San.Sec.	-	2.	-	-	-	-	2.
(O.C., A.S.C) Remainder from 4th Cav.Dn-Mhow Vet.Sec., Amb.C. Fd.Amblce.	1.	57.	67.	9.	11.	7.	

    @ Ambala

        Commence Entraining at 8-30-hours on 2nd March.
        Train leaves at 11-30-hours on 2nd March.

    (d) No 15 Train :- 1 Coach, 23 Covers and 24 Flats.

	B.O's.	O.R's.	Animals.	4-Wheels.	2-Wheels.	Motor Ambs.	Box Car.	Motor Car.
Sec.Fd.Amb.	1.	34.	67.	8.	9.	-	-	-
Mhow Fd.Amb.	-	50.	67.	8.	9.	7.	-	-
Signal Sqdn.	-	1.	-	-	-	-	1.	-
Divnl.H.Q.	-	2.	-	-	-	-	-	2.

        Commence Entraining at 17-30-hours on 2nd March.
        Train Leaves at 20-30-hours on 2nd March.

                                                Para 2.------

Continued :-

2. O.C,18th Lancers will detail officers to command Nos 12 & 13 Trains.
    Capt COLLET,A.V.C.will command No 14 train and the officer detailed by Sec.Field Ambulance will command No 15 train.

3. The remainder of the 18th Lancers will go to Marseilles with Group "B".
    O.C.,18th Lancers will hand to the Divisional Staff Officer at the station a statement showing the exact number of officers (Br.& Ind),O.R's and animals which are remaining behind.
    The O.R's 18th Lancers detailed for the D.A.C's in Franck (vide my A.8250 of 28th Feb:) will remain. Orders for their disposal will be issued on the 2nd.March.

4. O.C.Trains will take over three days iron rations in bulk.
    Each man will be in possession of the iron ration and the unexpended portion of the day's ration.

5. A.D.M.S.will make necessary Medical arrangements.

6. 2nd and 3rd blankets will be taken over by D.A.D.O.S.

7. An officer of the Divisional Staff will meet the O.C.Trains at the station at entraining times.

8. O.C.Trains will obtain from the R.T.O,a table showing Haltes Repas on the journey.

                                          H W Collie
                                          Lieut.Colonel.
                                          A.A and Q.M.G.5th Cav.Division.

Copy to Ambala Mot Vet Section
Mhow Cav. F.D Amb.
Signal Sqdn

No. CR/46.

To,
Mhow Brigade.   O.C. Det.Sialkot Bde. at BACOUEL.
Lucknow Brigade.   O.C. Ind.Vet.Sect. at BACOUEL.
A.D.M.S.   A.D.V.S.
O.C.,A.S.C.

---

1. Following will be at SALEUX Station at 1.0 p.m. to-morrow 23th instant to entrain for TARANTO.

	BO.	IO.	BOR.	IOR.	
Dethmt. 6th Cavalry.	1	2	-	97	) BACOUEL.
" 19th Lancers.	-	1	-	52	)
" 2nd Lancers.	2	2	-	50	
38th C.I.Horse.	-	6	-	81	
Sialkot C.F.A.	-	1	1	27	
Ambala C.F.A.	-	-	-	8	
Lucknow C.F.A.	1	2	6	75	
Jodhpur C.F.A.	-	-	-	20	
5th Cavalry Div.	3	2	2	138	
Total.	7	16	9	548	

2. A.D.M.S. will be responsible thuk for the arrival of Lucknow C.F.A. and details Ambala and Sialkot C.F.A. and Lucknow Brigade for Jodhpur C.F.A.

3. The nominal roll in duplicate of each party is required at the Station at time of entraining (4th Cav.Div. only).

4. O.C.,A.S.C. will detail lorries as follows :-

    H.Q. 38th C.I.Horse.   5 lorries at 11.0 a.m.
    H.Q. 2nd Lrs.   3   "   " 11.0 a.m.
    Maire at BACOUEL
    (for Ind.Vet Secs).   8   "   " 10.30 a.m.
    Maire at BACOUEL
    (for Sialkot Bde
    details).   1   "   " 10.30 a.m.

5. The 5th Cavalry Division are detailing O.C. train and Mhow Brigade an Adjutant and Q.M.

GRMaitland

Lieut-Colonel,
A.A.& Q.M.G. Cavalry Corps "Q" (Rear).

27/2/18.

Appendix 'B'

SECRET.   No Q-531/R/16.

Headquarters, 5th Cavalry Division.
2nd March 1918.

To
   Sec'bad Cavalry Brigade.
   18th Lancers.
   Camp Commandant.
   5th Signal Squadron.
   O.C., A.S.C.
   Sec'bad Mob.Vet.Section.
   A.D.M.S.
   D.A.D.O.S.
   B.T.O., Sec'bad Cavalry Brigade.
   French Mission.
   A.D.V.S., 4th Cavalry Division.
   4th Cavalry Division, "Q".
   Cavalry Corps, "Q", Rear.

Group "B", sailing from MARSEILLES on the 10th March 1918.

1. The details of the 5th Cavalry Division included in this Group will be:-

	B.O's.	I.O's.	O.R.B.	O.R.I.	Animals.	2-Whls.	4-Whls.	Motors.
(a) (Div.H.Q.	-	-	22.	7.	50.	2.	2.	2.
(5th Sig.Sq.	2.	-	22.	3.	24.	3.	-	1.
(Hqrs.A.S.C.	1.	-	15.	4.	15.	3.	1.	-
(b) 18th Lancers.	1.	4.	1.	130.	181.	-	-	-
(c) Sec'bad M.V.S.	-	-	3.	6.	2.	1.	-	-
34th Poona Hse.	1	-	32.	64.	14.	6.	-	-
20th Horse.	-	-	12.	24.	-	6.	-	-

Sec'bad Bde H.Q. 1 (The Brigade Transport Officer, who will be in charge of (c))

The remainder of the group will consist of details from 4th Cav.Divn.

2. Group "B" will commence entraining early on the 3rd March. The details of this Division will probably entrain on the 4th March.

H.E. Cochrane Lt.Col.
Lieut.Colonel.
A.A and Q.M.G., 5th Cavalry Division.

Appendix L

SECRET.   No Q-531/R/17.

Headquarters, 5th Cavalry Division.

3rd March 1918.

To
  Sec'bad Cavalry Brigade.
  18th Lancers Detachment.
  Camp Commandant.
  5th Signal Squadron.
  O.C., A.S.C.
  Sec'bad Mob.Vet.Sec.
  A.D.M.S.
  D.A.D.O.S.
  B.T.O., Sec'bad Cav.Bde.
  French Mission.
  A.D.V.S., 4th Cavalry Division.
  4th Cavalry Division.Q.
  Cavalry Corps Q, Rear.

---

1. This office No Q-531/R/16 dated 2nd March 1918 is cancelled and the following substituted:-

2. The details of the 5th Cavalry Division included in Group "B", sailing from MARSEILLES on March 10th 1918, will be:-

	B.O.	I.O.	O.R.B.	O.R.I.	Animals.	2-Whls.	4-Whls.	Box Car.	Motor Car.	Bikes
(a) (Div.H.Q.	-	-	22.	7.	50.	2.	2.	-	3.	-
(Sig.Sqdn.	2.	-	23.	3.	24.	3.	-	1.	-	5.
(Q.A.S.C.	1.	-	15.	4.	15.	3.	1.	-	-	-
(b) 18th Lancers.	2.	4.	1.	130.	186.	-	-	-	-	-
(c) 34th Horse.	2.	4.	-	200.	306.	13.	6.	-	-	-
(d) 20th Horse.	-	-	-	30.	62.	13.	6.	-	-	-
Sec.Mob.V.Sec.	-	-	3.	-	6.	2.	1.	-	-	-
Sec.Sig.Troop	-	-	2.	-	4.	2.	-	-	-	-
Sec.Bde.H.Q.	1(@)	-	8.	-	11.	5.	1.	-	-	-

(@) The B.T.O., who will be in charge of (d).

Remainder of this group will consist of details from 4th Cavalry Division

3. This will leave one water cart with the detachment of Poona Horse and one with the Deccan Horse. They will accompany them with Group "C".

4. Group "B" will probably commence entraining early on 5th March. The details of this Division will probably entrain on the 6th March (night) or early morning of 7th March.

Lieut.Colonel.
A.A and Q.M.G., 5th Cavalry Division.

Appendix D

SECRET. No Q-531/R/18.
　　　　　　　　　　　　　　　　Headquarters, 5th Cavalry Division.
To　　　　　　　　　　　　　　　5th March 1918.

　Sec'bad Cavalry Brigade.
　18th Lancers Detachment.
　Camp Commandant.
　5th Signal Squadron.
　O.C., A.S.C.
　Sec'bad Mob.Vet.Sec.
　A.D.M.S.
　D.A.D.O.S.
　D.A.D.O.S., 4th Cav.Divn.
　B.T.O., Sec.Cav.Bde.
　French Mission.
　A.D.V.S., 4th Cavalry Division.
　4th Cavalry Division."Q".
　Cavalry Corps,"Q", Rear.
----

1. The details of the 5th Cavalry Division proceeding with Group B, will entrain for Marseilles on the 7th March as follows :-

(a) No 25 Train – 1 coach, 30 covers and 17 flats.

	B.O.	I.O.	O.R.B.	O.R.I.	Animals.	4-Whs.	2-Whs.	Motor Car.	Box Car.
4th Cav.San.Sec.	1.	-	15	1.	-	-	-	-	2.
20th Horse.	1.	-	-	30.	62.	6.	13.	-	-
Sec.Bde.H.Q.	1(@)	-	8	-	11.	1.	5.	-	-
Sec.Sig.Trp.	-	-	1.	-	2.	-	2.	-	-
Sec.M.V.Sec.	-	-	3.	-	6.	1.	2.	-	-
5th Cav.Dn.Hqrs.	-	-	17.	9.	48.	2.	2.	2.	-

(@) The B.T.O.

　　Commence entraining 5-30-hours on 7th March.
　　Train leaves 8-30-hours on 7th March.

(b) No 26 Train – 1 coach, 35 covers and 12 flats.

	B.O.	I.O.	O.R.B.	O.R.I.	Animals.	4-Whs.	2-Whs.	Motor Car.	Box Car.
34th Horse.	2.	2.	-	112.	166.	6.	13.	-	-
H.Q., A.S.C.	-	-	19	-	15.	1.	3.	-	-
Sig.Sqdn.	1.	-	16.	-	24.	-	3.	-	1.
Div.Hqrs.	-	-	1.	-	-	-	-	1.	-

　　Commence entraining 8-30-hours on 7th March.
　　Train leaves 11-30-hours on 7th March.

(c) No 27 Train. – 1 coach and 47 covers.

	B.O.	I.O.	O.R.B.	O.R.I.	Animals.	4-Whls.	2-Whls.
34th Horse.	2.	2.	-	88.	140.	-	-
18th Lancers.	2.	4.	1.	130.	186.	-	-

　　Commence entraining 17-30-hours on 7th March.
　　Train leaves at 20-30-hours on 7th March.

2. Sec'bad Cav.Bde will detail officers to command Nos. 25 & 26 Trains. Major Howell, 18th Lancers will command No 27 Train.

3. The remainder of Divisional Hqrs. and Sec'bad Cav.Bde will go to Marseilles with Group "C".
　Sec'bad Cav.Bde., Camp Commandant, A.D.M.S., A.D.V.S., and D.A.D.O.S. will send to Div.H.Qrs by 6 p.m., on 6th March the exact number of Officers (Br and Ind), O.R's and animals which will remain for group "C".

4. O's.C.Trains will take over 3 days iron rations in bulk at the station. Each man will be in possession of the iron ration and the unexpended portion of the days ration.

5. A.D.M.S. will make necessary Medical Arrangements.

6. 2nd and 3rd Blankets will be taken over by D.A.D.O.S.

7. An officer of the Divisional Staff will meet O's.C.Trains at the station at entraining times.

8. O's.C.Trains will obtain from the R.T.O. a table showing Haltes Repas on the journey.

H.E. Cochran
Lieut for
A.A and Q.M.G., 5th Cavalry Division.

Appendix 'G'

SECRET.   No Q-531/R/19.

Headquarters, 5th Cavalry Division.

8th March 1918.

To
- Sec'bad Cavalry Brigade.
- Sec'bad C.Field Amb.
- Camp Commandant.
- 5th Signal Squadron.
- "X", Sound Ranging Section.
- Sec'bad M.V.Section.
- A.D.M.S.
- D.A.D.O.S.
- D.A.D.O.S., 4th Cav.Divn.
- French Mission.
- A.D.V.S., 4th Cavalry Division.
- 4th Cav.Divn.,Q.
- Cavalry Corps,Q,Rear.

---

1. The remaining details of the 5th Cavalry Division will entrain as follows :-

    Entraining station SALEUX. Dates and times will be notified later.

(a) Train No 28.- 1 coach, 47 covers.

	B.O.	I.O.	O.R.B.	O.R.I.	Animals.	2-whl.	4-whl.	Motor Cars.	Motor Ambs.
34th Horse.	8.	4.	2.	170.	320.	-	-	-	-

(b) Train No 29.- 1 coach, 6 flats, 41 covers.

	B.O.	I.O.	O.R.B.	O.R.I.	Animals.	2-whl.	4-whl.	Motor Cars.	Motor Ambs.
34th Horse.	1.	1.	-	31.	46.	1.	-	-	-
Sec.Bde.H.Q.	4.	1.	28.	7.	33.	-	-	2.	-
Sec.C.Fd.Amb.	1.	-	11.	23.	-	-	-	-	3.
20th Horse.	2.	3.	1.	89.	184.	1.	-	-	-

(c) Train No 30. 1 coach 47 covers.

	B.O.	I.O.	O.R.B.	O.R.I.	Animals.	2-whl.	4-whl.	Motor Cars.	Motor Ambs.
20th Horse.	5.	4.	2.	208.	312.	-	-	-	-

(d) Train No 31.- 1 coach, 17 flats, 30 covers.

	B.O.	I.O.	O.R.B.	O.R.I.	Animals.	2-whl.	4-whl.	Motor Cars.	Motor Ambs.
20th Horse.	3.	2.	2.	110.	118.	-	-	-	-
Divnl.H.Q.	2.	-	24.	2.	-	-	-	4.	-
5th Sig.Sqdn.	2.	-	20.	-	-	-	-	-	-
Sec.Sig.Troop.	1.	-	16.	1.	15.	-	-	-	-
2nd Lancers.	1.	-	-	32.	56.	14.	4.	-	-
X Sound Rg.Sec.	-	-	3.	-	-	-	-	3.	-

(e) Train No 32.- 1 coach, 47 covers.

	B.O.	I.O.	O.R.B.	O.R.I.	Animals.	2-whl.	4-whl.	Motor Cars.	Motor Ambs.
Sec.M.V.Sec.	1.	-	10.	6.	18.	-	-	-	-
2nd Lancers.	10.	-	-	170.	297.	-	-	-	-

2. Sec'bad Cavalry Brigade will detail officers to command Trains Nos 28, 29, 30 and 31.

H.E. Cochran
Lieut. for
A.A and Q.M.G., 5th Cavalry Division.

Appendix 'Y'

SECRET.   No. Q-531/R/20.

Headquarters, 5th Cavalry Division,

15th March 1918.

To,
Sec'bad Cavalry Brigade.
Sec'bad C.Field Amb.
Camp Commandant.
5th Signal Squadron.
"X" Sound Ranging Section.
Sec'bad M.V.Section.
A.D.M.S.
D.A.D.O.S.
D.A.D.O.S., 4th Cav.Divn.
French Mission.
A.D.V.S., 4th Cavalry Divn.
4th Cav.Divn. "Q"
Cavalry Corps, "Q", Rear.

Reference this office No.Q-531/R/19, dated 8th March 1918.

1. The remaining details of the 5th Cavalry Division will entrain on the dates and times as specified below :-

  (a) Train No.28.   1 coach, 47 covers.
        Train leaves 8.30 hours on 19th March.
        Commence entraining 5.30 hours on 19th March.

  (b) Train No.29.   1 coach, 6 flats, 41 covers.
        Train leaves 11-30 hours on 19th March.
        Commence entraining 8.30 hours on 19th March.

  (c) Train No.30.   1 coach, 47 covers.
        Train leaves 20-30 hours on 19th March.
        Commence entraining 17-30 hours on 19th March.

  (d) Train No.31.   1 coach, 17 flats, 30 covers.
        Train leaves 8-30 hours on 20th March.
        Commence entraining 5-30 hours on 20th March.

2. Lieut-Colonel A.N.FLEMING, I.M.S. will be in command of Train No.29. Sec'bad Cavalry Brigade will detail officers to command trains No.28, 30, 31, and 32.

3. O's.C. Trains will take over 3 days iron rations in bulk at the Station.
   Each man will be in possession of the iron ration and the unexpended portion of the day's ration.

4. A.D.M.S. will make necessary Medical arrangements.

5. 2nd and 3rd blankets will be taken over by D.A.D.O.S.

6. An officer of the Divisional Staff will meet O.C. Trains at the Station at entraining times.

7. O'sC Trains

No. O/595

Hdqrs. 5th Cavalry Divn
26th April 1918

To A.G. in India
Army Hdqs.
Simla.

Herewith Administrative war Diary for Advanced 5th Cavalry Divisional Hdqs. for month of March 1918.

[stamp: ARMY HEAD QUARTERS INDIA / SIMLA / 20. MAY 1918 / ADJUTANT GENERAL'S BRANCH]

[signature]
Major
for G.O.C. 5th Cavy Divn

Army Form C. 2118.

Headquarters, 5th Cavalry Division.
(ADMINISTRATIVE).

WAR DIARY
~~INTELLIGENCE SUMMARY~~

(Erase heading not required.)

Instructions regarding War Diaries and Intelligence Summaries are contained in F. S. Regs., Part II. and the Staff Manual respectively. Title pages will be prepared in manuscript.

Place	Date	Hour	Summary of Events and Information	Remarks and references to Appendices
TEL-EL-KEBIR	March 5th		Advanced Div'nl Headquarters opened at TEL-EL-KEBIR at 9.0 p.m. STAFF:— Brig-General G.A.H. Beatty, D.S.O., Commanding. Major H.B. Nutting, D.A.A.& Q.M.G. Major H.B. Clegg, S.S.O. Lieut. J.A. Ewart, A.D.C. to G.O.C.	
do.	March 21st		Director of Remounts, E.E.F., inspected the following Units, who have now become complete:— 6th Cavalry. 9th Horse. 19th Lancers. Ambala C.F.A. Sialkote C.F.A.	
do.	March 25th		The details already arrived of the 4th and 5th Cavalry Divisions inspected by the G.O.C., Force in Egypt.	
do.	March 27th		H.R.H., Duke of Connaught, met General Beatty and Staff, all C.O's of Regiments and Field Ambulances on the railway platform at TEL-EL-KEBIR. Jemadar Gobind Singh, V.C., was also present. The following numbers of horses, surplus to Establishment, were this day despatched to No.3 Remount Depot, BILBEIS:— 6th Cavalry: 35 Riding. 2 Draught. 4 Pack. 19th Lancers: 40 Riding. 4 Draught. 1 Pack. 9th Horse: 14 Riding. 6 Draught.	

Major,
D.A.A.& Q.M.G., 5th Cavalry Division.

WAR DIARY of INTELLIGENCE SUMMARY.

Headquarters, 5th Cavalry Division. (ADMINISTRATIVE).

Army Form C. 2118.

Place	Date	Hour	Summary of Events and Information	Remarks and references to Appendices

TEL-EL-KEBIR	March 5th		Advanced Div'nl Headquarters opened at TEL-EL-KEBIR at 9.0 p.m.
			
			 STAFF:
			     Brig-General G.A.H. Beatty, D.S.O., Commanding.
			     Major H.B. Nutting, D.A.A.& Q.M.G.
			     Major H.B. Clegg, S.S.O.
			     Lieut. J.A. Ewart, A.D.C. to G.O.C.	

do.	March 21st		Director of Remounts, E.E.F., inspected the following Units, who have now become complete:-
			
			   6th Cavalry. 9th Horse.
			   19th Lancers. Ambala C.F.A.
			                   Sialkote C.F.A.	

do.	March 25th		The details already arrived of the 4th and 5th Cavalry Divisions inspected by the G.O.C., Force in Egypt.	

do.	March 27th		H.R.H., Duke of Connaught, met General Beatty and Staff, all C.O's of Regiments and Field Ambulances on the railway platform at TEL-EL-KEBIR. Jemadar Gobind Singh, V.C., was also present.
			
			 The following numbers of horses, surplus to Establishment, were this day despatched to No.3 Remount Depot, BILBEIS:-
			
			   6th Cavalry: 35 Riding. 9th Horse: 14 Riding.
			                     2 Draught. 6 Draught.
			                     4 Pack.
			
			   19th Lancers: 40 Riding.
			                     4 Draught.
			                     1 Pack.
			
			 Muthrie, Major,
			 D.A.A.& Q.M.G., 5th Cavalry Division.	

149(1)

WAR DIARY.

E.E. FORCE

Unit A.D. 5th Cav. Division

From April 1st. To April 30/1918

Army Form C. 2118.

WAR DIARY
or
INTELLIGENCE SUMMARY.

Headquarters,
5th Cavalry Division.
(ADMINISTRATIVE).

(Erase heading not required.)

Place	Date	Hour	Summary of Events and Information	Remarks and references to Appendices
TEL-EL-KEBIR.	April 4th		Brig-General L.L. Maxwell, C.M.G., arrived and took over command of Advanced Div'nl Hqrs. this date.	MTM
do.	April 7th		1 B.O., 1 I.O. and 46 O.R.I. left for work at the No.1 Remount Depot, KANTARA, to-day.	MTM
do.	April 8th		Leave to India sanctioned for Indian Ranks on a percentage of 10% of strength. Numbers proceeded to India by 1st Batch to-day:- 24 Indian Officers. 631 Indian Other Ranks.	MTM
do.	April 11th		Orders received for the move of 6th Cavalry and 19th Lancers to KANTARA by route march. Date to be notified later.	MTM
do.	April 15th		6th Cavalry, 19th Lancers, Sialkote C.F.A. and Sialkote M.V.S. moved to day by route march to KANTARA en route for BELAH. (Administrative Instructions - Appendix "A".)	MTM
do.	April 16th		29th Lancers, 36th Jacob's Horse and Lucknow C.F.A. moved to-day by route march to KANTARA en route for BELAH. (Administrative Instructions - Appendix "B").	MTM
do.	April 19th		9th Horse, 18th Lancers, Ambala C.F.A. and Ambala M.V.S. proceeded by route march to KANTARA en route for LUDD. (Administrative Instructions - Appendix "C").	MTM
do.	April 21st		No.23 Field Veterinary Section proceeded to KANTARA by rail en route for LUDD.	MTM
do.	April 22nd		20th Deccan Horse and 34th Poona Horse proceeded to KANTARA by road en route for BELAH, and on arrival will come under orders of Desert Corps. (See Appendix "D").	MTM
do.	April 24th		Jodhpore Lancers and Jodhpore C.F.A. proceeded by road to KANTARA, en route for BELAH, to come under the orders of Desert Corps. (See Appendix "E")	MTM

Army Form C. 2118.

WAR DIARY
or
INTELLIGENCE SUMMARY.

(Erase heading not required.)

Instructions regarding War Diaries and Intelligence Summaries are contained in F.S. Regs., Part II. and the Staff Manual respectively. Title pages will be prepared in manuscript.

Place	Date	Hour	Summary of Events and Information	Remarks and references to Appendices
TEL-EL-KEBIR.	April 25th		2nd Lancers, 38th C.I. Horse, Mhow C.F.A. and Mhow M.V.S. proceeded by route march to-day to KANTARA en route for BELAH. On arrival at that place they will come under the orders of the Desert Corps. (See Appendix "F").	MF
	27th.		Secbad Cav.Field Ambulance marched to KANTARA today en route to BELAH to come under the orders of Desert Corps. (See Appendix "G" - Administrative Instructions)	MF
	28th.		Secbad Mobile Veterinary Section, Lucknow Mobile Veterinary Section and 4th.Sanitary Section marched today to KANTARA en route to BELAH. (Administrative contained in Appendix "H").	MF
			Orders issued for details of Sialkote, Lucknow and Secbad Brigade Headquarters and Signal Troops to concentrate at Divisional Headquarters prior to being broken up.	
	29th.		All horses of 5th.Signal Squadron, Lucknow - Sialkote and Secbad Signal Troops returned to No.3 Remount Depot. BILBEIS today. All harness and Ordnance equipment being handed in to the Ordnance Depot TEL-EL-KEBIR.	MF

Appendix 'A'

SECRET & URGENT.   No. Q.393.
                                    Headquarters, 5th Cavalry Division.
                                                        14th April, 1918.

To/

    Sialkot Cavalry Brigade.   A.D.V.S.
    O.C., A.S.C.   D.A.D.O.S.
    A.D.M.S.   Admin.Comdt. Tel-el-Kebir.

              Reference No.G.158 dated 14th inst.

1.   The unexpended portion of the day's rations and forage will be carried on men and horses.
    Rations will be delivered as under :-

    For 16th inst. - On arrival at QASSASIN.
    " 17th inst. - On arrival at ISMAILIA.

2.   Water carts will march full and all water-bottles are to be filled daily before leaving camp.

3.   No tents will be taken.
    All tents at present in use by units will be struck to-morrow morning and returned to D.A.D.O.S.
    The transport for return of tents will be supplied by Admin. Commandant and wagons will call for tents as under :-

    Tents of 6th Cavalry and 19th Lancers - 2 p.m. at Regtl Guard Rooms
    "   " Sialkot M.V.S. and C.F.A.   - at Hd.Qrs. of units at 2 pm

4.   The base kits of units clearly marked and securely packed will be handed over to the O.C., I.C.A.B.D. and Os.C. by 12 noon on 15th inst. under arrangements to be made with O.C., I.C.A.B.D. and Os.C Units.

5.   Baggage surplus to that carried on regimental wagons which it is desired to send to the forward area will be dumped by units, prior to marching out, at East end of No.1 Platform, Tel-el-Kebir Stn.
    Each unit will leave sufficient men to load and escort their own baggage. The baggage escort will travel with the baggage to KANTARA leaving Tel-el-Kebir on 16th inst. Time of train will be notified later.

6.   All personnel surplus to the mounted establishment of units will be left at Tel-el-Kebir and transferred to the I.C.A.B.D. on the morning of the 16th inst.
    Nominal rolls of such personnel will be rendered to the O.C. I.C.A.B.D.

7.   The dismounted personnel of the Sialkot C.F.A. will move to KANTARA by train on the 16th inst., time of departure to be notified later.

8.   ACKNOWLEDGE.

                                          Sgd. W.T. Hodgson,

                                                Lieut-Colonel,
                      for A.A. & Q.M.G. 5th Cavalry Division.

Copies to :-

        O.C., I.C.A.B.D.
        R.T.O. Tel-el-Kebir.

Appendix "B"

SECRET.

No. Q.423.

Headquarters, 5th Cavalry Division.
15th April, 1918.

To/
Lucknow Cavalry Brigade.
O.C., A.S.C.
A.D.M.S.
A.D.V.S.
D.A.D.O.S.
Admin. Comdt., Tel-el-Kebir.

Reference No. G.160 of to-day's date.

1. The unexpended portion of the day's ration and forage will be carried on men and horses.
Rations will be delivered as under :-

    for 17th inst. - On arrival at QASSASIN.
    " 18th inst. - On arrival at ISMAILIA.

2. Water carts will march full and all water bottles are to be filled daily before leaving the camp.

3. No tents will be taken.
All tents at present in use by units will be struck to-morrow morning and returned to D.A.D.O.S.
The transport for the return of tents will be supplied by Admin. Commandant and wagons will call for tents as under :-

Tents of 29th Lancers and 36th J.Horse - 2.p.m. at Regt'l
                                                           Guardrooms
" " Lucknow C.F.A.   at Hd.Qrs. of Unit at 2.pm

4. Baggage surplus to that carried on regimental wagons which it is desired to send to the forward area will be dumped by units prior to marching out at the eastern end of No.1 Platform, Tel-el-Kebir Stn.
Each unit will leave sufficient men to load and escort their own baggage. The baggage escort will travel with the baggage to KANTARA leaving Tel-el-Kebir on 18th inst. Time of train to be notified later.

5. All personnel surplus to the mounted establishment of units will be left in their present billets at Tel-el-Kebir and all Base kits of their units will be clearly marked and handed over to the O.C., of the Dismounted Party. This party will come the command of the O.C. I.C.A.B.D. Nominal rolls of such personnel being rendered to the O.C., I.C.A.B.D.

6. The Dismounted personnel of Lucknow I.C.F.A. will move to KANTARA by train on the 17th inst. Time of departure to be notified later.

7. ACKNOWLEDGE.

                                        Sgd. H. Nutting,

                                                  Major,
                              D.A.A. & Q.M.G., 5th Cav Div'n.

Copies to :-
    O.C., I.C.A.B.D.
    R.T.O., Tel-el-Kebir.

SECRET.   Appendix "C"   NO.Q.455.

Headquarters, 5th Cavalry Division,
17th April, 1918.

To/

Ambala Cavalry Brigade.   O.C., A.S.C.
Sec'bad Cavalry Brigade.   A.D.M.S.
A.D.V.S.   5th Signal Squadron.
D.A.D.O.S.   Admin.Comdt., Tel-el-Kebir.

Reference No.G.165 of to-day's date.

1. The unexpended portion of the day's rations and forage will be carried on men and horses.
   Rations will be delivered as under :-
   for 20th inst. - On arrival at QASSASIN.
   "   21st inst. - On arrival at ISMAILIA.
   "   22nd inst. - On arrival at EL FERDAN.

2. Water carts will march full and all water bottles are to be filled daily before leaving the camp.

3. No tents will be taken.
   All tents at present in use will be struck on the morning of the 19th inst., and returned to D.A.D.O.S.
   The transport for the return of these tents will be supplied by the Admin. Commandant and wagons will call for tents as under :-
   Tents of 9th Horse and 18th Lancers - 2 p.m. on the 19th at Regt'l Guard Rooms.
   Ambala C.F.A. and M.V.S. - at 2 p.m. on the 19th at Hd.Qrs of units.

4. Baggage, surplus to that carried on Regimental wagons, which it is desired to send to the forward area, will be dumped by units prior to marching out at the eastern end of No.1 Platform Tel-el-Kebir Station on the 19th inst.
   Each unit will leave sufficient men to load and escort their own baggage. The baggage escort will travel with the baggage to KANTARA leaving Tel-el-Kebir on the 20th inst. Time to be notified later.

5. All personnel surplus to the mounted establishment of units will be left in their present billets at Tel-el-Kebir and all base kits of their units will be clearly marked and handed over to the O.C. of the Dismounted Party. This party will come under the command of the O.C., I.C.A.B.D. Nominal Rolls should be forwarded to O.C. ICABD

6. The postal arrangements are as follows :-
   On 21st inst., units should call for mails at I.F.P.O.313, ISMAILIA.
   On 22nd inst., units will receive their mails at F.P.O.31 at KANTARA until such time as they entrain for BELAH.
   On arrival at BELAH mails will be delivered at the Ind. F.P.O. which is being opened there.

7. The dismounted personnel of Ambala I.C.F.A. will move to KANTARA by train on the 20th inst. Time of departure to be notified later.

8. ACKNOWLEDGE.

H. Nutting Major,
D.A.A.& Q.M.G., 5th Cavalry Division.

Copies to :-
   O.C., I.C.A.B.D.
   R.T.O., Tel-el-Kebir,
   F.P.O. No.99.

Appendix II

SECRET.   No. Q.517.

Headquarters, 5th Cavalry Division,
21st April, 1918.

To/
    Sec'bad Cavalry Brigade.   O.C., A.S.C.
    A.D.V.S.   A.D.M.S.
    D.A.D.O.S.   5th Signal Squadron.
    Admin. Comdt., Tel-el-Kebir.

Reference No. G.170 of to-day's date.

1. The unexpended portion of the day's rations and forage will be carried on men and horses.
    Rations will be delivered as under :-
    for 23rd inst. - on arrival at QASSASIN.
    " 24th inst. - on arrival at ISMAILIA.
    " 25th inst. - on arrival at   EL FERDAN.

2. Water Carts will march full and all water-bottles are to be filled daily before leaving the Camp.

3. No tents will be taken. All tents at present in use will be struck on the morning of the 22nd inst., and returned to D.A.D.O.S. The transport for the return of these tents (and also tables and lamps which have been supplied by Ordnance) will be supplied by the Admin. Commandant,
    Wagons will call at Regimental Guard Rooms of the respective Units at 2 p.m. on 22nd inst.

4. Baggage, surplus to that carried on regimental wagons, which it is desired to send to the forward area, will be dumped by units prior to marching out at the Eastern end of No.1 Platform, Tel-el-Kebir Station on the 22nd inst.
    Each Unit will leave sufficient men to load and escort their own baggage. The baggage escort will travel with the baggage to KANTARA leaving Tel-el-Kebir on the 23rd inst. Time to be notified later.

5. All personnel surplus to the mounted establishment of units will be left in their present billets at Tel-el-Kebir, and all base kits of their units will be clearly marked and handed over to the O.C., Dismounted Party. This party will come under the Command of the O.C., I.C.A.B.D. Nominal rolls will be forwarded to the O.C., I.C.A.B.D.

6. The postal arrangements are as follows :-
    On 23rd inst., units will call for mails at F.P.O.313 ISMAILIA.
    On 25th inst., units will receive their mails at F.P.O.31, KANTARA.
    On arrival at BELAH, mails will be delivered at F.P.O.18.

7. ACKNOWLEDGE.

                                                      Major,
                D.A.A.& Q.M.G., 5th Cavalry Division.

Copies to :-
    O.C., I.C.A.B.D.
    R.T.O., Tel-el-Kebir.
    F.P.O. No. 99.

Appendix E

SECRET No.Q.592.

Headquarters, 5th Cavalry Division,
26th April, 1918.

To/
Sec'bad Cavalry Brigade. O.C., A.S.C.
A.D.M.S. A.D.V.S.
D.A.D.O.S. 5th Signal Squadron.

Reference map 1/100,000, sheets C.11 and C.12.

1. Sec'bad I.C.F.A. will march to KANTARA in accordance with the attached March Table on Saturday, 27th inst., and subsequent days.
   On arrival at KANTARA, they will entrain for BELAH under orders to be issued later.

2. The unexpended portion of the day's rations and forage will be carried on men and horses.
   Rations will be delivered as under :-
   For 28th inst. - On arrival at QASSASIN.
   ." 29th " - " " " ISMAILIA.

3. Water carts will march full and all water bottles will be filled daily before leaving the camp.

4. No tents, except those which form part of their equipment, will be taken. All tents issued by local Ordnance Depot will be struck on the morning of the 27th inst. and returned to D.A.D.O.S.
   The transport for the return of these tents (and also tables and lamps) which have been supplied by Ordnance) will be supplied by the Admin. Commandant.
   Wagons will call at the Hdqrs. of the unit at 2 p.m. on 27th inst.

5. Baggage, surplus to that carried on regimental wagons, which it is desired to take to the forward area, will be dumped prior to marching out at the Eastern end of No.1 Platform, Tel-el-Kebir Station, on the 27th inst.
   Sufficient men should be left behind to load and escort the baggage. The baggage escort will travel with the baggage to KANTARA leaving Tel-el-Kebir probably on the 28th inst. Time and date will be notified later.

6. The dismounted personnel will move to KANTARA by train. Time and date will be notified later.

7. Postal arrangements are as follows :-
On 28th inst., F.P.O.313 ISMAILIA.
" 29th inst., F.P.O. 31 KANTARA.
" arrival at BELAH, mails will be delivered at F.P.O. 18.

8. ACKNOWLEDGE.

H Nuttma Major,
D.A.A. & Q.M.G., 5th Cavalry Division.

Copies to :-
R.T.O., Tel-el-Kebir.
Admin. Commandant, Tel-el-Kebir.
F.P.O. 99.

SECRET. Appendix "F" No.Q.555.

Headquarters, 5th Cavalry Division,
23rd April, 1918.

To/

Mhow Cavalry Brigade.   O.C., A.S.C.
A.D.V.S.   A.D.M.S.
D.A.D.O.S.   5th Signal Squadron.
Admin. Comdt., Tel-el-Kebir.

Reference No.G.174 of to-day's date.

1. The unexpended portion of the day's rations and forage will be carried on men and horses.
    Rations will be delivered as under :-

    For 26th inst. - On arrival at QASSASIN.
    "   27th   "   -   "   "   " ISMAILIA.
    "   28th   "   -   "   "   " EL FERDAN.

2. Water carts will march full and all water bottles will be filled daily before leaving camp.

3. No tents will be taken. All tents at present in use will be struck on the morning of the 25th inst., and returned to D.A.D.O.S.
    The transport for the return of these tents (and also tables and lamps which have been supplied by Ordnance) will be supplied by the Admin. Commandant.
    Wagons will call at the Regimental Guard Rooms of the respective units at 2 p.m. on 25th inst.

4. Baggage, surplus to that carried on regimental wagons, which it is desired to send to the forward area, will be dumped by units prior to marching out at the Eastern end of No.1 Platform, Tel-el-Kebir Station on the 25th inst.
    Each unit will leave sufficient men to lead and escort their own baggage. The baggage escort will travel with the baggage to KANTARA leaving Tel-el-Kebir on 25th inst. Time to be notified later.

5. All personnel, surplus to the mounted establishment of units, will be left in their present billets at Tel-el-Kebir, and all base kits of their units will be clearly marked and handed over to the O.C., Dismounted Party. This party will come under the Command of the O.C., I.C.A.B.D. Nominal rolls will be forwarded to the O.C., I.C.A.B.D.

6. Postal arrangements are as follows :-

    On 26th inst, units will call for mails at F.P.O.313, ISMAILIA.
    On 28th inst., units will receive their mails from F.P.O.31,
                                                            KANTARA.
    On arrival at BELAH, mails will be delivered at F.P.O.18.

7. ACKNOWLEDGE.

Major,
D.A.A.& Q.M.G., 5th Cavalry Division.

Copies to :-
    O.C., I.C.A.B.D.
    R.T.O., Tel-el-Kebir.
    F.P.O. No.99.

Appendix G

S E C R E T   No. Q.592.

Headquarters, 5th Cavalry Division,
26th April, 1918.

To/

    Sec'bad Cavalry Brigade.   O.C., A.S.C.
    A.D.M.S.   A.D.V.S.
    D.A.D.O.S.   5th Signal Squadron.

Reference map 1/100,000, sheets C.11 and C.12.

1. Sec'bad I.C.F.A. will march to KANTARA in accordance with the attached March Table on Saturday, 27th inst., and subsequent days.
    On arrival at KANTARA, they will entrain for BELAH under orders to be issued later.

2. The unexpended portion of the day's rations and forage will be carried on men and horses.
    Rations will be delivered as under :-
    For 28th inst. - On arrival at QASSASIN.
    " 29th " - " " " ISMAILIA.

3. Water carts will march full and all water bottles will be filled daily before leaving the camp.

4. No tents, except those which form part of their equipment, will be taken. All tents issued by local Ordnance Depot will be struck on the morning of the 27th inst. and returned to D.A.D.O.S.
    The transport for the return of these tents (and also tables and lamps) which have been supplied by Ordnance) will be supplied by the Admin. Commandant.
    Wagons will call at the Hdqrs. of the unit at 2 p.m. on 27th inst.

5. Baggage, surplus to that carried on regimental wagons, which it is desired to take to the forward area, will be dumped prior to marching out at the Eastern end of No.1 Platform, Tel-el-Kebir Station, on the 27th inst.
    Sufficient men should be left behind to load and escort the baggage. The baggage escort will travel with the baggage to KANTARA leaving Tel-el-Kebir probably on the 28th inst. Time and date will be notified later.

6. The dismounted personnel will move to KANTARA by train. Time and date will be notified later.

7. Postal arrangements are as follows :-
On 28th inst., F.P.O.313 ISMAILIA.
" 29th inst., F.P.O. 31 KANTARA.
" arrival at BELAH, mails will be delivered at F.P.O. 18.

8. ACKNOWLEDGE.

                                                        Major,
                          D.A.A. & Q.M.G., 5th Cavalry Division.

Copies to :-
    R.T.O., Tel-el-Kebir.
    Admin. Commandant, Tel-el-Kebir.
    F.P.O. 99.

5TH CAVALRY DIVISION.

March Table issued with No.G.532 dated 26th April, 1918.

Formation or unit.	Starting Point.	Date and Time.	Route.	Destination.	Remarks.
Sec'bad Cavalry Field Ambulance.		27th April. (after 3 P.M.)	All wheels by ISMAILIA CANAL ROAD.	QASSASIN BIVOUAC (9 miles).	
ditto.		28th April.	ditto.	ISMAILIA. (19 miles)	
ditto.		29th April.	SUEZ CANAL ROAD.	KANTARA. (22 miles).	

Appendix H

SECRET.
No. G.609.

Headquarters, 5th Cavalry Division,
27th April, 1918.

To/

    Lucknow Cavalry Brigade.   O.C., A.S.C.
    Sialkot Cavalry Brigade.   A.D.M.S.
    Sec'bad Cavalry Brigade.   A.D.V.S.
    5th Signal Squadron.   D.A.D.O.S.
    Admin. Commandant, Tel-el-Kebir.

Reference No.G.178 of to-day's date.

1. The unexpended portion of the day's rations and forage will be carried on men and horses.
    Rations will be delivered as under :-
  For 29th inst. - On arrival at QASSASIN.
  For 30th inst. - On arrival at ISMAILIA.
  For 1st prox. - On arrival at EL FERDAN.

2. All water bottles will be filled daily before leaving each camp.

3. No tents will be taken. All tents at present in use will be struck on the morning of the 28th inst. and returned to D.A.D.O.S. The transport for the return of these tents (and also tables and lamps which have been supplied by Ordnance) will be supplied by the Admin. Commandant.
    Wagons will call at the Headquarters of the Sec'bad and Lucknow M.V.Ss. at 2 p.m. on the 28th inst.

4. The horse ambulances of the Lucknow C.F.A. will proceed by rail on the 30th inst. A.D.M.S. will detail one man to travel with these vehicles as escort and will also arrange a loading party for entraining. R.T.O. will notify this office the time these vehicles should be loaded.

5. Postal arrangements are as follows :-
  29th inst. mails at F.P.O. 313, ISMAILIA.
  1st prox. at F.P.O.31, KANTARA.
  On arrival at BELAH at F.P.O. 18.

6. ACKNOWLEDGE.

                                     Major,
           D.A.A.& Q.M.G., 5th Cavalry Division.

Copies to :-
    R.T.O., Tel-el-Kebir.
    F.P.O. No.99.

SECRET.   No.Q.614.

                                    Headquarters, 5th Cavalry Division,
                                              27th April, 1918.

To/
    Sialkot Cavalry Brigade.
    Sec'bad Cavalry Brigade.
    Lucknow Cavalry Brigade.
    O.C., A.S.C.
    A.D.M.S.
    D.A.D.O.S.
    A.D.V.S.
    5th Signal Squadron.
    Admin. Commandant, Tel-el-Kebir.
    Captain P.T. SAENDERS, A.V.C.
    O.C., 4th Sanitary Section.

        Reference this office No.G.178 and Q.609 of to-day's date.

1.   4th Cavalry Sanitary Section will also march with the units mentioned.

2.   Major R.C. O'BRIEN, I.M.S. will now assume command of all units throughout the march.
        Para.2 of this office No.G.178 of to-day's date should be amended accordingly.

3.   Copies of this office Nos.G.178 and Q.609 are forwarded herewith to O.C., 4th Sanitary Section, who will acknowledge receipt.

                                                        Major,
                            D.A.A.& Q.M.G., 5th Cavalry Division.

Copies to :-
    R.T.O., Tel-el-Kebir.
    F.P.O. No.99.

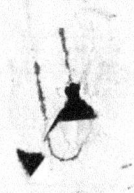

HEADQUARTERS, 5th CAVALRY DIVISION.

(ADMINISTRATIVE.)

1918.   APPENDIX.

March.   TEL-EL-KEBIR.

5th   Advanced Div'nl Headquarters opened at TEL-EL-KEBIR at 9 p.m.

STAFF: Brig-General G.A.H.Beatty, D.S.O., Commanding.
Major H.B.Nutting, D.A.A. & Q.M.G.
Major H.B.Clegg, S.S.O.
Lieut. J.A.Ewart, A.D.C. to G.O.C.

21st   Director of Remounts, E.E.F., inspected the following Units, who have now become complete :-

6th Cavalry.   9th Horse.
19th Lancers.   Ambala C.F.A.
    Sialkote C.F.A.

25th   The details already arrived of the 4th and 5th Cavalry Divisions inspected by the G.O.C., Force in Egypt.

27th   H.R.H., Duke of Connaught, met General Beatty and Staff, all C.O's of Regiments and Field Ambulances on the railway platform at TEL-EL-KEBIR. Jemadar Gobind Singh, V.C., was also present.

The following number of horses, surplus to Establishment, were this day despatched to No. 3 Remount Depot, BILBEIS:-

6th Cavalry: 35 Riding,
    2 Draught.
    4 Pack.

19th Lancers: 40 Riding.
    4 Draught.
    1 Pack.

9th Horse: 14 Riding.
    6 Draught.

H.NUTTING.
Major,
D.A.A.&Q.M.G., 5th Cavalry Division.

D.A.G. Ind Section, 3rd Echelon.

Headquarters, 5th Cavalry Division. (ADMINISTRATIVE).

1918.   Appendix.

April   TEL-EL-KEBIR.

4th   Brig-General L.L.Maxwell, C.M.G., arrived and
        took over command of Advanced Div'nl
        Hqrs. this date.

7th   1 B.O., 1 I.O. and 46 O.R.I. left for
        work at the No.1 Remount Depot, KANTARA,
        to-day.

8th   Leave to India sanctioned for Indian
        Ranks on a percentage of 10% of strength.
        Numbers proceeded to India by 1st Batch
        today:-   24 Indian Officers.
                    631 Indian Other Ranks.

11th   Orders received for the move of 6th
        Cavalry and 19th Lancers to KANTARA by
        route march. Date to be notified later.

15th   6th Cavalry, 19th Lancers, Sialkote C.F.A.
        and Sialkote M.V.S. moved to day by route
        march to KANTARA en route for BELAH.
        (Administrative Instructions - Appendix "A".)

16th   29th Lancers, 36th Jacob's Horse and Lucknow
        C.F.A. moved to-day by route march to
        KANTARA en route for BELAH. (Administrative
        Instructions - Appendix "B").

19th   9th Horse, 18th Lancers, Ambala C.F.A. and
        Ambala M.V.S. proceeded by route march to
        KANTARA en route for LUDD. (Administrative
        Instructions - Appendix "C").

21st   No.23 Field Veterinary Section proceeded
        to KANTARA by rail en route for LUDD.

22nd   20th Deccan Horse and 34th Poona Horse
        proceeded to KANTARA by road en route for
        BELAH, and on arrival will come under
        orders of Desert Corps. (See Appendix "D").

24th   Jodhpore Lancers and Jodhpore C.F.A.
        proceeded by road to KANTARA, en route for
        BELAH, to come under the orders of Desert
        Corps. (See Appendix "E")

25th   2nd Lancers, 38th C.I.Horse, Mhow C.F.A.
        and Mhow M.V.S. proceeded by route march
        to-day to KANTARA en route for BELAH.
        On arrival at that place they will come
        under the orders of the Desert Corps.
        (See Appendix "F").

27th   Secbad Cav. Field Ambulance marched to
        KANTARA today en route to BELAH to come
        under the orders of Desert Corps.
        (See Appendix "G" - Administrative Instructions)

1918. Appendix.

April.

28th   Secbad Mobile Veterinary Section,
Lucknow Mobile Veterinary Section
and 4th. Sanitary Section marched
today to KANTARA en route to BELAH.
(Administrative contained in
Appendix "H").
Orders issued for details of
Sialkote, Lucknow and Secbad
Brigade Headquarters and Signal
Troops to concentrate at Divisional
Headquarters prior to being broken up.

29th   All horses of 5th Signal Squadron,
Lucknow - Sialkote and Secbad Signal
Troops returned to No.3 Remount Depot
BILBEIS today. All harness and
Ordnance equipment being handed in to
the Ordnance Depot TEL-EL-KEBIR.

W.T.HODGSON,Lieut.Col.
for A.A.& Q.M.G.,
5th Cavy.Divn.

APPENDIX "A".

SECRET & URGENT.   No.Q.393.
Headquarters,5th Cavalry Division.
14th April, 1918.

To/
Sialkot Cavalry Brigade.   A.D.V.S.
O.C., A.S.C.   D.A.D.O.S.
A.D.M.S.   Admin.Comdt.Tel-el-Kebir.

Reference No.G.158 dated 14th inst.

1.   The unexpended portion of the day's rations and
forage will be carried on men and horses.
     Rations will be delivered as under:-

     For 16th inst. - On arrival at QASSASIN.
      " 17th inst. - On arrival at ISMAILIA.

2.   Water carts will march full and all water-bottles
are to be filled daily before leaving camp.

3.   No tents will be taken.

     All tents at present in use by units will be struck
to-morrow morning and returned to D.A.D.O.S.
     The transport for return of tents will be supplied
by Admin. Commandant and wagons will call for tents
as under:-
     Tents of 6th Cavalry and 19th Lancers - 2p.m. at
           Regtl Guard Rooms.
     Tents of Sialkot M.V.S. and C.F.A.   - at Hd.Qrs.of
           units at 2 pm

4. The base kits of units clearly marked and securely packed will be handed over to the O.C., I.C.A.B.D. ~~and Os.C.~~ by 12 noon on 15th inst. under arrangements to be made with O.C., I.C.A.B.D. and Os.C Units.

5. Baggage surplus to that carried on regimental wagons which it is desired to send to the forward area will be dumped by units, prior to marching out, at East end of No. 1 Platform, Tel-el-Kebir Stn.
   Each unit will leave sufficient men to load and escort their own baggage. The baggage escort will travel with the baggage to KANTARA leaving Tel-el-Kebir on 16th inst. Time of train will be notified later.

6. All personnel surplus to the mounted establishment of units will be left at Tel-el-Kebir and transferred to the I.C.A.B.D. on the morning of the 16th inst.
   Nominal rolls of such personnel will be rendered to the O.C. I.C.A.B.D.

7. The dismounted personnel of the Sialkot C.F.A. will move to KANTARA by train on the 16th inst., time of departure to be notified later.

8. ACKNOWLEDGE.

Sgd. W.T.Hodgson,
Lieut-Colonel,
for A.A.& Q.M.G. 5th Cavalry Division.

Copies to:-
O.C., I.C.A.B.D.
R.T.O., Tel-el-Kebir.

APPENDIX "B".

SECRET.   No. Q.423.

Headquarters, 5th Cavalry Division.
15th April, 1918.

To/
Lucknow Cavalry Brigade.
O.C., A.S.C.
A.D.M.S.
A.D.V.S.
D.A.D.O.S.
Admin.Comdt., Tel-el-Kebir.

Reference No.G.160 of to-day's date.

1. The unexpended portion of the day's ration and forage will be carried on men and horses.
   Rations will be delivered as under:-

   for 17th inst. - On arrival at QASSASIN.
   "   18th inst. - On arrival at ISMAILIA.

2. Water carts will march full and all water bottles are to be filled daily before leaving the camp.

3. No tents will be taken.
   All tents at present in use by units will be struck to-morrow morning and returned to D.A.D.O.S.

The transport for the return of tents will be supplied by Admin. Commandant and wagons will call for tents as under:-

 Tents of 29th Lancers and 36th J.Horse - 2 p.m. at
              Regt'l Guardrooms
 " " Lucknow C.F.A. at Hd.Qrs.of Unit at 2.pm

4. Baggage surplus to that carried on regimental wagons which it is desired to send to the forward area will be dumped by units prior to marching out at the eastern end of No.1 Platform, Tel-el-Kebir Stn.
 Each unit will leave sufficient men to load and escort their own baggage. The baggage escort will travel with the baggage to KANTARA leaving Tel-el-Kebir on 18th inst. Time of train to be notified later.

5. All personnel surplus to the mounted establishment of units will be left in their present billets at Tel-el-Kebir and all Base kits of their units will be clearly marked and handed over to the O.C., of the Dismounted Party. This party will come the command of the O.C. I.C.A.B.D. Nominal rolls of such personnel being rendered to the O.C.,I.C.A.B.D.

6. The Dismounted personnel of Lucknow I.C.F.A. will move to KANTARA by train on the 17th inst. Time of departure to be notified later.

7. ACKNOWLEDGE.

            Sgd. H.Nutting,
              Major,
       D.A.A.& Q.M.G.,5th Cav Divn.

Copies to:-
 O.C.,I.C.A.B.D.
 R.T.O.,Tel-el-Kebir.

APPENDIX "C".

SECRET.   No.Q.455.

       Headquarters, 5th Cavalry Division,
          17th April, 1918.

To/
 Ambala Cavalry Brigade.   O.C.,A.S.C.
 Sec'bad Cavalry Brigade.   A.D.M.S.
 A.D.V.S.   5th Signal Squadron.
 D.A.D.O.S.   Admin.Comdt.,Tel-el-Kebir.

Reference No.G.165 of to-day's date.

1. The unexpended portion of the day's rations and forage will be carried on men and horses.
 Rations will be delivered as under:-
  for 20th inst. - On arrival at QASSASIN.
  " 21st inst. - On arrival at ISMAILIA.
  " 22nd inst. - On arrival at EL FERDAN.

5.

2. Water carts will march full and all water bottles are to be filled daily before leaving the camp.

3. No tents will be taken.
All tents at present in use will be struck on the morning of the 19th inst., and returned to D.A.D.O.S.
The transport for the return of these tents will be supplied by the Admin. Commandant and wagons will call for tents as under:-

Tents of 9th Horse and 18th Lancers - 2 p.m. on the 19th at Regt'l Guard Rooms.

Ambala C.F.A. and M.V.S. - at 2 p.m. on the 19th at Hd.Qrs of Units.

4. Baggage, surplus to that carried on Regimental wagons, which it is desired to send to the forward area, will be dumped by units prior to marching out at the eastern end of No.1 Platform Tel-el-Kebir Station on the 19th inst.
Each unit will leave sufficient men to load and escort their own baggage. The baggage escort will travel with the baggage to KANTARA leaving Tel-el-Kebir on the 20th inst. Time to be notified later.

5. All personnel surplus to the mounted establishment of units will be left in their present billets at Tel-el-Kebir and all base kits of their units will be clearly marked and handed over to the O.C. of the Dismounted Party. This party will come under the command of the O.C., I.C.A.B.D. Nominal Rolls should be forwarded to O.C. I.C.A.B.D.

6. The postal arrangements are as follows:-
On 21st inst., units should call for mails at I.F.P.O.313, ISMAILIA.
On 22nd inst., units will receive their mails at F.P.O.31 at KANTARA until such time as they entrain for BELAH.
On arrival at BELAH mails will be delivered at the Ind. F.P.O. which is being opened there.

7. The dismounted personnel of Ambala I.C.F.A. will move to KANTARA by train on the 20th inst. Time of departure to be notified later.

8. ACKNOWLEDGE.

H.Nutting, Major,
D.A.A.& Q.M.G., 5th Cavalry Division.

Copies to:-
O.C., I.C.A.B.D.
R.T.O., Tel-el-Kebir,
F.P.O. No.99.

APPENDIX "D".

SECRET.　　　　　　　　　　　　　　　　　　　　　　　　　No.Q.517.

Headquarters, 5th Cavalry Division,
21st April, 1918.

To/
Sec'bad Cavalry Brigade.　　O.C., A.S.C.
A.D.V.S.　　　　　　　　　　A.D.M.S.
D.A.D.O.S.　　　　　　　　　5th Signal Squadron.
Admin. Comdt., Tel-el-Kebir.

Reference No. G.170 of to-day's date.

1. The unexpended portion of the day's rations and

forage will be carried on men and horses.

Rations will be delivered as under:-
for 23rd inst. - on arrival at QASSASIN.
" 24th inst. - on arrival at ISMAILIA.
" 25th inst. - on arrival at EL FERDAN.

2. Water Carts will march full and all water-bottles are to be filled daily before leaving the camp.

3. No tents will be taken. All tents at present in use will be struck on the morning of the 22nd inst., and returned to D.A.D.O.S. The transport for the return of these tents (and also tables and lamps which have been supplied by Ordnance) will be supplied by the Admin.Commandant.
Wagons will call at Regimental Guard Rooms of the respective Units at 2 p.m. on 22nd inst.

4. Baggage, surplus to that carried on regimental wagons, which it is desired to send to the forward area, will be dumped by units prior to marching out at the Eastern end of No.1 Platform, Tel-el-Kebir Station on the 22nd inst.
Each unit will leave sufficient men to load and escort their own baggage. The baggage escort will travel with the baggage to KANTARA leaving Tel-el-Kebir on the 23rd inst. Time to be notified later.

5. All personnel surplus to the mounted establishment of units will be left in their present billets at Tel-el-Kebir, and all base kits of their units will be clearly marked and handed over to the O.C., Dismounted Party. This party will come under the Command of the O.C.,I.C.A.B.D. Nominal rolls will be forwarded to the O.C., I.C.A.B.D.

6. The postal arrangements are as follows:-
On 23rd inst.,units will call for mails at F.P.O.313
ISMAILIA.
On 25th inst.,units will receive their mails at F.P.O.31,
KANTARA.
On arrival at BELAH, mails will be delivered at F.P.O.18.

7. ACKNOWLEDGE.

H.Nutting,Major,
D.A.A.& Q.M.G.,5th Cavalry Division.
Copies to:-
O.C.,I.C.A.B.D.
R.T.O.,Tel-el-Kebir,
F.P.O. No.99.

APPENDIX "E".

SECRET.   No.Q.592.

Headquarters,5th Cavalry Division
26th April,1918.

To/
Sec'bad Cavalry Brigade.   O.C.,A.S.C.
A.D.M.S.   A.D.V.S.
D.A.D.O.S.   5th Signal Squadron.

Reference map 1/100,000, sheets C.11 and C.12.

1. Sec'bad I.C.F.A.will march to KANTARA in accordance with the attached March Table on Saturday, 27th inst., and subsequent days.
On arrival at KANTARA, they will entrain for BELAH under orders to be issued later.

2. The unexpended portion of the day's rations and forage will be carried on men and horses.
   Rations will be delivered as under:-
   For 28th inst. - On arrival at QASSASIN.
   "   29th "   - "   "   " ISMAILIA.

3. Water carts will march full and all water bottles will be filled daily before leaving the camp.

4. No tents, except those which form part of their equipment, will be taken. All tents issued by local Ordnance Depot will be struck on the morning of the 27th inst. and returned to D.A.D.O.S.
   The transport for the return of these tents (and also tables and lamps) which have been supplied by Ordnance) will be supplied by the Admin. Commandant.
   Wagons will call at the Hdqrs. of the unit at 2 p.m. on 27th inst.

5. Baggage, surplus to that carried on regimental wagons, which it is desired to take to the forward area, will be dumped prior to marching out at the Eastern end of No.1 Platform, Tel-el-Kebir Station, on the 27th inst.
   Sufficient men should be left behind to load and escort the baggage. The baggage escort will travel with the baggage to KANTARA leaving Tel-el-Kebir probably on the 28th inst. Time and date will be notified later.

6. The dismounted personnel will move to KANTARA by train. Time and date will be notified later.

7. Postal arrangements are as follows:-
   On 28th inst., F.P.O. 313 ISMAILIA.
   " 29th inst., F.P.O. 31 KANTARA.
   " arrival at BELAH, mails will be delivered at F.P.O.18.

8. ACKNOWLEDGE.

H. Nutting, Major,
D.A.A.& Q.M.G., 5th Cavalry Division.

Copies to:-
   R.T.O., Tel-el-Kebir,
   Admin. Commandant, Tel-el-Kebir.
   F.P.O. 99.

APPENDIX "F".

SECRET.   No. Q.555.

Headquarters, 5th Cavalry Division,
23rd April, 1918.

To/
   Mhow Cavalry Brigade.   O.C., A.S.C.
   A.D.V.S.   A.D.M.S.
   D.A.D.O.S.   5th Signal Squadron.
   Admin. Comdt., Tel-el-Kebir.

Reference No. G.174 of to-day's date.

1. The unexpended portion of the day's rations and forage will be carried on men and horses.
   Rations will be delivered as under:-

   For 26th inst. - On arrival at QASSASIN.
   "   27th "   - "   "   " ISMAILIA.
   "   28th "   - "   "   " EL FERDAN.

2. Water carts will march full and all water bottles will be filled daily before leaving camp.

3. No tents will be taken. All tents at present in use will be struck on the morning of the 25th inst., and returned to D.A.D.O.S.

The transport for the return of these tents (and also tables and lamps which have been supplied by Ordnance) will be supplied by the Admin. Commandant.

Wagons will call at the Regimental Guard Rooms of the respective units at 2.p.m. on 26th inst.

4. Baggage, surplus to that carried on regimental wagons, which it is desired to send to the forward area, will be dumped by units prior to marching out at the Eastern end of No.1 Platform, Tel-el-Kebir Station on the 25th inst.

Each unit will leave sufficient men to lead and escort their own baggage. The baggage escort will travel with the baggage to KANTARA leaving Tel-el-Kebir on 25th inst. Time to be notified later.

5. All personnel, surplus to the mounted establishment of units will be left in their present billets at Tel-el-Kebir and all base kits of their units will be clearly marked and handed over to the O.C., Dismounted Party. This party will come under the Command of the O.C., I.C.A.B.D. Nominal rolls will be forwarded to the O.C., I.C.A.B.D.

6. Postal arrangements are as follows:-

On 26th inst., units will call for mails at F.P.O.313, ISMAILIA.
On 28th inst., units will receive their mails from F.P.O.31, KANTARA.
On arrival at BELAH, mails will be delivered at F.P.O.18.

7. ACKNOWLEDGE.

H.Nutting, Major,
D.A.A.& Q.M.G., 5th Cavalry Division.

Copies to:-
O.C., I.C.A.B.D.
R.T.O., Tel-el-Kebir.
F.P.C. No.99.

APPENDIX G.

SECRET.   No.Q.592.

Headquarters, 5th Cavalry Division,
26th April, 1918.

To/
Sec'bad Cavalry Brigade.   O.C., A.S.C.
A.D.M.S.   A.D.V.S.
D.A.D.O.S.   5th Signal Squadron.

Reference map 1/100,000, sheets C.11 and C.12.

1. Sec'bad I.C.F.A. will march to KANTARA in accordance with the attached March Table on Saturday, 27th inst., and subsequent days.

On arrival at KANTARA, they will entrain for BELAH under orders to be issued later.

2.   The unexpended portion of the day's rations and forage will be carried on men and horses.
   Rations will be delivered as under:-
   For 28th inst. - On arrival at QASSASIN.
   "   29th "   - "   "   " ISMAILIA.

3.   Water carts will march full and all water bottles will be filled daily before leaving the camp.

4.   No tents, except those which form part of their equipment, will be taken. All tents issued by local Ordnance Depot will be struck on the morning of the 27th inst. and returned to D.A.D.O.S.
   The transport for the return of these tents (and also tables and lamps) which have been supplied by Ordnance) will be supplied by the Admin. Commandant.
   Wagons will call at the Hdqrs. of the unit at 2 p.m. on 27th inst.

5.   Baggage, surplus to that carried on regimental wagons, which it is desired to take to the forward area, will be dumped prior to marching out at the Eastern end of No.1 Platform, Tel-el-Kebir Station, on the 27th inst.
   Sufficient men should be left behind to load and escort the baggage. The baggage escort will travel with the baggage to KANTARA leaving Tel-el-Kebir probably on the 28th inst. Time and date will be notified later.

6.   The dismounted personnel will move to KANTARA by train. Time and date will be notified later.

7.   Postal arrangements are as follows:-
On 28th inst., F.P.O.313 ISMAILIA.
" 29th inst., F.P.O.31 KANTARA.
" arrival at BELAH, mails will be delivered at F.P.O.18.

8.   ACKNOWLEDGE.

                                 H.Nutting, Major,
               D.A.A.& Q.M.G., 5th Cavalry Division.

Copies to:-
   R.T.O., Tel-el-Kebir.
   Admin. Commandant, Tel-el-Kebir.
   F.P.O. 99.

5TH CAVALRY DIVISION.

March Table issued with No.Q.592 dated 26th April, 1918.

Formation or unit.	Starting Point.	Date and Time.	Route.	Destination.	Remarks.
Sec'bad Cavalry Field Ambulance.		27th April (after 3 P.M.)	All wheels by ISMAILIA CANAL ROAD.	QASSASIN BIVOUAC (9 miles).	
ditto.		28th April.	ditto.	ISMAILIA. (19 miles)	
ditto.		29th April.	SUEZ CANAL ROAD.	KANTARA. (22 miles).	

APPENDIX "H".

SECRET.   No. Q.609.

Headquarters, 5th Cavalry Division,
27th April, 1918.

To/
   Lucknow Cavalry Brigade.   O.C., A.S.C.
   Sialkot Cavalry Brigade.   A.D.M.S.
   Sec'bad Cavalry Brigade.   A.D.V.S.
   5th Signal Squadron.   D.A.D.O.S.
   Admin. Commandant, Tel-el-Kebir.

Reference No. G.178 of to-day's date.

1. The unexpended portion of the day's rations and forage will be carried on men and horses.
   Rations will be delivered as under:-
   For 29th inst. - On arrival at QASSASIN.
   For 30th inst. - On arrival at ISMAILIA.
   For 1st prox. - On arrival at ELFERDAN.

2. All water bottles will be filled daily before leaving each camp.

3. No tents will be taken. All tents at present in use will be struck on the morning of the 28th inst. and returned to D.A.D.O.S. The transport for the return of these tents (and also tables and lamps which have been supplied by Ordnance) will be supplied by the Admin. Commandant.
   Wagons will call at the Headquarters of the Sec'bad and Lucknow M.V.Ss. at 2 p.m. on the 28th inst.

4. The horse ambulances of the Lucknow C.F.A. will proceed by rail on the 30th inst. A.D.M.S. will detail one man to travel with these vehicles as escort and will also arrange a loading party for entraining. R.T.O. will notify this office the time these vehicles should be loaded.

5. Postal arrangements are as follows:-
   29th inst. mails at F.P.O. 313, ISMAILIA.
   1st prox. at F.P.O. 31, KANTARA.
   On arrival at BELAH at F.P.O. 18.

6. ACKNOWLEDGE.

H. Nutting, Major,
D.A.A.& Q.M.G., 5th Cavalry Division.

Copies to:-
   R.T.O., Tel-el-Kebir.
   F.P.O. No. 99.

No. Q. 614.

SECRET.   Headquarters, 5th Cavalry Division,
                                    27th April, 1918.

To/
    Sialkot Cavalry Brigade.
    Sec'bad Cavalry Brigade.
    Lucknow Cavalry Brigade.
    O.C., A.S.C.
    A.D.M.S.
    D.A.D.O.S.
    A.D.V.S.
    5th Signal Squadron.
    Admin. Commandant, Tel-el-Kebir.
    Captain P.T.SAUNDERS, A.V.C.
    O.C., 4th Sanitary Section.

          Reference this office No. G.178 and Q.609 of to-day's date.

1.   4th Cavalry Sanitary Section will also march with the units mentioned.

2.   Major R.C.O'BRIEN, I.M.S. will now assume command of all units throughout the march.
        Para.2 of this office No. G.178 of to-day's date should be amended accordingly.

3.   Copies to this office Nos. G.178 and Q.609 are forwarded herewith to O.C., 4th Sanitary Section, who will acknowledge receipt.

                                    H. Nutting, Major,
                        D.A.A.& Q.M.G., 5th Cavalry Division.

Copies to:-
        R.T.O., Tel-el-Kebir.
        F.P.O. No.99.

www.ingramcontent.com/pod-product-compliance
Lightning Source LLC
Chambersburg PA
CBHW082010220426
43670CB00014B/2594